T0320315

The Competitiveness of European Industry

First published in 1989, *The Competitiveness of European Industry* helps in developing our understanding of the process of improving and measuring industrial competitiveness. The contributors focus on the competitiveness of European industry. Three main topics are discussed: the concept of competitiveness itself; what can be learned about competitiveness at the level of an individual national economy; and processes and strategies in forms which might contribute to improved competitive performance. The first two papers critically assess concepts and measures of national competitiveness and review the performances of the economies of Britain, France, and the Federal German Republic. Then follow accounts of industrial competitiveness in three smaller economies (Belgium, Switzerland, and Sweden), which develop a series of methods and techniques for the analysis of industrial structures and indicate significant policy implications. The three concluding papers look at the competitiveness of British industry at the firm level, focusing on the strategic changes, the competitive process, and technical innovation. This book will be of interest to policy makers, business school teachers, and researchers in the area of strategy, industrial economics, organization behaviour, and innovation management.

The Competitiveness of European Industry

Edited by Arthur Francis and P. K. M. Tharakan

Routledge
Taylor & Francis Group

First published in 1989
By Routledge

This edition first published in 2023 by Routledge
4 Park Square, Milton Park, Abingdon, Oxon, OX14 4RN
and by Routledge
605 Third Avenue, New York, NY 10017

Routledge is an imprint of the Taylor & Francis Group, an informa business

Publisher's Note
The publisher has gone to great lengths to ensure the quality of this reprint but points out that some imperfections in the original copies may be apparent.

Disclaimer
The publisher has made every effort to trace copyright holders and welcomes correspondence from those they have been unable to contact.

A Library of Congress record exists under ISBN: 0415031230

ISBN: 978-1-032-43995-2 (hbk)
ISBN: 978-1-003-36982-0 (ebk)
ISBN: 978-1-032-43997-6 (pbk)

Book DOI 10.4324/9781003369820

THE COMPETITIVENESS OF EUROPEAN INDUSTRY

Edited by Arthur Francis
and P. K. M. Tharakan

Routledge
London and New York

First published 1989 by Routledge
11 New Fetter Lane, London EC4P 4EE
29 West 35th Street, New York, NY 10001

Typeset by J&L Composition Ltd, Filey, North Yorkshire

British Library Cataloguing in Publication Data

The Competitiveness of European industry:
country polices & company strategies.
 1. Europe. Industries. Competitiveness
 I. Francis, Arthur II. Tharakan, P. K. M.
 338.6'048'094

ISBN 0-415-03123-0

Library of Congress Cataloging in Publication Data

The Competitiveness of European industry : country policies and
 company strategies / edited by Arthur Francis and P. K. M. Tharakan.
    p.   cm.
 Papers from a seminar held at the European Institute for Advanced
Studies in Management, Brussels.
 ISBN 0-415-03123-0
 1. Industry and state—Europe—Congresses. 2. Competition—
Europe—Congresses. 3. Europe—Industries—Evaluation—Congresses.
I. Francis, Arthur. II. Tharakan, P. K. M. III. European Institute
for Advanced Studies in Management.
HD3616.E8C65   1989
338.6'048'049—dc19   89-31168
                                                                    CIP

Contents

The competitiveness of European industry

Tables

Figures

Contributors

Luis Araujo was a research student in the School of Management at the University of Lancaster and is now a lecturer in the Department of Engineering in the University of Oporto, Portugal.

Mark Boden is a research associate within the Programme of Policy Research in Engineering Science and Technology (PREST) at the University of Manchester.

Silvio Borner is Professor at the Institut für Volkswirtschaft, Basle, Switzerland.

Gibson Burrell was a lecturer in the Department of Behaviour in Organizations at the University of Lancaster and is now Professor of Organizational Behaviour at the University of Warwick.

Geoff Easton is a senior lecturer and Head of the Department of Marketing, School of Management, University of Lancaster.

Janet Evans is a research associate within the PREST group at the University of Manchester.

Arthur Francis is senior lecturer in business policy and marketing in the Management School, Imperial College, and co-ordinator of the ESRC research programme on the competitiveness of British industry.

Hans-Peter Fröhlich is at the Institut der Deutschen Wirtschaft, Köln.

Michael Gibbons is Professor of Science and Technology Policy and co-director of the PREST group at the University of Manchester.

Christer Karlsson is Professor at the European Institute for Advanced Studies in Management, Brussels.

J. Stanley Metcalfe is Professor of Economics at the University of Manchester and co-director of the PREST group.

Andrew M. Pettigrew is Professor of Organizational Behaviour and director of the Centre for Corporate Strategy and Change, University of Warwick.

Tim Ray is a research associate within the PREST group at the University of Manchester.

Robert Rosenfeld is a senior research fellow in the Centre for Corporate Strategy and Change, University of Warwick.

Robert Rothschild is lecturer in economics at the University of Lancaster.

Santi Rothschild is a research associate in the School of Management at the University of Lancaster.

A. Sendhaji was research assistant at the Free University of Brussels and is now at the World Bank.

Claire Shearman was a research associate in the School of Management at the University of Lancaster and is now a lecturer in IT Policy at the Information Technology Institute, Salford University.

P. K. M. Tharakan is Professor of Economics at the University of Antwerp.

D. Verstralen was research associate at the University of Antwerp and is now working in the private sector.

J. Waelbroeck is Professor of Economics at the Free University of Brussels.

Richard Whipp is principal research fellow in the Centre for Corporate Strategy and Change, University of Warwick.

Acknowledgements

The symposium leading to most of the contributions in this volume was held at the European Institute for Advanced Studies in Management, Brussels, and the editors would like to express their thanks to the Director of the Institute at that time, Professor Herman Daems, and the administrator, Gerry Van Dyck. This symposium was only possible because of funds provided by the UK Economic and Social Research Council, who have also funded the research reported on in Chapters 6–8.

The production of the typescript was undertaken by Catherine Hill and Jane Lakey, each of whom displayed unfailing patience and efficiency with both authors and systems and to whom go the editors' warmest thanks.

Introduction

Arthur Francis

Worries about the competitiveness of European, and American, industries have been widespread for at least a decade. They are likely to remain for as long as Japanese and other Pacific rim companies continue to gain market share across a range of industries. Early hopes that the success of Japanese companies would be limited because it was based merely on their late development were shown to be in vain when in many sectors the Japanese not only caught up but overtook their western rivals. The euphoria expressed recently in some quarters of the UK political scene about the recent fast growth of Britain's economy is now muted by the rapid slide in that country's external trade balance.

In 1983, in response to this concern about the long-term competitiveness of industry in the UK, the Economic and Social Research Council (ESRC) of that country launched a substantial programme of research comprising over twenty research projects at several universities and other research centres. Three years into this programme an international seminar was held at the European Institute for Advanced Studies in Management in Brussels at which most of the contributions to this volume were presented.

The contributions address three main topics – the concept of competitiveness itself; what can be learned about competitiveness at the level of an individual national economy; and processes and strategies in firms which might contribute to improved competitive performance.

The first two chapters show just how far we still have to go to establish acceptable definitions and measures of competitiveness. In Chapter one Francis attempts to correct some of the more elementary mistakes often made in defining and measuring the competitiveness of a national economy. He shows that in a number of cases writers have failed to make the distinction between a country's slow rate of economic growth and the competitiveness of its industries. He argues that it is possible to conceive of an

1

economy remaining competitive though on a slow growth path. Similarly levels of industrial efficiency are conceptually distinct from degrees of competitiveness. Analysts and policy makers need to be clear about which symptoms are associated with each condition, for the policy implications may differ. This point is illustrated by his sketching four alternative scenarios with regard to growth rates and competitiveness in the UK economy.

Fröhlich, in Chapter two, endorses Francis' caution about leaping to early conclusions about a nation's competitiveness. His precise definition of competitiveness allows him to spell out just three options facing policy makers who wish to improve competitiveness. Two of these – wage reduction and devaluation – he rapidly dismisses. The third option is that of raising productivity and the major way of doing this is via innovations in products and production processes. Fröhlich then reviews the experience of the UK, France, and the Federal Republic of Germany in increasing their respective competitive positions, ending with a review of supply-side policies available to government to increase rates of innovation.

Pursuing the same theme of national industrial policies for increasing a country's industrial competitiveness is the work of Tharakan and colleagues reported in Chapter three. This chapter is of interest for at least two reasons. One is the innovatory econometric analysis they have developed to assess the revealed comparative advantage and profitability of particular industrial sectors. The other is the results this yields about the country they have subjected to the analysis – Belgium. This, they suggest, is to be seen as an example of a small, 'open' economy. They reach strong conclusions about the need to re-focus that country's industrial policies away from a bias which has favoured physical capital investment.

Another relatively small economy is the subject of the next chapter in which Borner examines the competitiveness and internationalization of the Swiss economy. However, he focuses directly on the firms themselves, rather than government industrial policies, arguing that the competitiveness of most firms in highly industrialized nations is linked to their ability to innovate and to transfer technology, both externally and internally. His thesis is that innovation and technology transfer do not rely on technological skills alone but on organizational and contractual innovations designed to adjust the scope of the firm to its economic and political environment. In the Swiss economy the international production of Swiss firms exceeds the total value of Swiss exports and so it provides an ideal context for Borner to explore his thesis.

2

The chapter painstakingly details types of internationalization strategies and factors associated with each type.

If Chapter four is the bridge between econometric analyses of industrial performance and studies of the strategies of individual firms, Chapter five takes us further into the territory of firm-level strategies. In this chapter Karlsson reports the results of his study of the start-up process of new, small, technology based companies in Sweden. His findings enable him to make a series of observations about the difficulties facing technical entrepreneurs and a set of recommendations for improving the chances of success for technology based small business start-ups. These recommendations span advice for the entrepreneurs themselves, advice to the business community trying to support them, and policy implications at industrial sector and societal levels.

Pettigrew is well-known for his detailed ethnographic researches into processes of organizational change. In Chapter six he and colleagues working with him on their research within the ESRC's Competitiveness Programme set out their approach to the study of strategic change and regeneration. They report on work they are undertaking in four industrial sectors, in each of which there are firms attempting to regain a competitive edge. A notable feature of this research is its attention not just to the content of change strategies but also to the social processes involved in the management of strategic change.

Chapters seven and eight also contain accounts of research being conducted under the ESRC initiative. Araujo and colleagues, authoring Chapter seven, comprise a multi-disciplinary team at the University of Lancaster. This multi-disciplinarity covers economics, marketing, and organizational behaviour. Rather than addressing themselves to the question of how competitiveness might be enhanced they have asked the prior question about the nature of the competitive process. By looking at the perceptions of competitors and customers in four industrial sectors of varying maturity they have developed a typology for this process. Sectors go through a life cycle, they suggest, beginning with firms in a particular sector belonging to what they term a community. They progress through an informal and then a more formal network, and end in a club-like relationship with each other. Araujo *et al.* illustrate each type from material from their study and deduce policy implications, one of which is to advocate a change in emphasis from 'industrial policy' to 'policies for industries'. These phrases are intended to signify the need for government to take note of the social organization of industry and intervene in more subtle and sophisticated ways.

3

Finally, in Chapter eight, Ray and colleagues deal at length and in depth with the implications for competitiveness of technical change. Building on Schumpeter and Nelson and Winter they develop a model built upon the evolutionary nature of technical change which aims to explain the process by which firms give economic weight to technical developments. They then test this model by applying it to the first three of ten technological advances they are studying. The technological trajectories of carbonless copy paper, home computers, and optical fibres are traced and firms' strategies in each of these sectors are analysed.

As Fröhlich observes in Chapter two, back in the 1950s and 1960s economists did not care much about a country's international competitiveness. This applies *a fortiori* to other social scientists, and even within the business schools those concerned with business policy limited themselves to the consideration of factors influencing a single company's economic performance. By the mid-1980s the position had changed radically. Improving competitiveness was an exhortation on nearly everyone's lips, but, as Fröhlich again observed, economists were not particularly well equipped to provide advice on how this should be done. Nor were those from other disciplines. The issue is now beginning to be tackled in a systematic way and it is our hope that this volume will make its own contribution to the development of our understanding of this process.

Chapter one

The concept of competitiveness

Arthur Francis

Introduction

In the early 1980s, after the second oil price shock, the USA and many European countries were greatly concerned about the competitiveness of their national economies. Official concern showed itself in the UK in the Report of the House of Lords Select Committee on Overseas Trade (HMSO 1985) and in the same year there was published in the USA the Report of the President's Commission on Industrial Competitiveness (US GPO 1985). The previous year the Brookings Institution had published Robert Lawrence's study *Can America Compete?* (Lawrence 1984). Mirroring the concern, the Economic and Social Research Council (ESRC) in the UK launched in 1985 a programme of research, of which the present author is Co-ordinator, on the competitiveness and regeneration of UK industry. Though worries about the competitiveness of British industry receded somewhat over the next three years in the face of record growth in productivity and output, the dramatic turnaround, indeed substantial deficit, of the UK overseas trade balance in 1988 has re-awakened the fears which were rife in the early 1980s.

However, what is meant by the competitiveness of the industry of a particular national economy, how it might be measured, and the extent to which lack of competitiveness poses a problem, are matters about which there is much less clarity and agreement than might at first be supposed. This chapter is an attempt to set out some of the current confusions and suggest some ways forward.

Why an interest in competitiveness?

One type of interest in the question of competitiveness at the level of the national economy (rather than at individual firm level) is that which has been expressed by economists over a long period,

5

namely the restricted question of price competitiveness. The variables usually taken to have a significant effect on price competitiveness are money wages, productivity, and the exchange rate. These can be combined to give an index of real efficiency wages (movements in money wages corrected for changes in labour productivity and the exchange rate) and hence movements in one country's competitive position versus others can be measured. It should be noted, however, that this measure only enables one to say whether any one country has become more or less competitive and does not enable one to evaluate an appropriate level of competitiveness. Similarly, changes in relative output prices, corrected for exchange rate movements, can be charted to give a broader measure of changes in price competitiveness.

Using these two measures it is possible to sound the alarm that any one country is becoming less competitive because of increasing labour costs or increasing prices. The former was of considerable concern in the UK in the period 1977–81 when relative unit labour costs rose by over 50 per cent (HMSO 1985: 29). They have since fallen back to 30 per cent above the 1977 figure. Price competitiveness fell in this same earlier period, and then rose again after 1981 (HMSO 1985: 29), but the fluctuations have not been so great as in the labour cost movements, presumably because profit margins were cut and then expanded.

Economists have also introduced the notion of non-price competitiveness as a way of coping with the fact that much international trade is in differentiated products (and services). Competition between such goods is not solely on the basis of price but on characteristics of the goods themselves, or the after-sales service associated with them. The notion, as usually formulated, is as described in Morris: 'Non-price competition may be just as important as price competition in determining the trade successes of a particular economy. Attention to product specification and quality, the marketing of a product, and the provision of a service can become the decisive features rather than price' (1985: 481). This seems a rather unsatisfactory way of expressing the matter. If one product is more competitive than another in non-price terms, this means that it is generally recognized that the more competitive product has a better specification, higher quality, more effective marketing, and/or more service provided with it than the less competitive product. Presumably the customer can put a price on each of these things, and the market place for many goods is filled with a range of differentiated products offering a variety of levels of quality at a range of market-clearing prices. The presumption underlying the concept of non-price competitiveness appears to be

6

that improvements to the less competitive product could be made at costs that would yield super-normal profits. (I am indebted to Paul Seabright for clarifying my mind on this point.) In other words, reasons for poorer quality and specification are more to do with incompetence and laziness rather than a sensible pitching of the product at the lower-quality end of the market place. The classic example of the non-price uncompetitive British good is, of course, the automobile, but it is difficult to find convincing evidence that this example is anything other than the result of the generally higher efficiency of the Japanese car industry.

A valuable research project, in my view, would be to attempt to assess the extent to which so-called non-price uncompetitiveness did have this market-failure characteristic, and, if the phenomenon is widespread, to establish why firms were not engaging in the cost-effective strategy of upgrading these non-price factors.

The other major source of interest in the competitiveness of particular national economies is rather less precisely formulated, and seems to stem more from a generalized fear that that nation is losing out to her international trading partners than from particular indicators. Such concern has found focus in the USA in the President's Commission on Industrial Competitiveness (US GPO 1985), in Britain in the House of Lords Select Committee on Overseas Trade (HMSO 1985), and in Europe in growing support for a more protectionist external trade policy (a policy subjected to critical review by Pearce *et al.* 1985). The one major trading nation apparently not involved in government level enquiries about national competitiveness is, of course, the source of much of this western concern, namely Japan.

Both the Report of the President's Commission and the House of Lords Select Committee Report (the Aldington Report, so named after the Committee chairperson) indicate general worries about the role of each respective nation in the world rather than specific worries based on economic indicators. The Presidential Report begins by noting that

the United States, which once dominated most major aspects of the world economy, is now a nation that must compete ... An internationally competitive US economy is a prerequisite for the national goals to which we aspire – a rising standard of living for all Americans, our position as leader of the free world, and our national security. (US GPO 1985: 5).

The Aldington Report's preoccupation was with 'the mounting deficit in the United Kingdom's balance of trade in manufactures' (HMSO 1985: 5) and concluded that

'British people must recognize that success in manufacturing and trade is the sine qua non both of their happiness and prosperity as individuals and of collective harmony and stability of the nation and its institutions. This calls for a fundamental change of attitude from all sections of society followed by a national effort of will to apply the creed in daily life' (HMSO 1985: 57).

The allegedly grave nature of Britain's economic position was graphically described by Lord Kearton, one of the Select Committee members, when interviewed on television on the day the Report was published. Britain was, he declared, on a slippery slope, held back from the abyss only by the drag anchor of North Sea oil.

Related concerns in Britain have been with the relatively slow growth of the UK economy (see, for example, Beckerman 1979), with de-industrialization (Blackaby 1978), and with the rate of innovation in Britain (Pavitt 1980, Carter 1981), and a commonly-held view has been that a lack of international competitiveness has been a major cause of slow growth and de-industrialization of the domestic economy. The slow growth has been deplored on several grounds – that it is denying feasible prosperity to the nation; that it makes it more difficult to sustain desirable levels of social welfare expenditure; and, perhaps most importantly, that it may lead to the economy spiralling downwards in a vicious circle in which slow growth results in a failure to have available the capital for investment in new process equipment and in innovation, with such investment failure further slowing down the growth rate.

Definitions of competitiveness

Virtually all of the debate about the competitiveness of national economies has been conducted using measures of competitiveness rather than definitions. Two such measures, price competitiveness and real efficiency wages, we have already mentioned. These are direct measures of the process of competition itself and are precise, though limited. The two major limits, as already noted, are that they only measure changes and not levels, and that they are alleged to neglect non-price factors.

As a result, a variety of alternative statistics, attempting to measure the output, or result, of the competitive process, have been suggested.

One very frequently used measure of this kind is the decline in a country's share in world trade. The Aldington Report, for example, shows that the UK share of world manufactures has dropped from

14.2 per cent in 1964 to 7.9 per cent by 1983, and Brown and Sheriff (1978) show that the UK share was 25.5 per cent in 1950. The US Presidential Commission reported that the US share of world trade in manufactured goods, measured in terms of value, had declined for more than two decades and, 'more disturbingly', that the US share of high-technology exports also declined between 1960 and 1980 (US GPO 1985: 14).

A second frequently used statistic in this debate is the rise in import penetration of manufactured goods. The very first chart in the Aldington Report shows that manufactured exports as a percentage of imports in the UK fell from just over 220 per cent in 1963 to under 90 per cent by 1984. The US Commission takes a similarly serious view about the growing US trade deficit in manufactured goods (US GPO 1985: 14, 33).

However, loss of share in world markets is an unsatisfactory measure of a lack of competitiveness of any one country's industry for a number of reasons. Indeed Harrod (1967) described this measure as 'surely the most absurd ever perpetrated in a diagnosis', adding that 'the British share of world export has declined, is declining and will continue to decline, hopefully at an accelerated pace' (quoted in Thirwall 1982: 238).

As Thirwall says, 'The health of the balance of payments depends on the relation between the absolute level of exports and imports associated with a given growth rate, not on the growth of exports relative to the growth of total world exports.' (op. cit.: 238). On this view the position of both Britain and the USA is still healthy and much, if not all, of the reason for their declining shares in world markets can be explained in terms of the increasing internationalization of world trade and relative growth rates of GDPs.

Britain, for example, has over a very long period had a more open economy than most of the industrialized countries with which she is currently compared. Over the last decade, for example, the proportion of Britain's GDP going to export has been steady at 25–30 per cent. This is higher than Italy (23–5 per cent), France (19–24 per cent), Japan (12–15 per cent), and the USA (7–10 per cent), and has only just been overtaken by West Germany (up from 26 per cent to 31 per cent over the decade). All these figures are approximate and taken from NEDC (1985). Equivalent comparative figures are not given in the more recent 1987 edition of this survey.

Though Britain has maintained a high level of exports, the effect of other countries becoming more international in their trade patterns (i.e. importing and exporting a higher percentage of their

GDP) has increased the volume of world trade and hence, by simple arithmetic, reduced Britain's share of it, even though the volume of Britain's exports has kept up to its historically high level.

A second reason for an increase in the volume of world trade has been the emergence of the newly industrializing countries. Even if these countries simply add to the volume of economic activity and world trade, and do not steal the markets of established industrialized countries, the effect of these new entrants will be to reduce the market share (though not necessarily the absolute market size) of those already trading internationally. A reduction in market share caused by either of these two factors is the likely result of a process that is to be welcomed as it increases the welfare of all trading countries.

A third contributing factor to the British and US falls in their shares of world markets has been the slower growth of the UK and US economies compared to that of their trading partners. If exports as a percentage of total GDP remain steady for all countries then those countries with a slower growth rate will lose market share pro rata with their relative growth rate. Falling share of world markets may thus be due merely to slow growth rather than uncompetitiveness. Some other measure of uncompetitiveness is needed to establish the extent to which slow growth is itself caused by a lack of competitiveness.

The rise in import penetration of manufactured goods as an output measure of lack of competitiveness is equally controversial. As the Aldington Report shows, imports of manufactures to the UK have almost trebled in volume since 1972, but it can be argued that there are at least three reasons for this increased import penetration, other than a lack of competitiveness. First, imports are likely to rise in volume due to economic growth and growth in the internationalization of world trade. Indeed, during the first half of the period shown in the Aldington Report's graph the rise in volume of UK exports of manufactures was as steep as that of imports. Second, a relatively high percentage of UK imports in the past were food and raw materials. If the income elasticity of demand for these is lower than that for more sophisticated items then one would expect, as GNP rose, an increase in the proportion of manufactures in total imports. Thus the rise in the volume of imports of manufactures is likely to be higher than the rise in the volume of imports overall.

A third reason for the increased volume of manufactured imports to the UK is, of course, North Sea oil. The UK government might have had both the power and the will to run a current account balance of payments surplus equivalent in value to the output of North Sea oil, in which case it would most likely have run a capital account deficit in much the way Japan is currently doing. However, this is not the only, or even the most obvious, policy choice for government to have made. The alternative would have been to choose to balance the current account at a higher exchange rate, in which case the export of North Sea oil would be balanced by a corresponding rise in imports. The most optimistic economic scenario for the impact of North Sea oil might have been one in which, with highly competitive UK exports, the medium-term outcome in terms of international trade would have balanced out at this higher exchange rate, with no diminution in manufacturing output or exports, and a higher GDP, possibly with a higher level of savings against the day when the oil runs out. But even on this view the net balance on the balance of payments current account implies a substantial rise in the volume of imports.

Instead, the current account has balanced out at a lower level of the exchange rate at a correspondingly lower level of GDP and an absolutely lower level of manufacturing output. The extra income from North Sea oil has been used to buy imports rather than continue manufacturing at home. To some extent this outcome is the result of government policy about the exchange rate and the money supply rather than an underlying uncompetitiveness of UK industry, a view that is supported by the second graph in the Select Committee's report which shows the rate of growth of imports to be balanced by that of exports until 1977. The acceleration in the growth of imports began to show through in the figures the year after the oil balance began to rise (HMSO, 1985: Figs 2.2, 2.6).

That manufacturing import penetration as a measure of lack of competitiveness is a matter of deep controversy was demonstrated in the columns of the *Financial Times*, when an article by Geoffrey Maynard, Director of Economics at Chase Manhattan Bank, entitled 'The UK's manufacturing deficit doesn't matter', (January 29 1986) led to a nearly month-long debate in the Correspondence columns.

A more sophisticated argument advanced in explanation of the UK's alleged lack of competitiveness is the so-called balance of payments constraint due to the non-price uncompetitiveness of UK produced goods and services. The argument was originally put by Kaldor, and has since been developed by Stout (1978) and Thirwall (1982). The suggestion is that, because of non-price factors, the income elasticity of demand in the UK for imports is relatively high, and the world income elasticity of demand for UK exports is relatively low. Thus with any expansion either of world

11

trade or of the UK economy, imports are sucked in faster than exports can be increased, that the exchange rate can not be adjusted enough to correct for this and so the UK develops a balance of payments crisis which stops further growth. The difficulty with this argument is the unsatisfactory nature of the supporting data. Thirwall, though arguing this position in the latter part of his book, suggests in the earlier chapters that the UK balance of payments crises in the 1960s and 1970s were due to such factors as Britain's position in the world's financial markets, sterling's role as a reserve currency, and government economic management rather than an underlying lack of competitiveness in trade. Moreover the data he provides, as opposed to his text, on income elasticity of import demand for the UK show that the UK ranks rather low among our major competitors, with a lower propensity for imports than West Germany, France, or Italy, and the same as the USA (Thirwall 1982: 256). He does not provide direct data on export elasticities but sets up an equation using percentage growth in exports as the measure. Britain's relatively poor showing on this can be accounted for in some measure by the high base point from which the UK started compared especially to the other European countries in the immediate post-war period.

Stout's data are rather more persuasive, particularly on the import side, where he shows a particularly steep curve of rise in imports of manufacturers against growth in GDP for the UK for the period 1968–76, compared to the 1951–73 period examined by Thirwall. However, this is a rather short period, and it is only for manufactures, and a shift from manufactures to services was occurring in the overall pattern of imports, exports, and patterns of UK domestic consumption. Stout's data on exports, in which he does not distinguish between manufactures and others, are less persuasive. Unlike his analysis of imports he does not present regression equations or R values and the graphs are much less tidy. Moreover the data are in terms of percentage growth in export volume and so the UK suffers from the same problem as that in Thirwall's analysis, viz. that it starts from a higher base of exports than the comparative countries.

A fourth suggested measure of UK and US uncompetitiveness is the declining percentage of domestic economic activity in the manufacturing sector as a higher percentage of GDP has become devoted to services. In Britain this decline in manufacturing activity appears to have been particularly steep, though from a higher level than many other economies, and, partly because of slow growth in the UK economy, has led to an absolute, and not just relative, decline in manufacturing output. This has caused concern on three counts. One is that it has been suggested that services are much less tradeable than manufactures, and thus will not meet the balance of payments gap which will emerge as North Sea oil output declines. A second is that many services ride on the back of manufacturing industry (the Select Committee reports a figure of 20 per cent of service industry output having manufacturing industry as its customer, para. 73) so that a decline in manufacturing feeds through into the service sector. The third is also to do with the fact that a high percentage of manufacturers are traded and suggests that the rapid decline in UK manufactured output is the clearest symptom of the uncompetitiveness of UK industry (Prowse 1985).

Caveats may be entered to each of these arguments. Though services are less tradeable than manufactures they account for 45 per cent of GDP in the UK and if, as the Select Committee suggests, 20 per cent are tradeable overseas (para. 74), this implies a tradeable services sector of 9 per cent of GDP compared to manufactures share of 20 per cent of GDP (NEDC 1985). Moreover the services sector is rising, and has moved from a net deficit on balance of payments current account of £31m in 1963 to a surplus of £3,902m in 1983 (Select Committee: Fig. 2.5). The dependence of services on manufacturing does not necessarily imply that a decline in manufacturing will lead to a decline in services if, as appears to be the case, some of the decline in manufacturing is the result of this sector buying in more services rather than producing them for themselves. The third part of the above argument, that the decline in manufactures is the clearest symptom of the overall problem, rests on the assumption that there is an overall problem of competitiveness. If the figures are better interpreted in some of the alternative ways suggested here, then the demonstrator argument falls.

Not only may one disagree about the importance of a decline in the manufacturing sector, there is also room for debate about the relative size of the decline. Though the Aldington Report (p. 12) shows that, on the measure of value added in manufacturing as a percentage of GDP in the G5 countries (UK, W. Germany, France, USA and Japan) plus Italy, Britain now has the smallest manufacturing sector (at 21 per cent of GDP in 1983) and has had the largest fall (11.1 percentage points since 1960), the NEDC survey (1985: 7) shows that growth in services as a percentage of GDP in the period 1962–82 to be bigger in each of the other G5 countries than in the UK. The relatively steep decline in the percentage of GDP from manufacturing occurred in the 1972–82 decade and is entirely attributable to an increase in 'Other' activities. This category includes North Sea oil production, and therefore at least some of the 'decline' in manufacturing is the result of a net addition to GDP in this 'Other' sector. The NEDC survey comments (p. 6) that this shift from manufacturing reflects, to some extent, structural adjustment resulting from increased North Sea oil production, and notes that the share of total output represented by manufacturing is now similar to that in the USA (which is, of course, itself a very significant oil producer). Moreover a more comprehensive set of OECD statistics, in Seabright (n.d.), shows that there has been a relative decline in manufacturing production over the period 1975–83 (change in manufacturing production over this period divided by the change in GDP) in all 20 of the countries for which data are given; that although the UK has had the fifth most steep decline (0.745) the steepest was Norway (0.590), which is also a beneficiary of North Sea oil but, unlike the UK, had a massive rise in GDP of 61 per cent over the same period; and that the correlation between decline in manufacturing production (adjusted for GDP growth) and GDP itself is very small.

The final argument within the Aldington Report is the suggestion that output measures do not reveal the extent to which the UK is uncompetitive because this fundamental weakness has been disguised by the advent of North Sea oil. It is argued that, as that resource diminishes, the balance of payments gap which will open up has no chance of being filled by a resurgence of UK industry in its present form. Something has to be done now, while there is still time, to rejuvenate industry so that it is ready to meet the challenge.

There are a number of difficulties with this analysis. One is that it assumes that the oil has saved the UK balance of payments from a crisis that would otherwise have occurred, rather than viewing North Sea oil as the cause of the more rapid decline of the manufacturing sector. There are strong arguments in favour of this latter view. Another is that it assumes that it has to be manufacturing industry which has to fill the balance of payments gap. Debate over the ability of the services sector, which has been growing fast in Britain, to fill a large part of the gap continues. Third, it assumes that manufacturing industry will find it harder to expand to fill the gap de novo than it would have done if it had continued to operate at a high level of activity throughout the period of North Sea oil production. Arguments can be put forward in support of the view that it will be easier for new manufacturing capacity to emerge from out of the whirlwind of the 'creative destruction' of 1979–81 than for manufacturing industry to have adapted from its previous inefficient ways in a gradual way. The successful rapid growth of West German industry after the Second World War has often been attributed to the fact that it could start again from scratch. Many companies in the UK today favour moving to greenfield sites to begin new ventures. The speed with which modern manufacturing industry in the UK is capable of adjusting capacity upwards may be worth researching. Fourth, a difficulty with the Select Committee's view that something should be done about the regeneration of manufacturing industry ahead of time is that it presumes people know now what should be done. If the suggestion is that government should do something, then the old arguments about civil servants' ability to pick winners will come out of the drawer. Finally, the relatively small scale of the problem should be emphasized. The oil balance in overseas trade swung from a deficit of £4bn in 1976 to a surplus of £8bn in 1984 (Select Committee: Fig. 2.6). This implies that ultimately, when all North Sea supplies are exhausted, there has to be a net increase in exports of £12bn. Though this is a large sum it should be set in the context of a UK GDP of £275bn. Even if all these extra exports were generated by a direct switch from domestic consumption rather than through economic growth it would result only in a one-off 4 per cent reduction in standard of living. To replace all the oil element in the trade balance would require an 18 per cent increase in the volume of exports which, assuming a steady deterioration in the oil balance back to the status quo ante within the next 15 years, implies an annual growth rate in exports of less than 1 per cent compound. It is hard to see that this poses a problem in adjustment. If UK manufacturing exports have decreased simply as an adjustment to North Sea oil then there seems little reason to suppose that there cannot be a smooth adjustment back up again.

The Report of the President's Commission also has unsatisfactory definitions of competitiveness. Although it does argue that 'competitiveness cannot be defined as the ability of a nation to maintain a positive trade balance' (US GPO 1985: 7), an understandable position to adopt given the current US success in generating a fast rate of economic growth on the back of a very substantial trade deficit, and that 'competitiveness is also not assured or reflected by the ability to maintain and increase employment in the manufacturing sector', and it does recognize that even in highly competitive economies some industries will become unviable and be replaced by others, it fails to suggest satisfactory alternative measures. It begins with a definition of competitiveness at the level of the individual firm which, though perhaps familiar to business strategists, would be unrecognizable to many economists. 'A firm is competitive', the Report suggest (p. 6), 'if it can produce products or services of superior quality or lower costs than its domestic and international competitors. Competitiveness is then synonymous with a firm's long-run profit performance and its ability to compensate its employees and provide superior returns to its owners.' 'The definition of competitiveness for a nation', it goes on to suggest, 'must similarly be tied to its ability to generate the resources required to meet its national needs.' The Report rejects the notion that the concept can be captured by the single process measure of changes in the terms of trade, arguing (p. 31) that there are structural determinants of competitiveness that cannot be corrected simply by adjusting the value of the dollar. Instead, it is suggested that competitiveness is best measured by four key indicators: '(1) labour productivity, (2) real wage growth, (3) real returns on capital employed in industry, and (4) position in world trade' (p. 8).

The fundamental difficulty with the notion of competitiveness at the level of the national economy comes out most clearly in the US report, probably because it addresses itself centrally to the question of competitiveness, takes trouble to assess a variety of definitions and explanations, and presents its own definition. The Aldington Report, by contrast, begins by examining reasons for the UK deficit in the balance of trade in manufactures and pulls lack of competitiveness out of the hat as its main conclusion (p. 56). The fundamental difficulty is, in my view, the use of the concept at an inappropriate level of analysis.

In the classical economist's definition of the term, competition is a process whereby many producers attempt to sell a particular product to many buyers. The quantity of the good to be produced, and the price it is sold at, are given by the operation of the market. A firm is competitive if it is willing to accept the returns available from selling the good at the prevailing market price. Uncompetitive firms make inadequate returns and therefore are forced to withdraw from the market. Often they go bankrupt. Though every economist would acknowledge that this model of perfect competition is often far removed from the reality of the competitive process in the real world it is hard to avoid the suspicion that it is precisely this simple model of competition which is at the back of the minds of most of those who speak of the uncompetitiveness of a particular national economy. Much of the debate, in the UK anyway, seems to be driven by the fear that in the international competition for the bundle of goods each nation has on offer some countries will fail to sell enough, or have to sell at below cost price, and thus the country goes into a vicious spiral of decline and eventual national bankruptcy – Lord Kearton's abyss. In the USA

16

the concern seems to be with maintaining a world lead in the economic league table. Not nearly enough is heard, in this debate, about the long-established economic concept of comparative advantage. Indeed, so muddled is the debate that the US report even translates the term into the Porterian notion (Porter 1980) of competitive advantage. The argument about international trade might do better to begin with a discussion about national comparative advantages, how these are shifting, and whether they are reflected in the operation of the market (including exchange rate adjustments) before moving on to discussions about national competitiveness. Moreover, the argument should embrace the question of distinguishing between slow growth and competitiveness. At the same time the role played by relative levels of economic efficiency must be tackled. A relatively low level of efficiency in the use of any combination of factors of production may lead to slow growth, and slow growth may, as is often argued, be either the cause or result of a lack of competitiveness, but these three variables are not necessarily linked. How important this linkage is at the present time for particular countries needs to be demonstrated, but before that can be done a more precise concept of competitiveness must be agreed upon. The US Commission's definition has, it will be recalled, four elements. Three of these, labour productivity, real wage growth, and real returns on capital employed in industry, are actually measures of either efficiency or rate of growth rather than of competitiveness.

Conclusions

The purpose of the chapter has been to clear the ground rather than suggest an alternative set of concepts and measures. My conclusion is not that there is not a problem about the competitiveness of particular national economies but that with greater precision in our use of the concepts, and with more careful analysis, we might be able to distinguish between inefficiency, slow growth, and lack of competitiveness and thus develop a more appropriate set of policy responses. In particular, the distinction between slow growth and lack of competitiveness is of vital importance in its research and policy implications. To illustrate this I end the chapter by briefly running through four possible scenarios with regard to slow growth versus lack of competitiveness as explanations.

Four scenarios

1. That there is no problem of competitiveness. Slow growth is revealed preference. Markets are all working smoothly, though with a bit of friction, and so there are unpleasant transitional effects.

Relevant research would be to see what social mechanisms might smooth market mechanisms to reduce friction; what social welfare actions might be taken which would not unduly disturb market mechanisms – such actions should not lead to market signals being misread. Research might be needed to help establish what the market signals were, so that government action on the social welfare front or on the economic adjustment front, was in line with market signals.

2. There is a problem with slow growth, but not competitiveness. Slow growth is not revealed preference but the result of people not being able to exercise their preference for greater intensity of effort (for higher reward) for whatever reason. The more important examples of people being blocked from doing what they wanted would probably not be that of trade union based restrictive practices but, for example, highly qualified people being willing to go into industrial management provided the terms and conditions of employment were acceptable, but such positions not being available either because of a managerial old guard or family ownership control. Similarly, there may be a reduced flow of the well qualified into specialist occupations like engineering because of out-dated forms of work organization, career paths, and so on. Entrepreneurial opportunities may be blocked for lack of available risk capital, conservatism on the part of existing companies not being willing to buy new goods/services from unknown suppliers, etc.

Relevant research would seek to identify thwarted objectives for high effort intensity/high reward, and those institutional features which do the thwarting. One might alternatively identify an 'ecology of micro-motives' whereby situations were structured so that individuals were making choices which in the light of the information available to them were entirely rational, but the sum of those choices added up to macro-outcomes which no one desired.

3. There is a problem of competitiveness for UK industry but it is a transitional/adjustment problem. The argument would be the well-rehearsed one that Britain's social and economic structure has been inherited from an imperial past and from being an early industrializer. The disappearance of those conditions only became a problem in the 1960s after the Empire had been disbanded, the post-war boom was beginning to run out, and trade was becoming much more intensively internationalized. Nevertheless much of the necessary restructuring has been going on for some time, more is going on now, the oil price shocks of the 1970s and the advent of North Sea oil in the late 1970s have disguised much of the great improvement that has been occurring (more professional management, degree-level engineers in more senior positions, internationalization of UK firms, rationalization of much UK production, closer links between banks and industry, phasing out of much third and fourth generation family ownership, closing down of old industrial sectors where the UK has lost any comparative advantage and emergence of new sectors in high technology and the services sector). What is necessary is for this task of re-construction to be speeded along.

Relevant research would be to identify where reconstruction is still needed, and to evaluate changes already made, recognizing that any one country's economic and social conditions are unique and that this process of adaptation should not follow slavishly the path taken by others. In other words, Japanese (and US) experience are not enough to guide UK practice.

4. There is a crisis now. We are, as Lord Kearton has said, on the slippery slope. Urgent action to restructure industry so that it can become more competitive should be a national priority.

Relevant research would be to indentify what that action should be and how it can best be taken. The point made in 3 above would stand, viz. that the UK situation is unique and solutions have to be found which take account of British cultural and institutional factors, and therefore there should be research which, while taking account of, for example, the Japanese experience, seeks to indentify what the uniquely British solutions might be. If the situation is as outlined in 4 then one might expect substantial government intervention and redirection of national resources.

The implications of each of these four scenarios for research and action are so different that it seems to me essential that some effort should go into attempting to establish which scenario is the most credible: hence this exercise in attempting to clarify some conceptual and measurement confusions.

References

Beckerman, W. (ed.) (1979) *Slow Growth in Britain: Causes and Consequences*, Oxford: Clarendon Press.

Blackaby, F. (ed.) (1978) *De-industrialisation*, London: Heinemann.

Brown, C. and Sheriff, T. D. (1978) 'De-industrialisation: a background paper', in F. Blackaby (ed.) (1978) *De-industrialisation*, London: Heinemann.

Carter, C. (ed.) (1981) *Industrial Policy and Innovation*, London: Heinemann.

Harrod, R. (1967) 'Assessing the trade returns', *Economic Journal*, September.

HMSO (1985) *Report from the Select Committee of the House of Lords on Overseas Trade*, the Aldington Report.

Lawrence, R. Z. (1984) *Can America Compete?* Washington, DC: The Brookings Institute.

Maddison, A. (1979) 'Long run dynamics of productivity growth', in W. Beckerman (ed.) (1979) *Slow Growth in Britain: Causes and Consequences*, Oxford: Clarendon Press.

Morris, D. (ed.) (1985) *The Economic System in the UK* (3rd edn), Oxford: Oxford University Press.

NEDC (1985) 'British industrial performance', London: NEDC.

Nossiter, B. D. (1978) *Britain: A Future that Works*, London: Andre Deutsch.

Pavitt, K. (ed.) (1980) *Technical Innovation and British Economic Performance*, London: Macmillan.

Pearce, J. and Sutton J. with Batchelor, R. (1985) *Protection and Industry Policy in Europe*, London: Routledge & Kegan Paul.

Porter, M. E. (1980) *Competitive Strategy*, New York: Free Press.

Prowse, M. (1985) 'Why services may be no substitute for manufacturing', *Financial Times*, 25 October.

Seabright, P. 'The future of manufacturing industry in the medium term', unpublished paper, All Souls, Oxford.

Stout, D. K. (1978) 'De-industrialisation and industrial policy', in F. Blackaby (ed.) (1978), *Re-industrialisation*, London: Heinemann.

Thirwall, A. P. (1982) *Balance-of-Payments Theory and the United Kingdom Experience*, London: Macmillan.

US GPO (1985) *The Report of the President's Commission on Industrial Competitiveness: Vol. II Global Competition, The New Reality*, Washington DC: US Government Printing Office.

Williams, K., Williams, J. and Thomas, D. (1983) *Why Are the British Bad at Manufacturing?*, London: Routledge & Kegan Paul.

Chapter two

International competitiveness: alternative macroeconomic strategies and changing perceptions in recent years

Hans–Peter Fröhlich

Introduction

Back in the 1950s and 1960s economists did not care much about a country's international competitiveness. Those were the heydays of solid growth and full employment. With the advent of high unemployment rates in most industrialized economies, that has changed profoundly. Economists began to devote an increasing amount of professional attention to the ability of national economies to compete successfully in international markets. In fact, one of the standard pieces of advice economists give to policy makers nowadays is to improve the international competitiveness of their country's industries.

That is easier said than done. Economists are not particularly well equipped to deal with this issue. For one thing, standard economic textbooks provide no specific theories on how to tackle the problem. For another, matters of international competitiveness belong, to a large extent, to the realm of business economics. After all, the competitiveness of a country essentially is the competitiveness of its businesses. If they satisfy consumers' wants at home and abroad with attractive products and at low costs, the country as a whole will be competitive. Hence the main determinants of international competitiveness are such factors as management, engineering skills, labour force efficiency, and so on. Overall economic developments enter the scene only indirectly. Depending on the applied macroeconomic policies, policy makers can make it either harder or easier for domestic companies to face up to foreign competitors. Put differently, while economic policy cannot transform poor domestic products into hot-selling items abroad, it can make a great difference to whether or not a company which is successful at home can also be successful internationally.

Definitions and concepts

Even with those limitations in mind, the topic is not easy to treat. The reason is that the concept of 'international competitiveness' is rather fuzzy. A survey of the literature comes up with a wide variety of definitions. Some of them are overly general while others focus on specific aspects. The following definition by Bela Balassa (1964) may be regarded as something like a smallest common denominator:

> We can say that a country has become more or less competitive if, as a result of cost-and-price developments or other factors, her ability to sell on foreign and domestic markets has improved or deteriorated.

The problem with this definition is that it is hardly operational. In other words: which criterion can be used to measure a country's international competitiveness at any given point in time, or at least to determine whether its competitiveness has deteriorated or improved over time? Without a clear idea about such a yardstick it is virtually impossible to conclude whether there is a need for governmental action, nor is it possible to identify alternative economic strategies to improve a country's international competitiveness or to judge their relative merits. Unfortunately, there is no single economic indicator which is universally accepted as the best guide for policy actions.

It is often suggested that the current account balance be used as such a criterion. A current account deficit, for instance, indicates that the amount of goods and services which a country's residents buy abroad exceeds the amount they, in turn, sell to foreigners during the same period. Many observers interpret such trade deficits as indicators of a loss of international competitiveness – at least in case the deficit is not merely due to the country's relative business cycle position, but rather extends over a protracted period of time. There are, however, two serious objections to this view. First, even substantial and continuing current account imbalances may stem from quite different factors, i.e. exogeneous developments. Good cases in point are the two oil price shocks of the 1970s. While they pushed the current account of many industrial nations into deficit, they are obviously unrelated to changes in international competitiveness.

Second, current account deficits must also be looked upon from a different angle. From a flow-of-funds point of view they represent a net inflow of capital from abroad. This is tantamount to an excess of the economy's volume of investment over domestic saving. In other words, more investment opportunities can be exploited without the need to curtail domestic consumption in order to increase saving. Hence current account deficits may turn out to be extremely beneficial, provided that those investment projects are profitable enough to cover the interest payments on the foreign debt. As a matter of fact, economic history demonstrates that many successful economies displayed substantial current account deficits over long periods of time. Only thus were they able to exploit fully their growth potential. National economies are no different in this respect to individual businesses. Incurring debt is by no means a sign of poor competitiveness. On the contrary, every healthy business will borrow funds to finance profitable investment projects rather than to restrict investment to the amount of self-finance. So one should be sceptical of measuring a country's international competitiveness by merely looking at the state of her current account.

Another criterion which is often regarded as an indicator for international competitiveness is change in a country's share of world markets or world trade. Regardless of the state of the current account, the argument goes, this indicator provides a reliable measure of sales success. That is true enough; yet at times this indicator may be misleading too. An obvious example is an increase in the number of international competitors, such as the newly industrialized countries. If these newcomers succeed in seizing a considerable share of world markets, the share of traditional producers will inevitably fall, without that signalling a genuine loss of competitiveness. Similarly, a country may lose market shares simply because it is not able to meet world-wide demand due to lack of production capacity. The most serious drawback of market shares, however, is the fact that they are a mere quantity index. Consider a country whose industry is gaining additional market shares as a consequence of slashing prices. If these price cuts squeeze profit margins, it is clearly not justified to regard this country as more competitive than before.

An alternative would be to look at price changes over time. Like in the case of an individual producer, the sales performance of a national economy depends, to a large extent, on its ability to satisfy demand at low prices. In order to make sensible comparisons internationally, one will obviously have to look at relative price movements in a common currency. In other words, exchange-rate changes will also have to be taken into account. One possibility is to look at relative national price movements, adjusted for exchange-rate variations. Another possibility is to reverse this procedure by looking at exchange-rate movements adjusted for differences in national price-level changes. This is tantamount to calculating 'real exchange rates' which are published regularly by a number of national and international institutions. They, too, are often used to evaluate changes in a country's international competitiveness. If the nominal exchange rate moves in such a way as to compensate inflation differences, the real exchange rate, and hence the international competitiveness, remains unchanged. By contrast, if a currency is devalued in real terms, the competitiveness of that country's industry improves, and vice versa. But this index, too, can give wrong signals, namely, if producers are not able to pass on cost increases to the consumer (e.g. due to government controls or fierce competition). The resulting loss of competitiveness is not reflected by real exchange rates.

After all that has been said so far, the ideal yardstick would be an index to measure changes of relative production costs internationally. Much to the economist's regret, such an index does not exist. Even for the industrial countries it is not possible to collect the relevant data. For all practical purposes, however, it will suffice to restrict the analysis to labour costs. The reason is that wages are the single most important cost component. (In Germany, they account for about 50 per cent of total production costs.) Note that in this context the term 'production costs' must be interpreted as per unit costs. After all, a rise in total production costs has no negative impact on competitiveness as long as physical output growth exceeds the increase in production costs. Hence in addition to changes in wages and exchange rates, variations in productivity must also be taken into account.

According to this criterion,

– the lower the level of nominal wages,
– the lower the external value of the currency,
– the faster the increase in productivity,

the greater will be the international competitiveness of the country's industry. By the same token, a country which has fallen behind in competitiveness must necessarily take steps to improve one or all of these factors. From that it follows that policy makers basically have three options:

– to lower wages
– to devalue the currency
– to raise productivity.

While all of these options are designed to improve a country's international competitiveness, they entail quite different costs and benefits.

Alternative macroeconomic strategies

Low-wage strategy

The first option is to lower nominal wages while leaving productivity and exchange rates basically unchanged. That is equivalent to a direct fall in production costs which will lead to higher sales volumes without lowering profit margins. Although this is clearly a feasible solution in theory, it is almost impossible in reality – at least in Western Europe. No policy maker will be able to persuade his electorate to compete internationally on the basis of low wages. The resulting fall in the standard of living simply is not acceptable. But even if it were acceptable, it would not be desirable. There are many countries – in fact, the majority of countries in the world – which have no choice but to earn their income based on low wage rates. A low-wage strategy in Western Europe does not make any sense in terms of international comparative advantages. It could adversely affect the international division of labour, thus impeding the development process in much of the Third World.

It is important to note that these remarks only refer to a strategy aimed at improving the international competitiveness by lowering nominal wages. Wage restraint in the sense of productivity-oriented wage increases is quite a different story. This point will be discussed in more detail below.

Devaluation strategy

By devaluing the home currency a country's industry is able to sell its products in foreign markets at lower prices. At the same time, sales in the domestic market will be facilitated because the price of foreign goods in terms of domestic currency goes up. In addition, this two-fold effect can be accomplished seemingly without much pain or sacrifice. All it takes – in the case of fixed exchange rates – is a formal notice by the government or the central bank; or – in the case of flexible exchange rates – some official statement which can reasonably be expected to cause a devaluation of that currency in the international money markets. Owing to those advantages, the devaluation strategy is most appealing to many policy makers around the world. In fact, it has adequately been referred to as a 'classical' instrument of economic policy. Governments made use of it routinely between the First and Second World Wars as they sought to provide their industries with an edge in competitiveness during the Great Depression.

It was also in those days when the term 'beggar-thy-neighbour' policy was coined, which hints to an important aspect of

25

devaluation: by devaluing the domestic currency, a country can improve its international competitiveness only at the expense of its trading partners. In all likelihood they will not be willing to tolerate such a strategy indefinitely. Instead, they will take appropriate steps to counteract that move, either by barring the devaluing country's industry from their markets by protectionist measures, or by devaluing in turn, thus re-establishing the original set of conditions.

But it is not only those international feedback effects which cast a dark shadow on the devaluation strategy. Even more important is the fact that it poses grave economic dangers domestically as well. The core of the problem is that devaluation implies a worsening of the terms of trade: domestic residents must pay a higher price for imports in terms of real goods, while sales abroad fetch a lower price, again in terms of real goods. The deterioration in the terms of trade is tantamount to a direct reduction in real incomes. The government is thus faced with a genuine dilemma. It either forces the population to accept the loss of real income, or it tries to reduce that burden through accommodating wage and incomes policies at home. In the first case there will be widespread discontent or even rebellion by the electorate. If the government sticks to its policies none the less, this will normally mean political suicide. In the second case, where domestic incomes and monetary policies are used to cushion the impact of the terms of trade deterioration, price increases throughout the economy will inevitably follow suit. Inflation at home will thus eat up the edge in international competitiveness which devaluation was originally meant to bring about.

One has to be even more sceptical about the devaluation strategy when the likely reactions of the international financial markets are properly taken into account. Empirical data suggest that immediately after devaluation, there is often an inflow of capital from abroad into that country. But this is only a short-lived phenomenon, representing a repatriation of capital which was previously transferred abroad in anticipation of impending devaluation. In the medium and long run, by contrast, capital must be expected to flow out of the country – unless exchange-rate expectations of market participants are highly stable. In the latter case devaluation will induce expectations of future currency appreciation, thus rendering financial investment in that country attractive.

Experience shows that this is an extremely unlikely case. More often than not, the opposite is true: devaluation is interpreted by international market participants as a sign of weakness of the country's government. Rather than making determined efforts to improve the international competitiveness of domestic industries, the government merely postpones the internal adjustment process, thus eventually creating even bigger problems. As a result, capital will leave the country in search of a safe haven abroad; the exchange rate will be pushed down even further. Under these circumstances, interest rates will have to be raised, or the exchange rate will have to drop to such low levels where expectations of appreciation will finally be brought about. The resulting inflationary impact lowers the country's international competitiveness thus rendering necessary another devaluation before too long. This is the well-known 'vicious circle' process where devaluation and inflation are feeding upon each other. The lesson of the past decade or so is that countries find it extremely difficult to overcome their economic problems once they have been caught in that vicious circle. At some point they will eventually have to adopt the third strategy mentioned above, i.e. to gear their efforts towards speeding up productivity growth.

Innovation strategy

This approach to improving a country's international competitiveness is different from both the low-wage strategy and the devaluation strategy in several respects. Whereas the latter are aimed at rendering domestic products in foreign markets cheaper, the innovation strategy aims at making them better. Typical elements of this strategy are, for example

- improvement in quality standards
- development of new products and production processes
- adoption of modern technology, etc.

An indispensable prerequisite for this strategy is a high degree of technological know-how and innovation potential, as well as flexibility and productive efficiency on the part of both a company's management and work force.

To adopt the innovation strategy is to rely on one's own strength rather than on the weakness of others. This is an offensive strategy. A country with an edge in international competitiveness resulting from product and process innovation does not negatively affect its trading partners. In this case, international trade is not a zero-sum-game in which one country can gain only at the expense of others. By increasing productivity in a country, more production is profitable, and hence incomes grow. Growing incomes, in turn, stimulate import demand. Through this channel the benefits of the innovation strategy will spill over to other countries as well.

In addition, the edge in competitiveness can be expected to serve as an incentive abroad, to the effect that there, too, efforts will be made to spur productivity growth. The end result of this process is more production and higher real incomes in all countries.

Note that the source of income growth here is an autonomous increase in productivity. In the real world, the chain of causality is often reversed: workers demand higher wages and as a consequence, employers are forced to step up productivity by substituting capital for labour. In this case, productivity growth is induced, namely by a change in relative factor prices. A mere glance at the statistics in retrospect will hardly tell the difference. In both cases, productivity and wages are up. With respect to international competitiveness both developments are basically equivalent. There is, however, a substantial difference with regard to the impact on the labour market. In the first case where productivity growth takes the lead, employment will tend to rise because overall output goes up. In the second case where productivity rises as capital is substituted for labour, employment will obviously tend to decrease. It goes without saying that only the first type of innovation strategy can be a desirable course of events.

Occasionally, some critics who doubt that innovation and productivity growth is the most promising way of improving a country's international competitiveness raise their voices. Paradoxically enough, it is precisely this strategy's good chance of success which makes them sceptical. Investors all over the world, so the thinking goes, will appreciate the vigour and determination of a country pursuing the innovation strategy. They will be eager to invest their funds in that country. In the process, the external value of that currency will be pushed up to the effect that domestic goods become more expensive on international markets. According to those critics, the competitive edge which was brought about with much effort by means of productivity growth will thus be offset by currency appreciation.

Indeed, this sequence of events cannot be ruled out. In the long run, it is even highly probable. However, there is no reason to be as pessimistic as these critics. In fact, their negative judgement seems to turn things upside down. Someone to whom potential creditors are eager to lend money because they think he can make better use of it than they can themselves, has no reason for complaining. That is true for individuals as well as for national economies, even under flexible exchange rates. If foreign investors rush to place their funds in a particular country, they force down interest rates. This is clearly a most beneficial effect, as low interest rates stimulate investment, growth and employment. The appreciation of the currency which goes hand in hand with capital inflows also entails some very positive aspects. One is that appreciation lowers the domestic price of imported goods. That holds down costs and prices, and hence tends to improve the country's international competitiveness. The other positive aspect is that appreciation is equivalent to an improvement in the international terms of trade, which corresponds to a direct increase in real incomes for the country's residents.

So in the final analysis, capital inflows and currency appreciation are far from being a counter-productive side-effect of the innovation strategy. The truth of the matter rather is that, due to those secondary developments, the fruits of increased efforts to raise production in the export sector will be spread throughout the economy. The innovation strategy indeed seems to be the only viable macroeconomic approach to improving the international competitiveness of a country's industry. There are numerous indications that policy-makers in most industrialized nations now share this view.

Recent experience in major European countries

Against this purely theoretical backdrop, it is instructive to look at the economic experience of the major European economies during the 1970s and 1980s. Figure 2.1 shows the behaviour of relative unit labour costs for the UK, France and the Federal Republic of Germany since 1970.

Except for the steep increase in unit labour costs in the UK towards the end of the 1970s, the time path of unit labour costs is strikingly similar in all three countries. At least there are no fundamental discrepancies. It is also worth mentioning that at the end of 1984 (the last year for which comparable data are available), unit labour costs in these countries were fairly close to their original level in 1970. In other words, these time series give the impression of close national similarities and relative stability over time. However, a more detailed analysis of the various determinants of relative unit labour costs, i.e. nominal wages, productivity and exchange rates, detects considerable national differences between the three countries.

United Kingdom

The state of the UK economy has often been described by the term 'British sickness'. The core of the problem is sluggish growth in productivity. In 1980, for instance, output per hour was up 30 per

The competitiveness of European industry

Figure 2.1 Relative unit labour costs (Indices 1970 = 100)

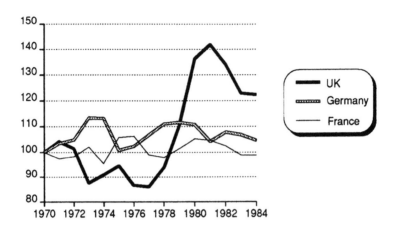

Source: OECD Economic Outlook

cent in comparison with 1970. By contrast, during the same period productivity rose by 55 per cent in Germany, and even by more than 60 per cent in France. Numerous arguments have been put forward to explain the poor UK performance. Some observers suggest that the management of British companies may be less successful in developing new products and applying modern technologies. Another factor may be social relations in British industry. Traditionally, there has often been more confrontation than cooperation between management and labour representatives, as is documented by the high amount of working days lost due to strikes. A third reason is government interference to the effect that many companies were at least partially protected from the cruel though beneficial forces of normal economic life: some ailing companies like British Leyland and Rolls Royce were nationalized, while subsidies in one form or another were given to virtually all industries. It stands to reason that this kind of economic policy hampers microeconomic efficiency and macroeconomic productivity.

Still, in spite of the poor productivity performance, British unit labour costs in terms of foreign currency did not go up for a long while. In fact, they actually declined somewhat until 1977. The reason is that the British pound fell sharply in international currency markets. Between 1970 and 1977 the pound lost more than one–third of its external value. In this respect the UK may be

30

considered to be a typical representative of countries pursuing the devaluation strategy in order to stay internationally competitive.

At least partially in response to the pound's fall, prices began to rise sharply. During the 1970s inflation in the UK was well above the average of all industrialized countries. Combined with low productivity, that implied modest, or sometimes even negative growth in real incomes. The resulting discontent amongst workers led to double-digit wage increases in the late 1970s. For instance, hourly compensation in manufacturing went up by 16 per cent annually between 1975 and 1980. Those wages increases were particularly disastrous for UK industries because beginning in 1977, the pound appreciated markedly as British exports of North Sea oil exerted a positive impact on the balance of payments. In 1981, relative UK unit labour costs were 65 per cent higher than in 1977. By that time they were 35 per cent above the corresponding figures for France and Germany, whereas four years earlier, they were 15 per cent below the French and German levels. The deterioration in the international competitiveness of British industries is also reflected in the volume of exports (excluding oil): from 1977 to 1980 exports of the manufacturing sector were almost constant (after 1980 they actually declined for three years).

Such was the state of the UK economy when the new government of Prime Minister Margaret Thatcher assumed power in 1979. She was determined to reverse those negative trends and to improve the international competitiveness of British industry. To this end, she focused on three policy priorities: first, drastically lowering the rate of inflation by strict control of the money supply process; second, redressing the government sector by reducing both public spending and budget deficits; third, revitalizing the private sector by improving supply-side conditions. A variety of steps was taken to this end, such as gradual shift from taxes on income towards taxes on spending, or a reduction in the top rate on earned income from 83 per cent to 60 per cent. Another important step was the move to reprivatize some previously state-owned companies like British Petroleum, Jaguar and British Telecom.

Those policies required painful domestic adjustment. Unfortunately, that process coincided with the beginning of the 1980–82 world recession. As a consequence, Britain suffered more than most other industrialized countries during those years. In particular, unemployment in the UK by far exceeded the levels of France and Germany (13 per cent versus 10 and 9 per cent respectively). By now, however, the situation has improved greatly: inflation is running at less than 5 per cent and productivity is rising more rapidly. The biggest problem is still unemployment, which is aggravated by excessive increases in real wages, as the OECD pointed out. A most recent problem is the fall in oil prices. As a result, the external value of the pound goes down in anticipation of a worsening of the balance of payments. This is one of the reasons why the government still hesitates to firmly peg the British pound to the EMS currencies. That strategy may well backfire, though. Fixing the pound's exchange rate is certainly painful, but by doing so the government could send a clear message to the international financial community that it no longer considers the devaluation strategy a viable policy option. The potential benefits should be worth it.

France

In many respects, France's economic problems were similar to those of Britain. Still, there are marked differences. As to the franc's effective exchange rate, there were no major changes up until 1976. France's productivity performance was also superior to Britain's, achieving approximately the same growth rates in output per hour as did West Germany.

During the second half of the 1970s, things turned worse. Inflation hovered at or above the 9 per cent mark. The government tried to offset the resulting deterioration in international competitiveness by devaluing the franc, i.e. by cancelling its commitment to co-operate under the European currency 'snake' arrangement. By looking at the franc's effective exchange rate, this devaluation cannot be fully appreciated due to the simultaneous decline of the US dollar. But a look at the franc/DM rate tells a different story. *Vis-à-vis* the D-mark, the franc lost more than one fourth of its value between 1975 and 1980. Yet in spite of this large devaluation, the international competitiveness of French industry as measured by relative unit labour costs hardly improved at all. On the contrary, devaluation fuelled price inflation thus providing an additional negative impact.

Those economic difficulties were one of the major reasons why the French electorate voted the left-wing coalition of socialists and communists into office in 1981. From the beginning, the new government under President Mitterrand had two major economic policy objectives. One was to stimulate domestic economic activity by stepping up both public and private spending. The other was to improve the international competitiveness of French industry. To some extent, however, the two objectives were in conflict with each other. For example, in order to add to the spending power of

French consumers, the government increased the minimum wage SMIC as well as a wide variety of social benefits. Combined with additional measures such as a reduction of the working week to thirty-nine hours and an extension of annual vacation from four to five weeks, these policies raised labour costs substantially. While domestic output achieved remarkable growth rates during a time of worldwide economic slump, the international competitiveness of French industry continued to deteriorate in spite of two devaluations in 1981 and 1982. France's external position – current account, foreign reserves – worsened rapidly.

The 'plan de rigeur' of March 1983, a harsh austerity programme, marks a fundamental turning point in the economic policies of the new government. The economic experiments of the first eighteen months or so obviously led policy makers to the conclusion that there is only one way of improving a country's international competitiveness: low inflation, moderate wage increases and high productivity growth. Ever since, the government has been sticking to this course with surprising steadfastness. The results so far are quite impressive: inflation is now lower than 5 per cent; the current account is more or less in balance; and there has been no need for any further franc devaluations.

One other aspect deserves mentioning in this context, in particular when compared to the United Kingdom. While the British government reprivatized state-owned companies in order to raise efficiency and productivity, the French government did exactly the opposite. Altogether, two steel concerns, five large industrial companies, as well as thirty–eight banks and other financial institutions were nationalized. Government control was presumed to be essential on the way back to international competitiveness. Indeed, the nationalized companies were intended to act as the 'spear-heads' of French industry in international markets. While the nationalizations attracted much attention from foreign observers, they are essentially a continuation of a long tradition in France. President Mitterrand's predecessors, de Gaulle, Pompidou and Giscard d'Estaing also made efforts to push French industries into the lead technologically. There are some quite impressive results of this policy, especially in the fields of communications, energy and transportation (Concorde, TGV). But those are mostly public goods. As far as consumer durables and private investment goods are concerned, the superiority of the French industrial policy has yet to be demonstrated.

None the less, French policy makers of all political parties are nowadays convinced that the key to international competitiveness is innovation and productivity growth. It seems that the times of frequent currency devaluations belong to the past. This positive impression is further reinforced by another shift in policies. Recently, an increasing number of subsidies are being devoted to modern industries rather than to the ailing sectors, even if that means a loss of jobs – and votes.

Federal Republic of Germany

Germany had almost totally different problems. During most of the last two decades, the D-mark was under upward pressure in international currency markets. In 1980, for example, the effective exchange rate was almost 60 per cent higher than in 1970. Therefore German companies were continuously forced to speed up productivity growth in order to maintain their competitiveness in international markets. On the other hand, the strong revaluation of the D-mark was probably the single most important factor contributing to Germany's high degree of price stability. German union officials could thus ask for comparatively moderate wage increases, while still enjoying satisfactory growth in real incomes.

In spite of the strong D-mark revaluation, the international competitiveness of German industry was for a long time no matter of concern for both policy makers and the public. Interestingly enough, that changed only in 1980–1 when the D-mark experienced a marked decline in international currency markets. For the first time in history, Germany's current account was deeply in the red at that time. There was virtually unanimous agreement that something had to be done in order to strengthen Germany's international competitiveness. In other countries, policy makers might have welcomed currency depreciation in such circumstances. The reaction in the Federal Republic was quite different though. There was a widespread fear of becoming engulfed in the vicious circle of devaluation and inflation. So in February 1981 the German central bank raised interest rates in a fairly dramatic action. The monetary authorities thus made it perfectly clear that they were not willing to resort to devaluation as a means of solving the economic problems.

As a consequence of this decisive action, the confidence of the international financial community with respect to the D-mark was quickly restored. The external value of the German currency began to rise again, and by 1982 the country's current account displayed a healthy surplus. Yet in spite of the prompt turnaround in the external position of the economy, the whole episode had a lasting impact on professional analysts as well as on the public. Obviously, the German economy was much more vulnerable than previously perceived. The large public budget deficits, in particular, came under attack. Towards the end of the 1970s public spending was increased sizeably in an effort to stimulate the economy – last but not least under heavy pressure from abroad. While this policy had only limited success in terms of fiscal stimulus, public debt went up substantially. Shortly afterwards, with the advent of the worldwide economic slump, the situation got even worse. It became increasingly obvious that public spending had to be brought under control, and that more emphasis had to be given to supply-side oriented policies rather than to aggregate demand management.

That, of course, requires painful policy decisions. The government of Helmut Schmidt at that time seemed unable to do what had to be done. As a consequence, the minor coalition partner changed alliance in the autumn of 1982, thus bringing the new government of Helmut Kohl to power. He promised to restore Germany's international competitiveness by a policy of fiscal and monetary restraint in conjunction with more incentives for the private sector. By and large, this approach has been quite successful: employment has been growing steadily in recent months; inflation is at a twenty-year low; and most of all public spending has been brought under control. Admittedly, not all groups of society have greeted the new policies with enthusiasm. Some people were severely affected by the spending cuts, especially in the field of social benefits. There is none the less a broad social consensus about the inevitability of the measures taken. The high public esteem for finance minister Gerhard Stoltenberg is certainly proof of that.

German workers and union officials also made an important contribution. For several years in a row they accepted slight reductions in net real take-home pay. By doing so, they have enabled businesses to finance new investments, thus improving efficiency and productivity, which is of paramount importance if the international competitiveness is to be maintained in the face of continuing currency appreciation. The recent success with respect to export and employment growth shows that this was the right strategy. While some slowdown in exports seems likely in the near future due to the decline of the dollar, that is only an additional reason to stick to the innovation strategy.

This brief survey of the major European economies reveals some striking similarities, their many differences notwithstanding. All three countries experienced a marked shift in economic policy in recent years, as it became increasingly evident that international competitiveness is a prerequisite for growth of output and income.

The major lesson was that in the long run, only the offensive strategy of innovation and productivity growth will lead to this end.

A look at countries beyond Europe tends to confirm this experience. Japan, which leads the industrialized countries in terms of productivity growth, is renowned all over the world for its ability to compete successfully in whichever markets it chooses to. The opposite is true for the USA, where productivity is growing slower than in most of the rest of the world. The poor state of the US economy's external accounts is well-known. It is certainly true that this development must be attributed to a large extent to the long overvalued dollar and the federal budget deficits. But it is equally true that this is not the whole story. It may be recalled that the US current account also was in deficit during the second half of the 1970s, i.e. at a time when the dollar was at a record low. Unless the USA succeeds in speeding up productivity growth, its current account may well be negative for a long time to come.

Key elements of the innovation strategy

So in theory and by experience, the case for the innovation strategy is overwhelming. There is much debate, however, about what the key elements of such a strategy ought to be. Many political and business leaders in Europe are calling for a 'new industrial policy', i.e. intensified government efforts to spur on R & D and to adopt modern technologies. According to those voices, that is the only way for Europe to be able to compete in tomorrow's 'high-tech' markets. They point out that both in Japan and the USA the government is actively involved in shaping the industrial future. There actually can be little doubt about that. Just think of the vast amount of research as well as product and process innovation which is being carried out in the USA in the name of defence or space programmes, most of it financed by the federal government. Therefore, a certain amount of public spending in this field may well be justified and desirable in Europe as well.

As an economist, one none the less has to be sceptical about too much enthusiasm in this respect. There is a very real danger of setting wrong priorities and wasting precious resources in the process. Even more importantly, industrial policy often is likely to include some form of protectionism or other. It can range from outspoken protection of a so-called 'infant industry' to preferential allocation of public contracts to domestic suppliers. However, history has taught that protectionism is always detrimental in the long run. Without the constant pressure of fierce competition from abroad, no industry is able to develop ever-better products and cost-saving manufacturing processes, thus raising efficiency and productivity.

While industrial policy may play some useful role, it clearly cannot be the cornerstone of a policy aimed at improving the international competitiveness of a national economy. The main policy task is to give adequate incentives, i.e. to stimulate the technological know-how and the entrepreneurial skills of the country's residents. Economic policy must create an environment in which innovation and investment can prosper. Investment is the very essence of competitiveness. Without continued increase and modernization of a country's capital stock, productivity cannot be raised sufficiently.

What many people often fail to see: of equal, or even greater, importance is disinvestment. Closing down low-productivity plants raises overall productivity in the economy as much as opening high-productivity plants. Those parts of the capital stock which are no longer efficient have to be eliminated. The problem is, of course, that transferring resources from inefficient to efficient uses is not a smooth process. Frictions cannot be avoided as factors of production have to adjust to changing circumstances. That may imply severe economic hardships for individuals as well as communities and regions. Therefore, there is widespread reluctance to perform rapid and effective disinvestment once a particular line of production has turned out to be no longer profitable. Yet ample historical evidence suggests that public subsidies, protection and favourable regulations cannot stem the tide in the long term if an industry is no longer competitive. In the end, the situation will be even worse if those who are negatively affected desperately cling to obsolete patterns of production.

The indispensable process of disinvestment can be greatly facilitated if the factors of production which are set free have a reasonable chance of finding employment opportunities in more productive sectors of the economy. The most important contribution of economic policy to this end is to create supply-side conditions which encourage new ventures. Hence a top priority for policy makers should be to abolish a host of regulations which again and again have turned out to be a major obstacle to investment. Moreover, businesses must have the chance to earn adequate profits. Otherwise, they won't be able to finance even the most promising of their investment projects, nor can they bear the financial consequences of unprofitable investments.

As was mentioned above, labour costs are of particular importance among the various cost components. Unless the growth of labour costs is lower than productivity growth, business earnings will go down. This is not, of course, primarily an issue of income distribution. It is rather an issue of income growth. Therefore, productivity-oriented wage increases are in the best interests of the work-force as well. There can be little argument about the basic chain of causality running from better earnings and more invest-ment to higher employment, even if some other factors matter too.

To be sure, management and labour alone cannot do the job. Fiscal and monetary policies also have to play a role. Fiscal policy has to make sure that the tax burden of businesses is not suppressive. In particular, retained profits should enjoy clear tax privileges. On the other hand, individuals must not be taxed excessively either (income tax plus compulsory social security contributions). One reason is that high marginal tax rates will discourage people in their work efforts. Another reason is that progressive taxation tends to lower growth of disposable income. Hence labour may be induced to ask for higher nominal wages, with the result that in the end business has to bear the brunt.

Not only with regard to receipts but also with regard to expenditures should the public sector restrict itself. Excessive expenditure makes recipients dependent and is counter-productive to private initiatives. That holds for social spending programmes as well as for subsidies to businesses. In addition, a slowdown in government spending is of the utmost importance in order to reduce public budget deficits. This is a crucial prerequisite to bringing down interest rates as a means of stimulating private investment.

Lower interest rates must also be the main objective of monetary policy. But low interest rates cannot be simply decreed by the central bank. The key factor rather is investors' confidence. Interest rates will come down lastingly only when and if investors have no inflationary expectations, and if they don't expect that currency to devalue on international currency markets. Investors' expectations, in turn, are essentially determined by the conduct of monetary policy. A central bank committing itself to price stability is certain to lower interest rates before too long. At the same time, price stability is a major prerequisite for both strong private investment and wage restraint. Monetary policy can thus help to hold down costs and to strengthen international competitiveness.

Wage policy, fiscal policy and monetary policy – those are the central issues for the supply side of an economy. A country which provides favourable conditions for innovation and investment will experience growth of output and income. Policy makers who pursue such a strategy need not be concerned about their country's international competitiveness. In fact, growth-oriented policies at home will automatically assure success in foreign markets as well. Seen against this background, we do not need any specific economic policies to improve international competitiveness. Rather, we need more international competition with respect to improving economic policies.

References

Balassa, B. (1964) 'Recent developments in the competitiveness of American industry and prospects for the future', in B. Balassa (ed.) (1980) *Changing Patterns in Foreign Trade and Payments*, New York: Norton, 26–33.

Beyfuss, J. (1981) 'Die Position der Bundesrepublik Deutschland im Welthandel', *Beiträge zur Wirtschafts und Sozialpolitik des Instituts der deutschen Wirtschaft*, no. 88, Köln.

Brittan, S. (1978) 'How British is the British sickness?', *Journal of Law and Economics*, vol. 21: 245–68.

Fels, G. (1982) 'Internationale Wettbewerbsfähigkeit: Japan, Vereinigte Staaten, Bundesrepublik – Fakten, Trends, Hypothesen', *Zeitschrift für betriebswirtschaftliche Forschung*, vol. 34: 8–24.

Fröhlich, H. P. (1986) 'Die Französische Wirtschaftspolitik unter Präsident Mitterrand aus Europäischer Perspektive', *Europa–Archiv*, vol. 41: 79–86.

Gehrke, B. and Heinemann, H-J. (1985) 'Internationale Wettbewerbsfähigkeit als Wirtschaftspolitische Aufgabe', *Wirtschaftswissenschaftliches Studium* vol. 14: 330–6.

Giersch, H. (1979) 'Aspects of growth, structural change, and employment – a Schumpeterian perspective', *Weltwirtschaftliches Archiv* vol. 115: 629–52.

Haertel, H. H. (1983) 'Wirtschaftspolitische Strategien zur Verbesserung der Wettbewerbsfähigkeit der Deutschen Wirtschaft', *Beihefte zur Konjunkturpolitik* no. 29: 145–58.

Horn, E-J. (1983) 'Bestimmungsgründe der Internationalen Wettbewerbsfähigkeit von Unternehmen und Industrien, Regionen und Volkswirtschaften', *Beihefte zur Konjunkturpolitik* no. 29: 35–53.

IMF (ed.) *International Financial Statistics*, various editions.

Juergensen, H. (1976) 'Über einige Kategorien einer Messung der Internationalen Wettbewerbsfähigkeit von Industrienationen', in H. Körner, P. Meyer–Dohm, E. Tuchtfeld and C. Uhlig (ed.) *Wirtschaftspolitik: Wissenschaft und politische Aufgabe*, Bern and Stuttgart, 467–82.

Langhammer, R. J. and Hiemenz, P. (1985) 'Declining competitiveness of EC suppliers in ASEAN markets: singular case or symptom?', *Journal of Common Market Studies* vol. 24: 105–19.

McKinnon, R. I. (1981) 'The exchange rate and macroeconomic policy: changing perceptions in recent years', *Journal of Economic Literature* vol. 19: 531–57.

Miles, M. A. (1979) 'The effects of devaluation of the trade balance and the balance of payments: some new results', *Journal of Political Economy* vol. 87: 600–20.

OECD (1985) *Economic Outlook*, no. 38, Paris.

Sachs, J. D. (1981) 'The current account and macroeconomic adjustment in the 1970s', *Brookings Papers on Economic Activity* no. 1: 201–820.

Seidler, H. (1983) 'Wirtschaftliche Strategien zur Verbesserung der Wettbewerbsfähigkeit der westdeutschen Wirtschaft', *Beihefte zur Konjunkturpolitik* no. 29: 159–71.

Stützel, W. (1973) *Währung in Weltoffner Wirtschaft*, Frankfurt.

Chapter three

Comparative advantage and competitiveness in a small, 'open' economy

P. K. M. Tharakan, J. Waelbroeck,
D. Verstralen and A. Sendhaji

Preliminary remarks

There is a well-established tradition of econometric analysis of the determinants of the comparative advantage of the trade in manufactures of various countries (see Tharakan 1985). A surprisingly large number of such studies have been carried out in the case of Belgium (see Culem 1984, Dreze 1960, 1961, Glejser, Jacquemin, and Petit 1980, Tharakan and Vandoorne 1979).

Some of these studies have attempted to verify the structure of the comparative advantage of Belgium on the basis of Heckscher–Ohlin–Samuelson (HOS) type of variables. Others have taken into account the role of imperfect competition variables and protection. They have also covered various trade flows of Belgium: for example, those with the European Community countries, the OECD countries and the developing world. The role of a number of organizational factors, particularly in the exports of Belgium has been taken into account.

The present study follows this tradition in the sense that it uses an econometric approach to analyse the comparative advantage of Belgian industrial sectors. However, it innovates in a number of respects in comparison with earlier work. For example, while the existing studies measure comparative advantage in terms of foreign trade performance, we use the rate of profit as a sort of alternative indicator of 'comparative advantage' or more precisely, of competitiveness. This variable is more interesting in a way than trade performance, which is strongly influenced by historical factors, as large capacities that were built up in better times are kept going in sectors that are no longer competitive. Profit, on the contrary, is a forward-looking indicator of economic performance: it is in profitable sectors that investments tend to be concentrated. The present study also takes into account empirical data pertaining to a larger number of years (6), industries (77) and variables (12 in alternative specifications) than most of the previous studies.

It is well to stress at the outset the limitations of the econometric approach used. Econometric estimation seeks general causes that influence all of the observations available. Causes that affect one observation only are reflected in the residual for that observation. As will be seen, it turns out that in this study, as in most applications of econometrics to industrial economics, the regression residuals are large: 'general causes' usually account for less than half of the variance of the data, quite a bit less sometimes. This is normal. The competitiveness of industries does depend on general economic forces, but for each of them the factors that are specific to it are even more important, which reflect historical accidents, the availability of specific raw materials, government industrial policies and the like. Curiosity about the causes of these residuals led to undertaking a group of simple case studies, designed to shed light on this topic through interviews with persons who are well informed about particular sectors.

A word of caution finally. This study should not be seen as an attempt to identify the 'strong points' of the Belgian economy, i.e. the sectors on which the government should concentrate its industrial assistance. There can be no such method. The success of any particular investment is too dependent on specific elements, such as the hazards of innovation, to be predicted accurately by econometric formulae. The method does, however, point to some interesting tendencies of the Belgian growth process, and seems to suggest that a general re-focusing of the pattern of Belgian industrial policies may be called for.

Some elements of theory, the variables, the data and the specification

At the very core of the factor proportions theory – the so-called Heckscher–Ohlin–Samuelson theory – is the proposition that trade between countries will be determined mainly by the concordance of the pattern of the factor endowment of trading countries with the factor intensities of the production processes of the commodities traded. This would suggest that capital or labour intensity would be an important determinant of the comparative advantage of any country. The neo–factor proportions theory suggests that the concordance between the endowment of human capital (as distinct from physical capital) and the human capital intensity of the production process is an important determinant of the commodity composition of trade. Given the high rank of Belgium in terms of per capita income, industrial growth and educational development, intuitively one would expect both the physical capital and the human capital variable to play a 'positive' role in the determination of the commodity composition of Belgium's international trade.

The simple account of the determinants of comparative advantage sketched above has been enriched in recent years mainly as a result of the findings emerging from the empirical tests concerning the commodity composition of trade.[1] This has led econometricians to look for other general causes that may account for the comparative advantages enjoyed by various industries. These include economies of scale, degree of concentration of production, commercial policy variables such as tariff and non-tariff barriers, etc. The use of profits as an alternative measure of 'revealed' comparative advantage necessitated, especially in the specification considered in the present study, one important modification. Profit rates could be, in principle, influenced by the degree of openness of the economy. This could particularly be the case when the currency is overvalued because then profits are likely to be higher in 'sheltered' sectors where trade is small than in industries whose trade is large.

The most regularly used measure of 'revealed comparative' advantage' in economic literature is the Balassa index. The version of the Balassa index (RCA) used in the present study was defined as:

$$RCA_i = \frac{x_i/m_i}{X_t/M_t} \tag{1}$$

where

RCA_i = revealed comparative advantage of sector i
x_i = value of exports of sector i $\qquad X_t = \sum_i x_i$

m_i = value of imports of sector i $\qquad M_t = \sum_i m_i$

This measure was calculated using Belgian export and import figures. Second, it was calculated for Belgium-Luxemburg (BLEU) for the same years. Third, RCA was calculated for the intra-European Community (EC) trade and extra-EC trade of the BLEU (separate data for these flows were not available for Belgium). These four measures were calculated using trade data for the years 1977–82.

The profits variable (PROF) was defined as:

$$\frac{Profits + depreciation \times 100}{turnover} \tag{2}$$

This is not an ideal measure of competitiveness, since other

43

things being equal, gross profits tend to be larger in capital intensive industries than in other sectors, so that regressions of profits on capital intensity should be interpreted prudently. There is, however, no reason to expect that the introduction of the capital coefficient in profit regressions will bias the coefficients of other variables.

Among the explanatory variables used, the first group consisted of the basic HOS determinants of comparative advantage. The following two measures were used alternatively for the physical capital intensity:

$$\text{Capital-labour ration (KA)} = \frac{\text{fixed assets}}{\text{number of workers}} \tag{3}$$

and

$$\text{Ratio of capital to turnover (KOR)} = \frac{\text{fixed assets}}{\text{turnover}} \tag{4}$$

The first is a better indicator of physical capital intensity. The second is, however, a useful variable in the profit regressions, which seeks to explain profits expressed as a ratio of turnover.

The human capital intensity (CHI) was quantified as:

$$\frac{\text{Number of white collar workers} \times 100}{\text{Total number of workers}} \tag{5}$$

The limitations of the above measure are obvious. The ratio of professional, technical and scientific personnel as a percentage of the industry's labour force would have been a better, and more conventional, proxy (see Hufbauer 1970) for human capital intensity. But the data necessary for calculating that particular index were available for only one year. The Spearman rank correlation coefficient between CHI and the above mentioned index for that particular year was 0.77 which of course is very highly significant for the sample that contained 77 observations.

The second group of variables used in our estimations represents aspects of reality which the HOS model assumes away. The first of these is economies of scale (EE) which was estimated as:

$$\frac{\text{Value added in the industry}}{\text{The total number of firms in the industry}} \tag{6}$$

The above index represents a sort of 'revealed' economies of scale, to the extent that firms are typically larger if economies of scale are available than not.

Industrial concentration was measured in two alternative ways (CON1, CON2):

$$CON1 = C_{4d} = \sum_{i=1}^{4} \left[\frac{To_i - x_i}{To_t - x_t} \right] \qquad (7)$$

where

To_i = total turnover of firm i,
x_i = exported turnover of firm i,
To_t = total turnover of the industry,
x_t = turnover exported by the industry

and

$$CON2 = \frac{C4 \text{ Firm}}{C4 \text{ Establishment}} \qquad (8)$$

where

C4 Firm = the share of the four biggest firms in the total turnover of the industry

C4 Establishment = the share of the four biggest establishments in the total turnover of the industry

The first of these two measures is standard in this type of work. The interpretation of the second is less obvious. A high value of that indicator suggests that co-ordination of various production units is easily achieved (Jacquemin, de Ghellinck and Huveneers 1978). It could be argued that multinational organization of economic activity is easily achieved in industries of this type.

The third group of variables allows for the impact of protection on the comparative advantage and profits. Tariff (TP_i) and non-tariff (QUOT) barriers were taken into account. They were defined as follows:

$$TP_i = \frac{DD_i}{mT_i} \times \frac{mTB_i}{mE_i} \times 100 \qquad (9)$$

where

DD_i = value of tariffs on the imports of sector i, into Belgium
mT_i = value of imports of sector i
mTB_i = value of imports of sector i for BLEU
mE_i = value of the imports from extra-EC countries in sector i in BLEU

The weighting procedure implied in equation (9) takes into account the fact that tariffs apply only to imports from extra-EC countries.

Non-tariff barriers (QUOT) were proxied by a dummy variable:

QUOT = 1 where non-tariff barriers exist;
QUOT = 0 where there are non-tariff barriers $\left.\right\}$ (10)

The second protection variable thus represents the presence of forms of 'new protectionism'.

The 'openness variable' was relevant only for the profit regressions. Two alternative measures were developed as follows:

$$OUV1_i = \frac{(x_i + m_i)/2}{To_i} \times 100 \qquad (11)$$

where

x_i = exports of sector i
m_i = imports of sector i
To_i = turnover of sector i

and

$$OUV2_i = \frac{m_i}{(To_i + m_i)x_i} \times 100 \qquad (12)$$

where the symbols have the same meaning as in equation (11).

Some idea of the intertemporal stability of 'revealed comparative advantage' index for Belgium for the period covered can be obtained from Figure 3.1, which plots the RCA indices observed for the first (1977) and the last year (1982) included in the sample. The correlation coefficient between the observations for 1977 and 1982 was as high as 0.898. Figure 3.2 shows that as could be expected the correlation between RCA and Profits, though positive was rather weak.[2] This of course makes it all the more interesting to verify the differences in the role played by the independent variables in explaining these two indices of performance.

The four basic regression equations formulated to explain the commodity composition of the Belgian trade were specified as follows:

$RCA_{BT} = f(CHI,KA,EE,CON1,TP,QUOT)$ (13)
$RCA_{BT} = f(CHI,KOR,EE,CON1,TP,QUOT)$ (14)
$RCA_{BT} = f(CHI,KA,EE,CON2,TP,QUOT)$ (15)
$RCA_{BT} = f(CHI,KOR,EE,CON2,TP,QUOT)$ (16)

where RCA_{BT} stands for the revealed comparative advantage for the total trade of Belgium. All the other symbols have the same meaning as explained above.

Figure 3.1 Structure of the revealed comparative advantage (RCA) 1977 and 1982)

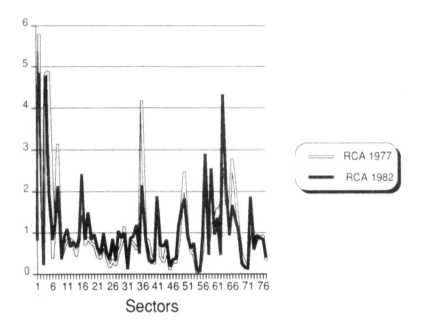

A number of regressions were also carried out to test the RCA with respect to intra- and extra-European Community trade. Since such a distinction was possible only with respect to BLEU trade data, and in order to ensure comparability, the basic regressions were carried out also using the BLEU trade data.

Given the heavy subsidies that were granted to loss-making industrial firms during the period under study, there was reason to suspect that eliminating the weakest sectors might make it possible to sharpen our view of the pattern of comparative advantages in Belgium. To investigate this possibility, the sample was split into four groups according to both the trade and the profits performance of the various industries. For each specification, regressions were then run both for the whole sample, and for the group of firms that had an above average performance during the

Figure 3.2 Structure of the revealed comparative advantage (RCA) and rate of profits in Belgian industrial sector 1982

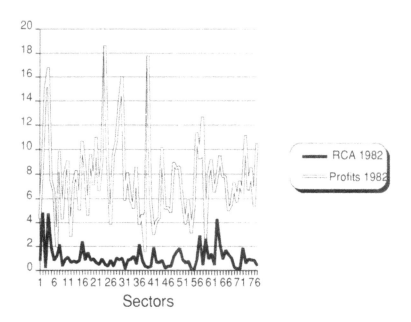

period under study in terms of both these criteria.

The basic 'profits regressions' were similar to the basic RCA regressions with the important difference that they also contained, alternatively, one or the other of the 'openness variables' ($OUV1_i$ or $OUV2_i$). The technique of 'pooling', i.e. a combination of time series and cross section, was made use of, except in the cases where the sample had to be split (e.g., the 'strong sector' regressions). This of course meant that the standard matrix form of the pooled specification looked as follows:

$$
\begin{matrix}
76 \times 1 \\
76 \times 1 \\
76 \times 1 \\
76 \times 1 \\
76 \times 1 \\
76 \times 1
\end{matrix}
\begin{bmatrix}
RCA_{77} \\
RCA_{78} \\
RCA_{79} \\
RCA_{80} \\
RCA_{81} \\
RCA_{82}
\end{bmatrix}
= \alpha_0
\begin{bmatrix}
1 \\
1 \\
1 \\
1 \\
1 \\
1
\end{bmatrix}
+ \alpha_1
\begin{bmatrix}
CHI_{77} \\
CHI_{78} \\
CHI_{79} \\
CHI_{80} \\
CHI_{81} \\
CHI_{82}
\end{bmatrix}
+ \ldots +
\begin{bmatrix}
\ \\
\ \\
\varepsilon \\
\ \\
\
\end{bmatrix}
$$

$$\text{Constant} \qquad (456 \times 1) \quad \text{Error term}$$

$= (456 \times 1)$

48

The results: interpreting the coefficients

It is usual in econometric studies to announce the expected signs of coefficients before presenting results. We prefer not to do this. What is studied is comparative, not absolute advantage.

Belgium is, for example, well equipped with physical capital, but will have a comparative advantage for products that use that factor intensively if it is not only well endowed with this factor, but better endowed than its competitors. As the most important of those are other industrialized countries which also have a large physical capital stock, this is far from certain.

For human capital, a quality element may come into play. A country's educational system may be expensive so that investment in human capital is large, but if it does not train workers well for work in production activities, that country may not have a comparative advantage in human capital-intensive industries. The system of taxation might likewise increase the cost of highly-skilled researchers and discourage international investors from setting up production units that are research intensive.

The early work of Drèze (1960, 1961) indicated that the interaction between economies of scale and product differentiation is an important determinant of comparative advantage, particularly that of a country such as Belgium. Since then an important branch of international trade theory has grown around the phenomenon of intra-industry trade which particularly stresses the role played by the economies of scale and product differentiation. A number of recent models of intra-industry trade suggest that some of the determinants of such trade and those of the modified versions of comparative advantage can be complementary (see Greenaway and Milner 1986, Part I). This is particularly relevant to economies of scale and product differentiation. Bergstrand (1983) has argued that in market equilibrium, the degree of increasing returns in the industry is a positive function of the degree of product differentiation and hence a proper econometric specification can include only one of these two variables. The econometric studies available so far have yielded mixed results for this particular variable (see Tharakan 1981).

For the industrial concentration variable (CON1), a positive sign would not be unexpected given the dominant role of three 'banques d'affaires' in Belgium's industrial growth until the Second World War, and the role which multinationals have played in recent decades. The second concentration index (CON2), which possibly reflects the case of management of large multi-branch firms and is interpreted as an indicator of the case of organizing

49

production on a multinational basis, indicates whether inter-national firms make a strong contribution to trade performance.

The sign of the protection variables can be positive or negative. Protection keeps imports out, so that it helps profits and improves the trade balance; thus it has a 'protective effect'.

Studies of protection, on the other hand, consistently point to a 'lobbying effect' which reflects the fact that for complex reasons, it is as a rule the weak sectors that obtain protection. As a result, protection is negatively correlated with comparative advantage. The sign of the coefficient of the protection variables indicates whether the protection or the lobbying effect predominates.

The alternative use of RCA or profits as a measure of 'compara-tive advantage' may lead to a change in the relevant regression results. Industrial concentration, for example, might enhance profits by making possible monopoly rents, without affecting trade performance.

The econometric results were on the whole strong. As usual in this type of cross-section analysis, the correlation coefficients obtained were not high. The regression results for different specifications were, however, mutually consistent, and the dif-ferences in signs can in most cases be explained in terms of the logic of the regressions specified.

In view of the large number of regression results involved (42 regressions using in most cases 9 variables) we limit the presenta-tion here to the most important ones in terms of policy implications. The robustness of the results is such that such a selection gives a good overall view of the underlying pattern. In fact the results are so much alike within each group that this choice does not convey a misleadingly flattering impression of the outcome of the empirical exercise.

Table 3.1 presents the results of the regressions in which the dependent variable reflects the overall trade performance of individual sectors (RCA_{BT}). The coefficient of human capital is systematically negative, that of physical capital systematically positive. In terms of trade theory this would suggest that Belgium is relatively better endowed in physical capital than its competitors and less well endowed in human capital. Although some such suggestion was implied in the results of earlier studies (see Culem 1984), the discrepancy is hardly sharp enough to justify the strong regression results obtained in the present study. This raises the question of alternative explanations.

It could of course be that the quality of Belgian education is inadequate. If this is so, it is not due to not spending enough, if we believe not the education lobby but the Belgian government,

Table 3.1 Regressions for the trade indicators of the comparative advantage of Belgium (t ratios)

Dependent Variable	Human Capital CHI	Physical Capital KA	KOR	Scale Economies EE	Concentration Variables CON1	CON2	Protection Variables TP_i	QUOT	R^2	No. of Observations
[1] Revealed Comparative Advantage of Belgium: all sectors, all destinations	-3.80		4.67	0.10	1.73		-1.46	2.30	0.11	456
[2] Ditto	-2.87		4.93	0.38		5.38	-0.47	0.39	0.16	456
[3] Ditto	-6.15	7.24		0.63	1.08		-0.77	3.03	0.17	456
[4] Ditto	-5.28	6.78		0.75		4.29	-0.12	1.39	0.20	456
[5] Revealed Comparative Advantage of Belgium: 'strong sectors', all destinations	-6.34		4.97	2.83	1.04		-4.59	-0.41	0.65	70
[6] Ditto	-6.18		5.24	3.50		1.80	-4.68	-1.21	0.66	70
[7] Ditto	-5.29	2.08		1.81	1.60		-3.91	-0.45	0.50	70
[8] Ditto	-4.99	2.61		2.27		2.25	-3.53	-1.50	0.52	70

which obviously does not feel that there is any underspending in this area. Do Belgian schools fail to produce economically productive workers? The country's educational system does impose high standards. Particularly at the secondary and post-graduate levels the Belgian system is probably more rigorous than its counterparts elsewhere in the industrialized world. But it tends to be rather rigid and 'academic'. It could well be that there is an overemphasis of factual knowledge to the detriment of the acquisition of an ability to learn, although it should be acknowledged that those who followed the 'classical' formation – specially of the 'Latin-Maths' variety – were drilled somewhat mercilessly to attain a high level of intellectual flexibility. Perhaps such formation remained rather elitist and did not contribute to building up a work-force with the necessary technical formation and flexibility. But such a hypothesis cannot be empirically verified. But what is well known is that the very high levels of taxation (the second highest in the world) prevailing in Belgium have led to a number of talented and highly motivated technical personnel seeking greener pastures elsewhere.

The authors, not being education experts, will not hazard strong pronouncements on the quality of Belgian education. But as economists they would suggest another explanation for the intriguing result yielded by the human-capital variable. It involves the longstanding emphasis in Belgium's industrial policies on subsidizing the creation of physical capital, and the limited support that has gone to research. The share of research in the country's GNP is one of the lowest among the advanced countries. The adoption of the 'Lois d'Expansion Economique' in the late 1950s and early 1960s led to heavy subsidization of investment in steel and heavy chemicals industries during the crucial decades of the 1960s and 1970s when Belgian industry was extensively restructured. This could have highly biased the physical capital intensity to the relative detriment of human capital.

The scale economies did not yield a significant result. But one of the concentration variables (CON2) which was tentatively identified with a sector's accessibility to multinational operations has a positive and significant coefficient. This is reasonable in view of the role of multinationals in recent Belgian industrial history.

As could be expected given the rather liberal trade policies of Belgium, the results of the protection variables are not strong. The 'protective effect' sometimes dominates, yielding a positive sign. In other instances, the 'lobbying effect' is predominant, and the sign is negative.

The correlation coefficients are not high although interestingly,

Table 3.2 Regressions for the trade indicators of the comparative advantage of BLEU, by geographical areas (t ratios)

Dependent Variables	Human Capital CHI	Physical Capital KA	Scale Economies EE	Concentration Variables		Protection Variables		R^2	No. of Observations
				CON1	CON2	TP,	QUOT		
[1] RCA of BLEU: all sectors, all destinations	-4.52	7.35	0.60	1.03		0.45	2.74	0.15	456
[2] Ditto	-3.79	7.09	0.74		3.05	0.59	1.52	0.16	456
[3] RCA of BLEU, 'strong sectors', all destinations	-5.26	2.78	1.21	2.27		-2.92	0.23	0.54	79
[4] Ditto	-6.17	4.69	4.24		-1.63	-2.01	0.277	0.53	79
[5] RCA of BLEU: all sectors, internal EC trade	-5.00	6.34	0.17	0.14				0.10	456
[6] Ditto	-4.54	5.78	0.96		2.83			0.12	456
[7] RCA of BLEU: 'strong sectors', internal EC trade	-7.89	3.48	2.97	1.35				0.51	85
[8] Ditto	-7.91	3.33	4.03		-1.40			0.51	85
[9] RCA of BLEU: all sectors, extra-EC trade	-4.17	10.93	-3.58	0.75		-1.08	-1.34	0.27	456
[10] Ditto	-3.71	10.90	-3.58	1.81		-0.75	-1.91	0.27	456
[11] RCA of BLEU: 'strong sectors', extra-EC trade	-0.60	7.19	-1.45	0.79		0.90	-3.58	0.69	49
[12] Ditto	-0.46	7.27	-1.29	-0.78		0.55	-3.48	0.69	49

they are systematically higher for the 'strong sectors' sub-sample than for the whole group of industries investigated. The regressions do reflect overall factors that contribute to trading success, but the fits obtained are not high enough to make them into effective predictors of that success. Any support that the government might decide to grant to a particular project should be justified far more in terms of the specific aspects of the investment than of the general factors which this study investigates.

Table 3.2 gives the results of the analysis of the patterns of comparative advantages with respect to two geographic areas: the European Community (EC) and the non-EC area. As mentioned earlier, because of the lack of data for Belgium alone, the dependent variable used reflects the trading performance of the Belgium–Luxemburg Economic Union (BLEU). The Belgian economy is far larger than that of Luxemburg, and hopefully those results do provide indications that are valid from the Belgian point of view. In fact the results obtained using BLEU data for total trade practically replicated those obtained for the total trade of Belgium, although the correlation coefficients were somewhat lower. Before turning to the interpretation of the results it is worth noting that trade with Belgium's historical hinterland (the Netherlands, France and the Federal Republic of Germany) accounts for a large fraction of the trade with EC, while the trade with the developing countries accounts for an important share of 'extra-EC' trade.

Apparently due to the last mentioned factor, the human capital turns out to be less significant in the extra-EC regressions than in the intra-EC ones. For the same reason, it is reasonable to find that the physical capital variable is more significant in the extra-EC regressions than in the others. Once again, the protection variables do not yield strong and consistent results. They are of course relevant only for extra-EC trade. For tariffs, the 'protection effect' dominates. For non-tariff barriers, the 'lobbying effect' prevails. This last result is consistent with the view of many trade economists that today's 'new protectionism' that uses trade barriers other than tariffs, has in practice little effect on trade flows.

Table 3.3 presents the results of the regressions that use profits as the dependent variable. Not surprisingly, the correlation coefficients are lower than for the trade indicators, because profits are more sensitive to random short-term forces than trade shares. Significance levels are thus less satisfactory than in Tables 3.1 and 3.2.

As could be expected, the physical capital variable yields a postive sign. But in contrast to the regressions for RCA, the

Table 3.3 Regressions for profit rates as indicators of competitiveness (t ratios)

Dependent variable	Human Capital CHI	Physical Capital KOR	Concentration Variables CON1	CON2	Protection Variables TP_i	QUOT	Openness Variables OUV1	OUV2	R^2	No. of Observations
[1] Profit rates: 'all sectors'	3.76	9.07	−1.06		−0.07	0.19	−0.07		0.18	456
[2] Ditto	3.76	9.08	−1.07		−0.07	0.22		−0.16	0.18	456
[3] Ditto	1.79	2.40	0.53		−0.94	1.24	−0.04		0.045	456
[4] Ditto	1.81	2.51	0.52		−0.95	1.34		−0.58	0.046	456

human capital variable turns out to have a positive and significant coefficient. This is indeed a very interesting finding. We believe that the opposing signs of human capital in the two regressions reflect policy distortions that characterize Belgium. As mentioned earlier, these go back to the crucial error at the end of the 1950s, when a system of industrial subsidy which was heavily biased in favour of physical capital was adopted by the Parliament. Investment in research, in contrast, remained – and still is – the weak point of industrial policy making. The capital intensive 'smoke-stack industries' of course did badly and market forces would normally have wiped out quite fast the capacities that had been built up mistakenly in the earlier period. But the subsidies granted to the firms experiencing difficulties froze in effect the unbalanced pattern of production, freezing also in the process the resulting pattern of trade. Whereas the trade regressions reflect a distorted pattern of trade, the profits regressions bring to light the pattern of competitiveness more or less as the market reveals it. The basic reason for this is that the profits index reflects the fact that the domestic competition cancels out the subsidy effect while that effect distorts the foreign trade figures which form the basis of the RCA variable. This interpretation suggests that Belgium would be well-advised to shift to a more balanced pattern of industrial policies as far as the physical and human capital variables are concerned.

A comparison of the results for all sectors and for the strong sectors reveals that in every case the results for the 'strong sectors sub-sample' are sharper than those for the whole sample. In particular, the correlation coefficients obtained are notably higher. We interpret this also as suggestive of the distorting impact of subsidizing weak industries, that has insulated them from competitive forces in a haphazard way that characterizes such defensive policies. The other independent variables show no significant impact on the inter-industry composition of profits.

Beyond regression analysis: the role of industry specific factors

It has been emphasized repeatedly that an econometric approach such as the present one misses – 'throws into the residuals' – the main causes of industrial success, which are industry specific. An R^2 of 0.2, the kind of value obtained in our study, implies that 80 per cent of the variance of a variable is accounted for by factors that are specific to each variable. What are these factors?

As a rather rough and ready way of shedding some light on this problem, a set of interviews was carried out to complement the econometric investigation. Ten sectors were selected, chosen mainly among the 'strong industries' that have both strong trade and profit performance. They were:

– cement, lime, and gypsum
– glass
– chemical products for industry and agriculture*
– agricultural machines and tractors
– electronic equipment*
– shipbuilding
– sugar
– beer
– carpets
– veneered and treated wood, chipboards.
(*not one of the 'strong sectors', but one that is often regarded as a growth industry)

The interviews reveal that industrialists are indeed largely unaware of the 'general' forces to which the study points as causes of industrial success, and stress only the 'specific' factors that are relevant to their own branch. This should not be taken to mean that they attach no importance to the macro forces. It seems rather that they take them for granted, as factors that they cannot influence, but focus their attention on the factors which they hope are to a certain extent under their control.

It is not possible, due to space limitation, to present in detail the full information gathered through the case studies. However, examples of the factors gathered which are listed below do shed some light on the factors that are reflected in the large regression residuals.

Locational advantages: The Belgian cement industry is located close to Belgium's border with Holland and France. In an industry characterized by heavy transportation costs, this locational advantage was grasped by the Belgian entrepreneurs who developed exports mainly to these neighbouring countries. The Belgian cement industry is also organizationally highly concentrated with high fixed costs acting as a sort of entry barrier. Faced with some overcapacity, the industry has undertaken steps for restructuring by means of the closing down of some units and at the same time improving productivity by adopting new production techniques.

History and restructuring: For the glass sector the Belgian specialization is the continuation over many decades of a nineteenth-century specialization in the production of blown glass. But by the 1970s the Belgian glass industry's competitive position had been seriously eroded. The industry went through a painful but effective restructuring process. The work-force in the industry dropped from 10,000 to 4,000. A new production process which increased the productivity and decreased the energy consumption was adopted. The output was diversified to meet the new pattern of demand arising due to the increased attention paid by consumers to safety, insulation and decorative uses of glass. The industry currently channels about 2 per cent of its profits into research and nearly 80 per cent of its turnover is accounted for by exports. The devaluation of the Belgian franc in 1982 also gave the industry a slight and temporary cost advantage particularly over its Dutch competitors.

Location, research and natural resource content: Chemical products for industry and agriculture have performed well in terms of exports but their profit margins have not been high. The locational advantages play an important role in the chemical industry as it includes both intermediate products and finished ones and in this respect the Belgian chemical industry (as well as that of Holland) has a definite advantage over its main competitors in France and the Federal Republic of Germany. In the sub-sector of finished chemical products, considerable research is carried out by the Belgian firms such as Solvay, Union Chimique, Gevaert, etc. But the high cost of human capital and the fiscal burden in Belgium erode some of this advantage. For example, a Belgian researcher with a gross salary of BF 2 millions per year earns in effect only 44.8 per cent of it, while his counterparts with a similar income would retain 75 per cent of the salary in the USA, 72.4 per cent in France and 61.2 per cent in the Federal Republic of Germany. The Belgian firms also face a disadvantage in terms of the natural resources and intermediate products which together make up an important part of the production cost of some of the basic chemical products.

Locational advantages and multinational activity: The agricultural machines and tractors industry in Belgium is dominated by two multinational companies: Sperry and Ford. For these companies, Belgium is a natural location as a place where components brought in from elsewhere can be assembled and re-exported to buyers in Belgium's hinterland. During the early years of the 1980s, considerable rationalization took place in these sectors. The foreign investment has brought in its wake the experience and technical knowledge of the parent companies and helped the performance of this industry. Nearly 90 per cent of the output of the above companies in Belgium is exported.

Hedging and geography: In the electronics equipment industry one Dutch firm – Philips – has become the largest producer in

Europe. It found it convenient to locate part of its production capacity in Belgium. The geographical proximity must have played a role in that decision. It was also possibly an effective way to hedge against the fluctuations of the guilder and the franc. The Belgian domestic sector of electronic goods is largely dominated by Philips. The performance of the Belgian industry in this highly competitive sector has not been very impressive in recent years. The adverse impact of the economic difficulties in the early 1980s on the purchasing capacity of the Belgian consumers and the high proportion of social security contributions have apparently restrained the performance of this industry.

Disappearance of the subsidy prop, re-emergence of the comparative disadvantage: The Belgian shipbuilding industry showed up in the list of 'strong sectors' (high profits and high revealed comparative advantage) during the years 1977, 1978 and 1979, but then disappeared from the list for the rest of the years included in the sample. Reasons for this somewhat curious phenomenon were mainly the disappearance of the direct subsidies and the development of internationally competitive shipbuilding industries in countries such as South Korea in this relatively labour intensive sector. The situation had deteriorated to such a point that by the early 1980s there was only one Belgian firm left in the industry (Boelwerf) and that too with a 40 per cent stake by the Belgian government. Neither the hopes which were placed on the possible development and use of new materials in shipbuilding nor the use of CAD-CAM methods in production has led to any noticeable results or stemmed the surge of the forces of comparative advantage.

Quotas, price guarantees and geography: Belgium has excellent natural conditions for growing sugar beet. But it is able to export in competition with cane sugar producers only because of a complex European Community system of production quotas and price guarantees. At least part of the cost of this system is paid through a production levy calculated on the basis of the guaranteed price. The high profits are a direct result of the guaranteed price which is calculated on the basis of the average production costs. Two important elements in the production costs are labour costs and energy costs. Efforts have been made to reduce both; the former through increased automation and the latter through energy-saving methods and alternative sources of energy. The industry is also putting considerable hope on promotional campaigns and product-diversification efforts.

History, locational factors and good management: Some of Belgium's best known varieties of beer date back to the Middle Ages. Since transport costs play an important role, the Belgian exports of beer, which account for about 10 per cent of the output, go mainly to the nearby countries, particularly France. The management has made some imaginative moves which have apparently helped to sustain the strong position of the Belgian beer industry. Thus, for example, while there is intense competition between the different firms in the domestic market, two of Belgium's largest beer producers have joined up to pool their export market strategy and efforts. Production methods have been updated. The producers of 'special beer' manage to earn higher profits on the basis of their higher price for the high quality beer.

Geography, good management and know-how and a smattering of subsidies: The Belgian carpet industry which was facing major problems during the second half of the 1970s managed to restructure the sector so remarkably that by the mid-1980s Belgium had emerged as the leading world exporter and the second biggest producer of carpets. The management correctly perceived that Belgium's comparative advantage lay mainly in tufted rather than woven carpets. The former sub-sector now accounts for 65 per cent of the exports of the sector. The world's leading producer of carpet-making machines is Belgian (Van De Wiele) and the close co-operation between the carpet producers and the machine makers has led to the development of machines particularly suited to the industry's requirements and their prompt maintenance. The industry is characterized by a number of relatively small and dynamic units which compete intensely internally, but co-operate to some extent in the export promotion and in the organization of research (at Centexbel), thus providing the benefits of scale in these activities which the small units could not have otherwise reaped. The sharp appreciation of the value of the dollar against the Belgian franc during the first half of the 1980s helped the Belgian exporters against their US competitors. The devaluation of the Belgian franc in 1982 also helped. Apparently the assistance provided to the industry by the Belgian government within the framework of the Textile Plan was made good use of by the industry in this particular case to improve its competitivity. Around the mid-1980s the Belgian carpet-making industry exported 90 per cent of its output.

History, restructuring and competition: The successful Belgian 'chipboard' industry was set up to use by-products of the production of flax fibres. The industry shifted to other raw materials as flax production dropped drastically. The sector, which also includes, in addition to chipboards, furniture and veneered and treated wood, faced serious difficulties during the 1970s. It went through a painful process of restructuring. Employment in the sector dropped by 24 per cent. The number of firms declined but the ones that emerged out of the period of crisis have sharpened their competitiveness through a process of intense internal competition. In turn this has helped the export capabilities of some of the sub-sectors of this industry. Imports still remain an important factor in the woodworking industry which is thus characterized by considerable intra-industry trade.

Conclusions

Combining econometrics and case studies, we have analysed the determinants of the comparative advantage and competitiveness (profitability) of the Belgian industries. The general causes appraised through the econometric approach yield some intriguing results. By far the most striking among them is that the human capital variable is negatively and signficantly correlated with the 'revealed' comparative advantage of Belgium while it gives a positive and significant coefficient for the profit rate of the same sample of industries. These results as well as the positive and significant performance of the physical capital variable, both for the comparative advantage and profits proved to be highly robust in different regressions and hence cannot be ignored. One possible explanation for the apparent paradox concerning the performance of the human capital variable is that the Belgian industrial policy since the early 1960s has been biased in favour of physical capital investment to the relative detriment of human capital investment. This interpretation suggests that Belgium would be well-advised to shift to a more balanced pattern of industrial policies as far as the physical and human capital variables are concerned.

The reasons behind the individual industrial performance – whether in terms of revealed comparative advantage or profitability – have to be sought of course in terms of industry specific factors as distinct from the general causes analysed in the econometric exercise. Case studies which covered 10 of the sectors – 8 of them 'strong sectors' in terms of comparative advantage and profitability – suggest a variety of reasons. One striking factor is that none of these successful 8 sectors belongs to the 'new technology' group while they have used what they consider to be the best or the most suitable technology available for their purpose. In fact when a sector with comparative disadvantage for Belgium sought to overcome this problem by the use of highly advanced new technologies, it does not appear to have succeeded at all (e.g. the shipbuilding industry).

The case studies also highlight the role of a number of other specific determinants of industrial success. Locational advantages repeatedly emerge as an important factor in the successful performance of a number of industries. Some industries went through a painful process of restructuring and emerged as much better competitors. A shrewd combination of intense domestic competition and close export co-operation by Belgian firms yielded good results in certain cases. Good management made such strategies as well as the identification and development of branches with potentialities possible. In the final analysis, in Belgium as well as elsewhere it is apparently an interesting combination of history and geography, economics and management, foresight and flexibility that makes successful industrial performance possible.

Notes

1 For a survey of this literature, see Tharakan (1985).
2 The correlation coefficient between the two amounted to 0.144.

References

Bergstrand, J. N. (1983) 'Measurement and determinants of 'intra-industry international trade', in P. K. M. Tharakan (ed.) (1985) *Intra-Industry Trade: Empirical and Methodological Aspects,* Amsterdam: North-Holland, 201–62.
Culem, C. (1984) *Comparative Advantage and Industrial Restructuring – The Belgian Case 1970–1980,* Centre d'Economie Mathématique et d'Econométrie, ULB, Brussels.
Drèze, J. (1960) 'Quelques réflexions sereines sur l'adaptation de l'industrie Belge au Marché Commun', *Comptes Rendus de Travaux de la Société Royale d'Economie Politique de Belgique* no. 273, December.
Drèze, J. (1961) 'Les exportations intra-CEE en 1958 et la position Belge', *Recherches Economiques de Louvain* 717–38.
Glejser, H., Jacquemin, A. and Petit, J. (1980) 'Exports in an imperfect competition framework: an analysis of 1446 small country exporters', *Quarterly Journal of Economics* May 1980: 507–24.
Greenaway, D. and Milner, C. (1986) *Economics of Intra-Industry Trade* Oxford: Blackwell.
Hufbauer, G. C. (1970) 'The impact of national characteristics and technology on the commodity composition of trade in manufactured products', in R. Vernon (ed.) *The Technology Factor in International Trade,* New York 145–231.
Jacquemin, A., de Ghellinck, E. and Huveneers, C. (1978) *Concentration Industrielle en Economie Ouverte: Le Cas de la Belgique,* UCL, CRIDE, Etudes Statistiques, no. 53: 45–7.
Tharakan, P. K. M. (1981) 'The economics of intra-industry trade: a survey', *Recherches Economiques de Louvain* vol. 47, nos 3–4.

Tharakan, P. K. M. (1985) 'Empirical analyses of the commodity composition of trade', in David Greenaway (ed.) (1985) *Current Issues in International Trade: Theory and Policy* London: Macmillan, 63–79.

Tharakan, P. K. M. and Vandoorne, M. (1979) 'Structure of Belgium's comparative advantage vis-à-vis the developing world', *Cahiers Economiques de Bruxelles* no. 82: 213–34.

Chapter four

Competitiveness and internationalization of industry: the case of Switzerland

Silvio Borner

Despite growing politicization of international markets and rising levels of government intervention, the internationalization of entrepreneurial activities is becoming more accentuated, albeit in a variety of forms. Just as increasing trade restrictions led to the expansion of international production, so too will increased government intervention, export requirements, and regulations regarding local production usher in a new phase of internationalization: bilateralism, direct barter agreements, re-export regulations, and local production requirements are making what is already a tough life even harder both for the pure exporters and the traditional multinationals. The precarious balance of payments and debt situation of many countries is increasing the incentive to pass on the heightened financial risks wherever possible to a local partner, the host country, or an international financial organization. Last but not least, the high political risk of Foreign Direct Investment (FDI) can be fobbed off on local firms or governments. A comparative analysis of exports and direct investments reveals that they are both extreme cases of a wide spectrum of forms of international operations. Between the two lies a broad gamut of internationalization options which may be termed 'New Forms of Internationalization'.

Whilst export transactions at arm's length can be carried out with a relatively low risk factor, foreign direct investments involve a long-term, sometimes even permanent, commitment of the parent company to assume all risks. Seen in this light, international transactions within the framework of 'New Forms of Internationalization' may be placed somewhere between the two extremes. This becomes even clearer if we also consider the aspect of controlling the product and process know-how, which is particularly important for maintaining firm-specific competitiveness. The direct investor does not abandon his control of knowledge either in regard to the product or in regard to the production technique. The exporter, on the other hand, loses all control over his products. 'New Forms of Internationalization', however, allow many combinations of risk sharing, transfer of know-how, and profit splitting between the various partners. New forms aim at reducing transaction costs of both markets and hierarchies.[1]

Depending on the strategy chosen, we can designate forms of internationalization either primarily as export financing strategies or primarily as international investment strategies (cf. Table 4.1).[2]

Table 4.1 Taxonomy of new forms of internationalization

New forms of international investment (NFII)
New forms of export financing (NFEF)
Licensing
Barter
Sub-contracting
Long-term commercial framework agreement
Consulting
Counter delivery
Contractual co-operation
Offset
Joint ventures
Junktim
Group investment
Turnkey
Buy-back

Any discussion of competitiveness has to go far beyond the traditional export-import framework. If, as is the case in Switzerland, international production of Swiss firms alone exceeds the total value of exports, traditional (national) market-share analysis overlooks right from the start the largest part of international operations. Furthermore, it is well established that the growth of a highly industrialized nation is inextricably linked to the successful transfer of technology by all means and in all possible forms. 'Nevertheless, economists have been remarkably slow in addressing themselves to the economics of international technology transfer' (Teece 1977: 242). The explanation for this misdirection of research efforts is easily discovered. Industrial branch data on trade, production, and consumption are readily available, whereas other forms of international operations and technology transfer are hard to grasp conceptually, let alone to measure empirically. '(S)hortcomings of the data have blocked the right kinds of research design' (Caves 1985: 45). Modern enterprises are multi-product firms generating and exploiting know-how. World trade for modern industry is based more on differences in technological, managerial, and marketing skills than on differences in endowments. 'Indeed, the importance of technological or organizational factors (i.e. intangible assets) continues to increase' (Kojima and Ozawa 1984: 2). In a small and highly interdependent country like Switzerland, it should surprise no one that internationalization of practically all entrepreneurial functions is the logical response by firms faced with tougher competitors on the one hand and higher barriers to entry in world markets on the other. The competitiveness debate should therefore be focused on the following aspects:

1. Except for dying industries producing standardized products and/or operating with degenerated technologies, competition is dynamic and innovative. It takes substantial resources to make a new process or product economically feasible, i.e. profitable for the firm.
2. Technological and managerial know-how has very little to do with national endowments. It is neither 'given' nor 'immobile'. On the contrary, it is generated by costly R&D as well as systematic learning and then deployed globally by international firms.
3. Competitiveness is, therefore, primarily firm-specific. What really determines the winner of the innovation-imitation race is the absolute advantage of one firm over the other(s).
4. Competitive (absolute) advantage can only remain firm-specific as long as it can be 'protected'. Know-how is not primarily owned by individuals, nor is it primarily embodied in technological hardware (be they processes or products). Know-how is a bundle of skills, developed, packaged, and exploited by a managerial system.
5. Expected competitive advantages are highly uncertain. Competitiveness strategies are, therefore, heavily influenced by perceptions of and attitudes toward risks. The function of competition is mainly to select those organizations which are best adjusted to the environment of markets and regulations.
6. Innovation must be interpreted as any adjustment to new requirements in the relevant environment. Strategies of innovation have three distinct but at the same time closely interrelated dimensions (Borner 1986):
   - the development of firm-specific skills
   - the organizational bundling of these skills into entrepreneurial scope through internalization/externalization
   - the global exploitation of skills and scope through all channels of technology transfer according to the costs associated with the various alternative modes of transactions.

From these six premises the following central hypothesis can be formulated: innovation cannot be understood in terms of skills or even technological skills alone. On the contrary, organizational and contractual innovations designed to adjust the scope of the firm to its economic and political environment are more important for international competitiveness. Only adequate modes of international transactions allow a multitude of technology transfers in bundled or unbundled form. Both scope of internalization and/or contractual co-operation and transaction risks place the problem of competitiveness advantage in a firm-specific 'intangible asset' setting.

Empirical results on new forms of international investments (NFII)

Data base and research concept

The data used for our empirical study of New Forms of Internationalization among Swiss industrial firms were generated by a survey in the spring of 1984 in the following industries:

- the textile industry (including the apparel and shoe industries)
- the chemical industry (including basic chemicals and pharmaceuticals)
- the machinery industry.

Altogether 1,456 questionnaires were sent out, 281 were returned and 272 were included in the evaluation process (18.7 per cent). The sample consists of 44 textile firms, 44 chemical firms, 177 machinery firms, and 7 firms not assignable to any particular industry.

An overview of international activities

Two hundred and thirty firms or 85 per cent reported export activity. An additional 4 per cent were planning to export in the near future. Ninety four per cent of the exporting firms made sales in Western Europe and/or North America, 37 per cent in the developing countries, 15 per cent in the Newly Industrialized Countries (NICs) and Japan, and 14 per cent in Eastern European countries. The unweighted average of exports as a percentage of total turnover (1983) was 56 per cent. A quarter of the firms showed an average export level of under 20 per cent and another quarter of over 80 per cent. Twenty nine per cent of the small firms, 48 per cent of the middle-sized firms, and 63 per cent of the large firms exported over 60 per cent of output.

With regard to FDI, we asked firms to distinguish between minority, majority, and 100 per cent ownership on the one hand and joint ventures on the other. The responses clearly indicated that they prefer 100 per cent ownership: 39 per cent had minority ownership, 27 per cent majority ownership, and 71 per cent had activities with 100 per cent ownership. For the individual branches these figures were: textiles 46–9–64; chemicals 40–26–65; machinery 30–28–76. As for geographical distribution, the OECD countries dominate. Between 85 per cent and 90 per cent of majority (including 100 per cent) ownership activities are located within OECD countries. However, only two-thirds of the minority holdings are located in OECD countries (cf. Table 4.2).

The rather high number of firms with minority holdings in developing countries is due to the ever growing legal restrictions in the field of capital participation. Whether or not entrepreneurial control of 'core skills' is really hampered by such legislation is another question. But it seems that only when forced by host governments do Swiss firms forgo investment with 100 per cent ownership.

One hundred and twenty-nine firms, or 47 per cent of the respondents, reported New Forms of International Investment (NFII). Sixty three firms (23 per cent) had experience with New Forms of Export Financing (NFEF). Forty–eight firms (18 per cent) indicated experience with both forms, 54 firms (20 per cent) experience with international investment alone, and 14 firms (5 per cent) experience with export financing alone. This means a total of 143 firms or 53 per cent had some kind of involvement with New Forms of Internationalization (NFI). If we include firms which have had such involvement in the past but not at present, then the figure is 60 per cent or 163 firms.

Of the 129 firms with experience in NFII we distinguish between 'inward' and 'outward' forms of activity. In the case of an inward form, the firm is on the receiving end of an arrangement, i.e. licensing-in. With an outward form the firm is 'selling' or 'giving', i.e. licensing-out (see Table 4.3). All in all our survey results indicate a relatively high frequency of NFII among Swiss firms.

Table 4.2 Geographical distribution of equity participation in per cent of occurrences in each category

Ownership	Industrial Countries	NICs + Japan	Developing Countries	Total
Minority (up to 50%)	66	13	21	100
Majority (51–99%)	88	8	4	100
100%	90	6	4	100

Table 4.3 Outward and inward forms of international investment among firms in the sample

	%	n
Outward and inward	47	129
Outward	38	102
Inward	32	86
Inward and outward	23	62

New forms of international investment and traditional categories of industrial analysis

In this section we investigate NFII in relationship to exports, FDI, size of firms, industrial branch of activity, technology, and host countries.

New forms of international investment and exports

The average export share of our sample oscillates for the period 1970–83 between 52 per cent and 58 per cent. Firms without any NFI show exports shares of between 31 per cent and 36 per cent. The average for firms with NFII (but without NFEF) fluctuates between 47 per cent and 65 per cent. Lastly, companies employing NFEF instead of NFII have a very high quota – between 69 per cent and 74 per cent. If both NFII and FDI are used, they correlate with an export share in the middle range, for NFII alone the figure may even be lower. Firms engaged in NFII are evidently located somewhere in the middle range, which leads us to the conclusion that firms 'select' between three basic strategies: (1) a supplementary export strategy, (2) an all-out export strategy, and (3) an internationalization strategy. The first approach is characterized by a basically domestic orientation. Exporting has a buffer function and export shares in total turnover may be erratic. Strategy number (2) is employed by firms for which the domestic market is far too small and for which foreign production is not a viable alternative. In this context countertrade solutions (NFEF) are often unavoidable. Finally, the third strategy comprises both FDI and NFII.

The results are in harmony with a similar study by the Ifo-Institute for the Federal Republic of Germany: 'In the course of export growth companies supplement their exports or maintain some degree of export stability by employing various forms of foreign engagement. The most intense engagement in foreign countries is shown by firms with an export quota of between 31 per cent and 50 per cent' (Berger and Uhlmann 1983: 33). Taking into account the generally lower average export quota of German firms (cf. Table 4.4) we would stretch this range to 60 per cent. The data suggest that Swiss firms have a higher level of 'internationality'. Only 21 per cent of the German firms reported current or planned application of what we call NFII. Among the Swiss firms, 38 per cent currently employed NFII and another 9 per cent planned to engage in such activity in the future, thus totalling 47 per cent.

Against the backdrop of the macroeconomic export quotas for Switzerland and the FRG, these data become even more meaningful. Where hardware exports are concerned, these quotas are roughly alike. Hence, we assume that the international relations of German industry are heavily concentrated among large firms, whereas Swiss companies are forced to go international at a much earlier stage of development and/or smaller scale of operation.

Table 4.4 Comparison of export shares of our study for Switzerland and the Ifo-Institute study for the Federal Republic of Germany 1982 (Firms in per cent)

	Export shares up to					
'Switzerland'	20%	40%	60%	80%	more than 80%	Total
With international investment	17	17	13	16	37	100
Without international investment	34	15	9	18	24	100
'Federal Republic of Germany'	20%	30%	50%	75%	more than 75%	Total
With international investment	33	22	28	23	5	100
Without international investment	76	11	9	3	1	100

Note: The export percentages shown are not the same: 20%, 40%, 60%, and 80% in the case of Switzerland; 20% 30%, 50%, and 75% for the FRG.

New forms of international investment and foreign direct investment

According to Table 4.5, the relative frequencies of NFII and FDI are practically the same. That small firms show less financial and personal freedom in undertaking foreign activities – especially in the form of direct investment – seems logical. Yet there is a great deal of variation in the success with which small firms penetrate into other cultural zones – like Japan or Brazil – and a great variety in the form such engagements take. For very small firms NFII seem to be preferred as a route to internationalization. In general, medium-sized firms as well as the textile and apparel industries seem to prefer FDI. Of all the firms reporting equity participation (FDI) abroad, only one-fifth do not employ NFII.

Since the subsidiary or branch plant must be licensed to use technology, designs, moulds, dies, etc., licensing as one type of NFII must come into use.[3] The corollary is that about one-fifth of FDI occurrences are exclusively designed for international marketing purposes. We think that this is particularly true for medium-sized enterprises.

Table 4.5 Internationalization by direct investment and new forms of international investment: a comparison according to industrial branch and size of firm, 1983 (in per cent of all firms)

	Industrial branch			Size of firm (no. of employees)				Total
	Tex	*Che*	*Mach*	*10–49*	*50–499*	*500–999*	*1000+*	
Foreign direct investment	25	46	40	11	48	78	100	39
New forms of international investment	18	43	39	21	37	72	100	38

Note: Tex = textiles Che = chemicals Mach = machinery

The Swiss textile firms possess hardly any production facilities abroad; their FDI activities are in the field of marketing and distribution. In other branches and for both small and large firms NFII and FDI seem to go hand in hand.

The relationship between FDI and NFII shows that majority ownership is less common than minority or 100 per cent ownership. Reasons for this finding may include the following: majority participation is simply unusual for the foreign partner of local enterprise. Where the laws allow, 100 per cent ownership is sought. In regard to the question of control, the difference between majority and minority holdings is minimal. The preference for 100 per cent ownership is obvious. Hunziker (1983: 155) confirms this result and remarks that Swiss industry, by clinging to complete ownership, reduces its own elbow-room. We are led to infer from our data that FDI in the form of 100 per cent ownership is also preferred to NFII.

New forms of international investment and the size of the firm

Table 4.6 confirms that the 'internationality' of firms is a function of size. This is true for exporting, FDI, and of course NFII. Our sample consists of 229 smaller firms (109 firms with 10–49 employees and 120 firms with 50–499 employees). Twenty nine per cent of the smaller and 86 per cent of the larger firms employ NFII. The overall average is 38 per cent. For the smallest firms equity participation is of marginal importance, but more than one-fifth of these firms are engaged in NFII. In general, NFII are employed more frequently than 100 per cent ownership. The output imputable to NFII is, however, nearly impossible to measure, whereas the generation of jobs and value added by the subsidiaries of Swiss multinational corporations is voluminous and measurable (Borner and Wehrle 1984).

Table 4.6   Internationalization by size of firm (in per cent of all firms)

Number of employees	NFII	Equity participation			Exporting	Export share for 1982 in %
		Minority	Majority	100%		
10–99	21	6	3	3	74	43
50–499	37	14	12	35	90	57
500–999	72	33	28	56	100	57
1000+	100	53	26	100	100	68
10–499	29	10	7	20	83	
500+	86	43	27	78	100	

New forms of international investment and industrial branch

The majority of textile companies is not in touch with the final consumer as foreign sales are primarily executed by specialized trading companies and converters. The industry is highly capital-intensive and oriented toward maintaining flexibility and producing very specialized, high-quality products. Production outside Switzerland is rare and limited to apparel and shoe manufacturers. As a consequence, we cannot expect a high level of NFII. FDI is limited to marketing and distribution as well as to some service-like manufacturing activities, e.g. sewing of garments for interior decorating purposes.

The chemical and pharmaceutical industry shows a high level of international commitment, both in the realm of FDI and NFII. Case studies suggest extensive international co-operation, particularly in pharmaceuticals. Despite the fact that product and process technologies are easily diffused, a tight patent-protection policy within a number of western countries allows extra-firm realization of firm-specific advantages. Outside these countries NFII operations are more delicate. Here FDI or 'no-shows' are prevalent. Co-operation occurs mainly as a means for overcoming smallness, be it the small size of the firm, of the product, or of country markets.

In the chemical industry NFII mainly cover process know-how. The 'intimacy' of co-operation is a function of the degree of experience-intensity of the technology transferred and of the potential of the local market. Markets characterized by intense competition, e.g. household chemicals, cosmetics, and OTC-drugs, are conducive to the use of NFII. In such cases NFII extend to the products themselves. As our case studies suggest, a number of manufacturers producing such products rely on NFII and show few hardware-oriented exports.

Table 4.7 Internationalization according to industrial branch (in per cent of all firms)

Branch	NFII	Equity participation			Exporting	Export share for 1982 in %
		Minority	Majority	100%		
Textiles	18	11	2	16	73	59
Chemicals	43	18	11	30	89	44
Machinery	39	15	11	30	84	55

In the case of the machinery industry, the adjective 'new' in 'New Forms' is most misleading. New Forms have a long history here. Sub-contracting appears to have an old tradition as a trade-cycle buffer. The other New Forms have had a significant impact on internationalization behaviour because processes are highly divisible compared to the batch and bulk production in the chemical industry. Owing to the idiosyncratic nature of many Newtonian technologies, control is ensured without recourse to patenting. In electronics and telecommunications, resistance to NFI is high because of the abstract and scientific character of the technology. But local production is bound to increase *vis-à-vis* world trade in markets where suppliers are abundant and where technology is dispersing rapidly. Where high-tech is involved, countries go out of their way to acquire and master know-how. All these factors contribute to a high level of NFII in the entire machinery industry.

New forms of international investment and host countries

The industrialized or OECD countries are the primary host countries for Swiss firms. If our exports go mainly to European countries and if most FDI takes place there too, one has to expect a large percentage of NFII to be hosted in western Europe also. However, the larger the firm, the more evenly distributed are its NFII in the world's regions. This is an obvious result of the financial and managerial limitations of smaller companies. They have to select carefully where they commit their resources, while large enterprises can afford to be represented in more regions. Owing to the higher transaction costs, small firms are less inclined to get involved in culturally distant countries (cf. Carlson 1975 and Robinson 1981).

For the chemical branch the eastern bloc plays a much greater role as a host region than the developing countries. We assume this is due to the technical competence of some of these countries as well as to the existence of the necessary infrastructure, particularly in heavier chemicals. Additionally, demand in these countries is similar to that in the west.

Table 4.8 Geographical distribution of new forms of international investment according to industrial branch and size of firm (in per cent: base = firms currently engaged in NFII)

				Current engagements (in %)			
	Tex	Che	Mach	10–49	50–499	500–999	1000+
Industrial countries	75	95	90	83	89	92	89
NICs + Japan	50	47	48	39	39	54	72
Developing countries	38	21	29	13	27	38	50
Eastern European countries	25	42	26	22	36	8	39

Note: Multiple entries possible: figures do not add up to 100 per cent

New forms of international investment and the level of technology

Our hypothesis was that NFI would be ruled out in the high-tech area. It was very difficult to collect information about the relationship between the speed of technological development and the use of NFII as judged by the firms themselves. Nevertheless, we can say that the firms with FDI or NFII have a different perception of technological change than the rest in the sample: they observe a faster pace of technological change. Our explanation for this situation is threefold: (1) firms employing NFII are more market-oriented, (2) proximity to the market forces firms to make a more realistic estimate of exogenous factors, (3) in order to keep up with the pace of progress without sacrificing market proximity, firms are forced to co-operate internationally and to participate more intensively in foreign markets.

The various new forms of international investment

Clearly, the most common NFII is licensing, followed by different forms of contractual co-operation. 'The basic statement about size-specific differences in respect to foreign engagement is that firms with 10 to 499 employees are less active than companies with 500 or more employees' (Berger and Uhlmann 1983). We want to test to what extent the various forms follow this pattern. Using an indicator developed by Berger and Uhlmann (1983), we compared the number of occurrences of one form (of the NFII) in two size categories: 'more than 500 employees' and 'less than 500 employees'.

This figure was then corrected by the cell count in each size category:

$$(A_l/k)/(A_s/i)$$

'A_l' is the frequency of a particular NFII among large firms, 'A_s' the same for the small firms. 'k' is the number of large firms in the sample, 'i' the number of small firms. Thus, the higher the indicator, the more active the larger firms are (cf. Table 4.9).

Table 4.9 Indicator of the relationships between size of firm and new forms of international investment

	Industrial countries	NICs + Japan	Developing countries	Eastern European countries	Future plans
Licensing	1.6	3.2	3.8	2.6	1.1
Sub-contracting	0.9	1.3	(0.7)	(0.4)	0.9
Management consulting	2.4	–	–	–	(0.4)
Technical consulting	1.1	1.9	2.16	(0.03)	0.7
Joint ventures	1.7	–	–	–	1.2
Contractual co-operation	0.9	3.6	1.8	(0.9)	1.6

Direct investment:
– Minority ownership: 1.5
– Majority ownership: 1.3
– 100% ownership: 1.4
Legend: () = small cell count; – = cell count equals zero
Note: The indicator was computed from the number of occurrences of a certain NFII employed by larger firms divided by the number of occurrences of the same NFII employed by smaller firms: the higher the value above unity, the greater the lag of small firms.
Source: framework taken from Berger and Uhlmann (1983).

As expected, most entries in the matrix are dominated by larger firms. This is particularly true for licensing and management consulting and, in terms of regions, the NICs and the developing countries. All forms of direct investment are a domain of the larger units. These findings of course are not surprising. In the case

The competitiveness of European industry

of management consulting, management capacity is the crucial limitation for the smaller firm. This explains why technical consulting is also dominated by the larger companies. The know-how of smaller enterprises often rests in one or a few persons. Hence, it cannot be codified and is, therefore, not transmittable internationally.

More surprising and interesing, however, is the relative lead of the smaller firms in sub-contracting, contractual co-operation, and in activities in the eastern bloc countries. It is typically the 'looser', more informal, NFII through which these firms – via personal contacts – establish an advantage. Although joint ventures are well suited to this size category, this form is met with suspicion. Since dealing with culturally more distant regions causes higher transaction costs, larger firms will be more numerous here again. Licensing and contractual co-operation tend to be the first NFII chosen by firms, especially for geographically distant operations. For all regions and for all types of firms these two forms are the most frequent. Where higher frequencies occur, technical consulting is significant. Sub-contracting shows a middle frequency, whereas management consulting and joint ventures are reserved for the well-versed internationalists.

Table 4.10 Firms' perception of the future role of new forms of international investment (in per cent)

Significance of NFII	Total	Tex	Che	Mach	A	B	C	D
All firms								
Insignificant	8	16	14	4	7	8	22	0
Diminishing	0	0	0	0	0	0	0	0
No change	10	2	25	9	13	9	6	11
Increasing	55	55	41	61	48	58	56	79
Heavily increasing	5	2	9	5	2	8	11	5
No opinion	22	25	11	22	30	18	6	5
Firms with experience in NFII								
Insignificant	5	13	11	3	9	5	8	0
Diminishing	0	0	0	0	0	0	0 .	0
No change	10	0	26	7	4	14	8	11
Increasing	66	88	42	73	61	64	62	78
Heavily increasing	11	0	16	10	4	16	15	6
No opinion	8	0	5	9	22	2	8	6

A: Firms with 10–49 employees
B: Firms with 50–499 employees
C: Firms with 500–999 employees
D: Firms with 1,000 and more employees

76

New forms of international investment in the future

The response to our question about future plans suggests increasing activities of SMEs in NFII. The figures reveal furthermore that firms with experience in NFII foresee a greater future role than firms with no experience, with the exception of large firms all of which anticipate an increasing role for NFII. The respondents from the chemical industry perceive a relatively lesser role for NFII than representatives from the textile and the machinery industries.

Empirical estimates for new forms of export financing (NFEF)

Forms and frequencies of countertrade

Table 4.11 shows the frequency with which the 56 Swiss firms engaged in countertrade (i.e. about 25 per cent of the exporting firms in our study) employed the various types of countertrade. It is not surprising that pure barter is not used more often given the high level of risks involved. Twenty six per cent of the respondents are involved in compensation. The high level of standardization of contracts, the experience in east-west trade, and the opportunities for sharing risks account for the attractiveness of commercial compensation. Counter delivery – 17 per cent of the responses – has the advantage of including the legal separation of the two halves of the contract, but the disadvantage of a medium-term obligation for fulfilling the terms of the contract. The difficulty of finding markets for goods received, as well as the general reluctance of Swiss firms to carry out an active countertrade strategy, explains why junktim was not mentioned even once.

Commercial compensation (i.e. barter, counterdelivery, junktim, multilateral countertrade) was indicated by 63 per cent and industrial compensation by 37 per cent of the respondents. This means that in a little more than one-third of the cases, an exchange of commodities which was tied to know-how transfer (industrial compensation) took place. Firms engaging in industrial compensation considered themselves as technologically more sophisticated than the average sample firm.

Geographical distribution of countertrade

For Swiss firms countertrade has become a global phenomenon. As shown in Table 4.12, about one-half of the respondents did business in the eastern European countries. The developing

The competitiveness of European industry

Table 4.11   New forms of export financing: frequency of application

Type of countertrade	Number of occurrences in % (Base 100% = 119 responses)
Classical barter	3.4
Barter with third parties/parallel barter	26.0
Counterdelivery	16.8
Junktim	0.0
Long-term commercial framework agreements	5.0
Buy-back	3.4
Turnkey	28.6
Multilateral countertrade	16.8

Table 4.12   Frequency of new forms of countertrade according to regions of the world

	Number of occurrences in % (Base 100% = 119 responses)
OECD without Japan	20.2
NICs including Japan	11
Developing countries	20.2
COMECON	48.6

countries and the NICs (cf. Blum 1983), together with Japan, accounted for another third. The OECD countries (North-North countertrade) accounted for only 20 per cent of the responses. Belgium, Denmark, France, Norway, Portugal, Australia, Canada, China, New Zealand, and last but not least the Latin American NICs and Indonesia are central to the growing countertrade activities. In the case of the developing countries,[4] it is above all the nations in the Near East and the Middle East (Iran, Iraq) and in Africa which have countertrade relations with Swiss industrial enterprises.

Theoretical analysis of countertrade implies that the geographical pattern of commercial and industrial compensation is dependent on the economic system on the one hand and on the state of development on the other. In the COMECON area, more than 80 per cent of all items concern commercial compensation. This is due to the fact that technology transfer is excluded or minimized for security reasons (e.g. COCOM). From the point of view of Swiss firms, transfer of know-how is not desirable since neither property rights nor contractual guarantees are considered to be sufficient. LDCs are involved in both categories, depending on the type of economic system and the country-specific locational advantages. This is illustrated by the role played by buy-back/ turnkey agreements with low-cost and/or resource-rich LDCs or NICs. With a high share of industrial compensation the OECD countries and the NICs seem to be 'partners of a higher order'. The technological, socioeconomic, and political conditions in the OECD, Japan, and the NICs allow forms of countertrade which combine financing with technology transfer and thus establish qualitatively different, more permanent ties of co-operation.

In our survey we asked firms to give the percentage of exports which were financed through any of the several forms of counter-trade. Twenty-nine firms responded to this question (cf. Table 4.13). From 1980 to 1983, the mean value of the export share of firms employing countertrade was 28.75 per cent higher than the figure for the other firms. If one also takes indirectly induced exports into consideration, then we can accept our working hypothesis that New Forms of Export Financing do induce higher levels of exports in the world of rising government interference.

Table 4.13 The relative importance of countertrade as a percentage of export volume

	1970	1975	1979	1980	1981	1982	1983
Number of responses	10	18	20	20	21	20	23
Yearly mean of countertrade activities as a % of exports	6.45	6.41	6.45	7.31	9.32	9.34	10.07
Standard deviation	8.99	8.86	10.73	15.24	14.30	16.11	15.73

Table 4.14 Frequency of new forms of export financing according to size of firm

Number of employees	Number of occurrences in % (Base 100% = 119 responses)
5–50	11.5
51–500	46
501–1,000	12.6
1,000 and more	29.9

Are Swiss firms affected by government assistance of their competitors? If so, how much and in what ways? More than 50 per cent of all exporters listed a total of 133 specific examples of such 'new protectionism'.

Countertrade according to the size of the firm

Table 4.14 gives an overview of the survey responses according to size of firms. Fifty-seven and a half per cent of the firms employing

New Forms of Export Financing were small and medium-sized firms, one-third of the firms had more than 1,000 employees. Our evaluation of future plans indicates that this situation is most likely to remain stable in the near future. Further, firms with more than 500 employees accounted for 58 per cent of commercial compensation agreements, small and middle-sized firms for only 30.2 per cent. The smaller firms use industrial compensation to take advantage of market niches; they use countertrade framework-agreements, buy-back, and turnkey in about 55 per cent of the cases. In general, these results supported our hypothesis that industrial compensation is primarily an instrument of internationalization employed by small and medium-sized companies in the marketing process in general and in the marketing of their core in particular (cf. Schlemper 1978, 1979).

Classical exports and new forms of export financing

One of our working hypotheses was that the defence and expansion of existing export markets or the opening up of new markets would be more successful among firms employing New Forms of Export Financing. To test this hypothesis we examined the export quotas for firms which had – or had not – employed innovative forms of countertrade. We found that the firms using countertrade showed a considerably high export quota. One-third of this difference can be considered to stem directly from the use of NFEF. There are indications that the amount of exports indirectly induced by NFEF is significant.

On the other hand there are three major risks faced by firms engaged in the various forms of countertrade: (1) quality of the

Table 4.15 Export quotas as a function of new forms of internationalization

Year	Export quota: the yearly mean in %			
	Firms with NFEF and classical exports	Firms with NFEF and NFII and classical exports	Firms with NFII and classical exports	Firms with only classical exports
1970	64.5	56.7	49.5	45.3
1975	67.9	66.5	57.8	46.8
1979	65.8	59.9	52.7	46.2
1980	66.5	67.0	57.9	46.6
1981	65.5	60.0	52.6	46.8
1983	66.4	64.3	57.0	46.5

goods received in exchange, (2) delays in delivery time, and (3) marketing risks for the goods received in exchange. Depending on the form of countertrade employed, these risks can either occur individually or in addition to the various risks already faced by firms engaged in traditional export activity. The possibilities of covering these risks are listed in Table 4.16.

Table 4.16 Insurance for types of countertrade risks(%)

	Poor quality of goods received	Time delays	Marketing risks
Base (100%) = 56 firms with 98 responses			
Risk does not exist	51	56.3	60.6
Shifting of risk to contractual partner	9	9.4	3
Risk not insured although possible	15	12.5	12
Risk cannot be insured	24.2	21.9	24.2

Results of surveys of Swiss multinationals

Foreign employment, FDI, and international production by Swiss multinationals

Switzerland is the 'number five' home country of multinational corporations with very high levels of FDI. In blatant contrast to the extensive export activities carried out by all sizes of Swiss firms, Swiss Foreign Direct Investment consists almost entirely of the foreign operations of only about 50 multinational corporations (multis) whose headquarters are located inside Switzerland.[5]

The results concerning employment of the 1980 survey are presented in Table 4.17. Nine of the 15 multis employ more than two-thirds of their personnel outside Switzerland. Thus the foreign employment of the 'top 15' – 483,000 – was equivalent to 70 per cent of the total number of industrial jobs inside Switzerland. Of the 100,000 employees in the Third World, almost 50,000 are to be found in the seven NICs: Brazil, Mexico, Argentina, Hong Kong, Taiwan, South Korea, and Singapore.

It is interesting to note that the declining watch industry has hardly any employees abroad. Also the design-oriented textile and garment industries in Switzerland are characterized by small companies producing inside Switzerland.

Levels of investment and investment growth for the 1970s are presented for the 15 largest Swiss multinationals in Table 4.18. We

Table 4.17 The geographical distribution of employment in the 15 largest Swiss industrial multis 1980

	Switzerland	Industrialized countries	Developing countries	Of which NICs	Total abroad	Total employment
Nestle	7,400	99,600	46,000	20,100	145,000	153,000
Ciba–Geigy	22,900	12,520	45,770	6,830	58,290	81,190
BBC	21,760	8,900	74,640	5,500*	83,540	105,300
Alusuisse	8,650	3,710	32,720	2,000*	36,430	45,080
Roche	9,610	25,220	8,820	3,150	34,040	43,650
Sandoz	9,830	19,240	6,390	2,290	25,630	35,460
Largest 6	80,150	297,190	86,340	39,870	383,530	463,680
Oerlikon-Buhrle	15,300	19,080	2,830	2,770	21,910	37,210
Sulzer	20,180	11,930	2,820	1,730	14,750	34,930
Holderbank	2,060	11,850	4,820	2,770	16,670	18,730
Georg Fischer	8,030	9,250	–	–	9,250	17,280
Schindler	6,010	12,660	2,990	2,310	15,650	21,660
Asuag**	12,830	2,740	–	–	2,740	15,570
Landis & Gyr	6,480	9,740	–	–	9,740	16,220
Von Roll	5,760	490	–	–	490	6,250
Hesta	3,840	8,040	570	570	8,610	12,450
Largest 15	160,640	382,970	100,370	50,020*	483,340	643,980

* Estimates
** Today: SMH (Schweizerische Gesellschaft für Mikroelektronik und Uhrenindustrie AG)
Source: calculations by the authors

Table 4.18 The geographical distribution of investment of the 15 largest Swiss industrial multis (1970*–80)

	Switzerland		Industrialized countries		Developing countries		Total abroad		Total investment	
	Mio.Fr	%	Mio.Fr	%	Mio.Fr	%	Mio.Fr	%	Mio.Fr	%
1970*	10,900	34.3	18,300	57.5	2,600	8.2	20,900	65.7	31,000	100.0
1980	17,800	32.4	32,300	58.5	5,000	9.1	37,200	67.6	55,000	100.0
1970–1980	+6,900	+63.6	+13,900	+76.0	+2,400	+92.3	+16,300	+78.0	+23,200	+73.0

* For 3 multis the data do not refer to 1970
Mio.Fr = millions of francs

note that domestic investment still accounts for about 33 per cent of total investment, while domestic employment is only 25 per cent of total employment. Yet investment in other industrialized countries was twice as high as in Switzerland during the 1970s. Only one-tenth of total investment went to the developing countries. Total European investment of the 15 largest Swiss multinationals is just about equal to total investment within Switzerland. The concentration of investment among the 6 largest multinationals is even greater than the concentration of personnel: 81 per cent of total investment – or 44 billion francs – is accounted for by the 6 largest companies.

New forms of international investment by Swiss multinationals

The year 1980 was a turning point in the history of the Swiss multinationals in industry. After two decades of growth and market-share oriented strategy more weight and attention is being given to the profit goal. In this context it is particularly pertinent to investigate whether the Swiss MNEs were switching from FDI to NFII. Table 4.19 confirms that NFII are significant for the 11 firms participating in our survey.[6] None of the various NFII will become less important for the strategies of Swiss multinational firms. Some of the NFII will definitely become more important, especially licensing, joint ventures, and contractual co-operation.

An even better impression of what our Swiss MNEs expect for the future can be gained from examining the geographical distribution of NFII. The highest potential for NFII is perceived for the USA on the one hand and for the NICs on the other. Finally, the most important correlations between forms and regions are

- licensing with the USA, Japan, and the NICs
- joint ventures with the USA and the NICs
- sub-contracting with the NICs
- contractual co-operation with European, US, and Japanese firms.

Table 4.19 Relative importance of NFII in 1984

	Total:11
Insignificant	0%
Of little significance	31%
Significant	69%
Highly significant	0%

These findings seem to be compatible with our theoretical hypotheses, namely that NFII are primarily seen as a means to establish a foothold in new and dynamic markets and/or to promote technology transfers both into and out of Switzerland. The contribution of various NFII to different dimensions of microeconomic competitiveness could be marked on a scale ranging from 1 (insignificant) to 6 (highly significant). The most interesting results are: (see Table 4.20)

Figure 4.1   Importance of NFII in the future

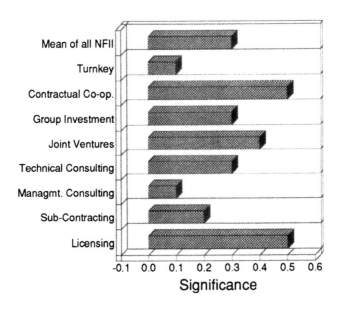

Notes: −1 = significance will decrease
          0 = significance will not change
          1 = significance will increase

1. In comparison with all other forms, both exports and FDI show the highest rating (4.3, 3.8), NFII are clearly viewed as contributing less to overall competitiveness (2.5). Individual forms such as licensing with 3.3, and joint ventures with 2.8 come relatively close to the preferred classical forms of internationalization.
2. Very interesting correlations between NFII and aspects of competitiveness become visible when we disaggregate. While exports rank highest with regard to job security in the home country, NFII engagements get top ratings in view of opening up new markets. FDI is primarily associated with high returns. At the same time, FDI contributes least to the security of jobs in the home country and – not surprisingly – NFII seem most threatening to entrepreneurial independence. NFII are also perceived as threats to the security of jobs in the home country.

Table 4.20   Influence of NFII on competitiveness

	Dimensions of competitiveness					
	Return on investment	Entre-preneurial inde-pendence	Potential for innovation	Security of jobs in the home country	Access to new markets	Mean of all dimensions
Exports	4.4	3.2	4.2	5.1	4.7	4.3
Licensing	3.6	3.0	3.3	2.8	3.9	3.3
Sub-contracting	2.6	2.2	2.1	1.8	2.6	2.3
Management consulting	2.2	1.9	1.9	1.6	2.2	2.0
Technical consulting	2.8	1.9	2.4	2.5	2.6	2.4
Joint ventures	2.8	2.5	2.8	2.4	3.7	2.8
Group investments	2.5	2.1	2.3	2.3	3.1	2.5
Contractual co-operation	2.3	2.4	2.3	2.0	3.2	2.4
Turnkey	2.5	2.1	2.6	2.4	2.9	2.5
FDI	4.6	4.0	3.4	2.9	4.3	3.8
Mean of all NFII	2.7	2.3	2.5	2.2	3.0	2.5

These results fit quite nicely into our conceptual and theoretical framework. This is especially true for the association of all New Forms of International Investment (NFII) with the strategic goal of penetrating into new markets. With the exception of technical contracts, this aspect dominates very clearly. Other rather interesting and at the same time consistent findings are:

1. the relatively high contribution of licensing and consulting activities to returns on investment
2. the relatively high contribution of both joint ventures and licensing operations to innovation potential.

The first finding conforms to our view of the firm as a (multiple) seller of firm-specific 'skills'; the latter demonstrates the importance of organizational aspects of 'scope' for innovative activity.

Foreign trade policy and new forms of internationalization

Small, open economies with highly internationalized firms view the demand side of their markets as part of the exogenous environment and not as a task of national economic policy. Demand management by way of international policy co-ordination is, of course, of decisive importance – but out of reach of both the policy maker in the (small) home country and the entrepreneurial strategist. Neither business leaders nor political elites in Switzerland develop a demand for a national macro perspective with regard to economic policies. What dominates political as well as entrepreneurial thinking is microeconomic integration into the international division of labour. Naturally, there are some minimal requirements for national macro policies, especially with regard to a stable and steady monetary policy. On the supply side, policy issues include incentives with respect to taxes, regulations, etc.

But the focus of corresponding economic policies is always international. This implies that the question of international competitiveness is primarily one of adjustment, adaptation, innovation, and specialization of business enterprises. The replacement of a narrow trade perspective by the 'internationalization paradigm' forces us, however, to view this structural adjustment in all dimensions of international transactions: trade, factor income, FDI, technology transfer, countertrade, etc. National strategies to improve international competitiveness must therefore focus on all possible comparative (national) advantages and all absolute (entrepreneurial) advantages resulting from all possible types of international operations.

But this goal can and usually will clash with internal, national policies of guaranteeing welfare standards, of insuring all sorts of risks (including the risks of world-wide and/or technological changes), of redistributing income vertically and regionally, of protecting locational and/or size structures of certain industries, etc. (cf. Hesse *et al.* 1985: 137–9).

The main conclusion to be drawn is that it is analytically impossible to distinguish between economic and political aspects of adjustment. The more global/economic forces disrupt political structures, the more these market forces will mobilize political counterforces. And these in turn can, as Olsen (1982) has convincingly argued, finally lead – via bureaucratization and interest-group haggling – to social sclerosis. Thus, any rational discussion of costs and benefits of adjustment policies must necessarily encompass the interdependencies between economic and political criteria of success and failure. Despite these limitations, the economic cost of government interventions intended to defend or even to extend the reach of national policies is associated with two different kinds of economic costs. The first kind obviously refers to the direct costs associated with 'closing' the economy. The second type results from indirect effects. Not only is international instability increased by uncoordinated national policies, adjustment problems will also be shifted from one group to another within an individual country. International trade and global allocation are, therefore, two quite different things (cf. Hesse *et al.* 1985: 141–2).

If access to world markets is sought by a greater and greater variety of strategies, designed and chosen by internationalized firms, and if this access is increasingly regarded as a privilege to be granted (or not) according to national(istic) preferences, then rules of trade alone will no longer suffice. Trade rules alone will do justice neither to the complex nature of international inter-dependence nor to the interdependence among national policies – regional policy, social policy, educational policy, R&D policy, industrial policy, etc. Thus we are confronted with the need of international policy co-ordination either in the form of global rules about fair and unfair practices in all these fields or in the form of functional (rather than territorial) authorities which would take over clearly defined (functional) sovereignty rights (cf. Hesse *et al.* 1985: 141). Neither is likely to happen. Since all these dimensions of economic policy are relevant for establishing comparative advantage at the national level, as well as for the absolute competitive advantage of individual firms, it is impossible to draw a sharp line between foreign and domestic policy or between market-conform and interventionist measures. As foreign govern-ments set up whole arsenals to fight imports, to regulate FDI, and to profit from NFI, the home country government is bombarded with two kinds of demands. The first is the demand to make competition fair, that is, to compensate the disadvantaged home country firms. The argument allows those asking for subsidies, or other indirect regulations which represent an implicit subsidy, not to lose their straight liberal faces. Industry would, they argue, fight it out without any government assistance, but since other national governments are helping their firms, a fair chance in international competition means government aid. The second demand arises from the policy distortion affecting home country firms with different core skills, different scope, and varying international profiles. This problem arises in the context of export risk insurance or other forms of export promotion. If these insurance schemes are subsidized by tax money or if promotion expenses one-sidedly benefit classical export activities in comparison to FDI or NFI, then distortions occur. Again, it is extremely difficult to draw a sharp line between efficient compensation for exporters, who are mostly SMEs, more vulnerable to protectionism and often creating more value-added and employment than NFI operations, on the one hand, and just plain old export subsidies on the other. We could produce a lengthy list of reasons for and against any specific home country policy in favour of NFI. On analytical grounds, there is no compelling case for or against NFII or NFEF promo-tion policies.

The more traditional exports are replaced and/or complemented by all kinds of NFI, the more Gross Domestic Product and Gross

National Income will diverge. More and more of the components for foreign income will no longer mirror current production but rather the income from previously transferred assets: real capital in the case of FDI, 'human capital' in the case of technology and know-how sales, and 'returns to scope' in the case of co-operation among independent firms.

As our empirical research has demonstrated, Switzerland is still a very good home country for firms specializing in various forms of internationalization. Orientation toward open world markets for final and intermediate goods, for the flow of capital and know-how, and for a set of general rules representing a collective good will remain the first best foreign policy option for Switzerland. Whenever and wherever these ideal conditions are violated, Swiss firms will, by themselves, try to find ways and means around the obstacles. Downhill and slalom are two different alpine sports. But gifted skiers will perform well in both of them – if we let them practice and experiment. Swiss industrial firms, be they large or small, do not expect active government assistance for restructuring. They themselves view the adjustment problem mainly as a strategic challenge at the level of the firm. The firms will be more than pleased if the present institutional framework can be maintained.

Notes

1 See for theoretical underpinnings Borner (1986), Chapters 7, 8, 9, and the literature cited there.
2 For detailed description see Borner (1986), Chapters 5 and 6.
3 There are exceptions, cf. Hämisegger (1986).
4 Basic aspects of North–South countertrade are described in Schwenk (1985), Jones (1984), Outters-Jaeger (1979), Business International (1983). For the East–West countertrade cf. for example, Economic Commission for Europe (1979, 1981, 1983) and Dizard (1983), Kaikati (1976, 1981). Fisher and Harte (1985) discuss countertrade as a global phenomenon.
5 For the complete reference see Borner and Wehrle (1984), Wehrle (1984).
6 Four firms refused to answer because they felt the questions on 'countertrade' (not reported here) touched 'sensitive' or 'secret' areas.

References

Berger, M. and Uhlmann, L. (1983) 'Kleine und mittlere Unternehmen und Auslandsinvestitionen', Ifo-Institut, Munich.
Blum, G. (1983) 'Die Finanzierung von Schwelländergeschäften unter erschwerten Bedingungen', Vortrag, gehalten an der HSG-Weiterbildungsstufe.

Borner, S. (1986) *Internationalization of Industry – An Assessment in the Light of a Small Open Economy (Switzerland)*, Berlin, Heidelberg: Springer.

Borner, S. and Wehrle, F. (1984) *Die Sechste Schweiz. Überleben auf dem Weltmarkt*, Zürich: Örell Füssli Verlag.

Bürgin, R. (1986) 'Multifunktionaler Countertrade als Internationalisierungsinstrument der Schweizer Industrie: Ausprägungen, Determinanten, Bedeutung und aussenpolitische Beurteilung', dissertation, Basel.

Business International (1983) *Countertrade with Developing Countries*, Geneva.

Carlson, S. (1975) *How Foreign is Foreign Trade*, Uppsala: Acta Universitatis Upsaliensis.

Caves, R. E. (1985) *Multinational Enterprise and Economic Analysis*, Cambridge: Cambridge University Press.

Dizard, J. W. (1983) *The Explosion of International Barter*, Fortune.

Economic Commission for Europe (1979) *Countertrade Practices in the ECE Region*, Trade/R. 385, Geneva.

Economic Commission for Europe (1981) *Reciprocal Trading Arrangements at the Western Enterprise Level with Special Reference for East-West Trade*, United Nations Trade AC. 18/R. 2, Geneva.

Economic Commission for Europe (1983) *Compensation Trade in the ECE Region: A Survey of Quantitative Estimates*, Trade/AC, 19/R.1, Geneva.

Fisher, S. and Harte, K. M. (eds) (1985) *Barter in the World Economy*, New York: Praeger.

Hämisegger, K. (1986) 'Neue Formen des Auslandengagements – Erhöhte Interdependenz in einer fragmentierten Weltwirtschaft', dissertation, Basel.

Hesse, H., Keppler, H. and Preusse, H. G. (1985) *Internationale Interdependenzen im weltwirtschaftlichen Entwichlungsprozess*, Göttingen: Verlag Otto Schwartz.

Hunziker, E. (1983) *Auslandsmarktstrategien*, Zürich: Verlag Industrielle Organization.

Jones, S. (1984) *North/South Countertrade: Barter and Reciprocal Trade with Developing Countries*, London: Economist Intelligence Unit Limited.

Kaikati, J. G. (1976) 'The reincarnation of barter trade as a marketing tool', *Journal of Marketing*, no. 40.

Kaikati, J. G. (1981) 'The international barter boom: perspectives and challenges', *International Marketing*, no. 1.

Kojima, K. and Ozawa, T. (1984) 'Micro- and macro-economic models of direct foreign investment: towards a synthesis', *Hitotsubashi Journal of Economics*, no. 25.

Olsen, M. Jr (1982) *The Rise and Decline of Nations*, Yale: Yale University Press.

Outters-Jaeger, I. (1979) *The Development Impact of Barter in Developing Countries*, Paris: OECD.

Robinson, R. D. (1981) 'Background concepts and philosophy of international business. From World War II to the present', *Journal of International Business Studies*, Spring/Summer.

Schlemper, A. (1978) 'Die Bedeutung des Warenverkehrs mit der DDR für Klein- und Mittelbetriebe', Essen: East-West Co-operation.

Schlemper, A. (1979) 'Gegengeschäfte: Wiedergeburt eines Absatzinstrumentes oder Rückfall in veraltete Handelsformen? Eine theoretische Analyse unter besonderer Berücksichtigung kleiner und mittlerer Unternehmen', in *Festschrift für Mattias E. Kampf. Perspektiven der Mittelstandspolitik und Mittelstandsforschung*, Göttingen.

Schwenk, M. H. (1985) 'North-south barter trade', in S. Fisher and K. M. Harte (eds) (1985) *Barter in the World Economy*, New York: Praeger.

Teece, D. J. (1977) 'Technology transfer by multinational firms: the resource cost of transferring technological know-how', *The Economic Journal*, June.

Wehrle, F. (1984) 'Die Sechste Schwiez. Bestandesaufnahme und Analyse der Dritt-Welt-Aktivitäten der Schweizer Industriemultis', in *Jahrbuch Schweiz – Dritte Welt*, Geneva: Institut universitaire d'études du développement.

Abbreviations

DCs	Developing Countries
FDI	Foreign Direct Investment
GDP	Gross Domestic Product
LDCs	Low Developed Countries
MNEs	Multinational Enterprises
NFI	New Forms of Internationalization
NFII	New Forms of International Investment
NFEF	New Forms of Export Financing
NICs	Newly Industrializing Countries
OMAs	Orderly Marketing Agreements
R&D	Research and Development
SMEs	Small and Medium Enterprises
VERs	Voluntary Export Restraints

Chapter five

Hindering and supporting factors in the start-up of new, small, technology based firms

Christer Karlsson

Introduction

The role of this chapter is to discuss different measures which can be taken to stimulate and improve technology based entrepreneurship in a society. Such an activity contributes in a variety of ways to the growth and vitality of the economy and will therefore significantly contribute to the competitiveness of the industry in different countries. One major base for this chapter is a study of the start-up process of new, small technology based firms in western Sweden. The study was initiated by the Swedish Academy of Engineering Sciences. The intentions were to gain more general knowledge of conditions for technology based entrepreneurship as well as creating a base for concrete actions to promote this.

The study covers start-up periods from fairly concrete ideas of a business mission to companies that have been in operation for a couple of years. The coverage of the study is also limited to companies that are managed by individuals or small groups of individuals who are both owners and actively working in the company. New businesses that are a result of investments in large corporations are not included.

The importance of technical entrepreneurship

Technology based entrepreneurship contributes in a variety of ways to the growth and vitality of an economy and will therefore contribute heavily to the competitiveness of the industry in different countries. For many regions and countries, the start-up of technically innovative companies is seen as a source of continuing technical and economic vitality, and possibly even the source of technical renaissance. All start-ups create jobs and, in the long term, technical firms seem to perform particularly well in this regard (Eisenhardt and Forbes 1984).

There are discrepancies between countries which should be

observed. While the USA is the outstanding example of the importance of technology based entrepreneurship, the same thing is to a lesser extent true for Europe but not a common pattern at all in Japan.

How to measure the importance of technical entrepreneurship to the competitiveness of the industry of a country can also be debated. The two most common factors mentioned are number of employees and innovations. A recent study (Gallagher 1986) on job generation in the UK between 1982 and 1984, found that the smallest companies (1–19 employees) were the only net creators of jobs during the period, with a 3 per cent annual growth. Larger firms just held their positions and in firms with over 1,000 employees employment decreased 6 per cent annually.

Small firms also hold a leading position in studies of the role of different firms as innovators, although there is a considerable difference between industries. But just as with employment figures, it is very difficult to get a comprehensive conclusion of the role of firms which are both new, small and technology based since most studies focus only on size. However, these remarks don't change the total impression of the role of these firms and many governments are running programmes to support this kind of activity.

Hindering and supporting factors

An essential starting point in an analysis of conditions for technology based entrepreneurship is to try to identify what forces influence the start-up process in hindering and supporting directions. The factors studied are summarized in Figure 5.1.

The same factor can sometimes have a supporting and sometimes a hindering influence. However, it must be observed that hindering and supporting factors do not always have opposite values, i.e. whatever efforts are made to eliminate a hindering factor, one cannot turn it into an advantage.

Another starting point has been to study the process as overlapping phases with slightly different characters, i.e. the idea phase, the development phase, the commercializing phase, and the expansion phase.

Methodology

The analysis is made from four perspectives, i.e.

– the individuals
– the businesses
– institutional factors
– society and culture.

Figure 5.1 A model of phases and influencing in the new business creation process. (N.B. Forces (arrows) can show up on both sides and in different phases)

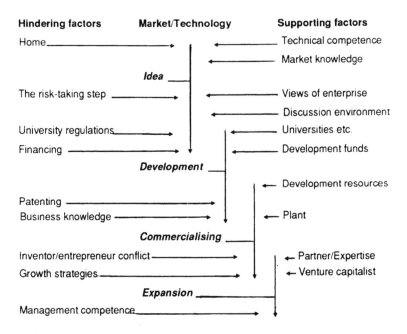

This analysis is based on interviews, literature studies and the researcher's knowledge and experience in numerous cases. Aggregate knowledge has been collected through interviews with 'significant actors', e.g. individuals with experience from numerous projects. Five cases of special significance were studied in more depth.

The whole study has been carried through in an explorative and holistic way with the purpose of identifying as many factors as possible and reaching conclusions on their relevance rather than reaching statistically significant conclusions of frequency of presence of factors.

Results

The results are presented following a classification in four different perspectives starting with the individual.

Individual factors

Why start your own business?

The outstanding and most frequent reason for starting your own business is a wish for autonomy. One could say that 'employment conditions' mean far more than business possibilities. This is well in line with conclusions from studies of entrepreneurship. The entrepreneur wants to be his own manager. He will often find that there is no room for him and his ideas in the organization where he is employed.

It is frequently mentioned that promotion of individual efforts to set up your own business would be one method of dealing with unemployment, for example in a region after a closure of a major establishment. In reality that is not a very good instrument. There is a great risk for negative selection of candidates as well as for a 'save our jobs' attitude which is not healthy for entrepreneurship.

Lacking in competence

The most common lack of knowledge is about the market. This is enhanced by the fact that we study technology based firms. A business idea should be based on knowledge of a potential market demand as well as of technical opportunities. In technology based new firms we find ideas which are based on very advanced product technology and often also advanced manufacturing technology. The entrepreneur might also have a good idea about what needs his product will fulfil. But there is a high risk that he might not be so familiar as to how to reach the potential customer and make them buy his product.

The most important lack of competence concerns the enterprise. To have a complete enterprise perspective means that one has a comprehensive understanding of product technology, manufacturing technology, market research, marketing, financial planning, accounting, legal aspects, contracts, and so on. The complete perspective of all aspects of enterprise is of course difficult if this is the first attempt of the entrepreneur. More serious is the lack of understanding of the need for gathering such knowledge.

The fact that there are different organizations that can help the individual with advice might not be so well-known by the first-time entrepreneur. There are signs that this is more often true for the technology based entrepreneur who is more concerned with technological possibilities than with economics.

A special condition that is often not noticed by an external observer is that the technology based entrepreneur is usually reluctant to share his idea with others because of the fear of it being stolen and exploited before he can develop it himself. Patenting is often not appropriate or sufficient to get protection against very big industrial powers. Besides, patenting is often not possible or feasible at an early stage of development. For this stage there should be some other form of protection, for example, an early stage temporary 'idea patent'.

The most advanced inventor in our study had a consultancy activity to help other inventors in their process. Among other instruments he had a contract that he presented to potential companies to exploit his inventions. He had even managed to make the president of a large multinational sign his contract ensuring him the right to his idea. It turned out to be an internationally successful innovation.

The situation of the inventor

The inventor often feels that he has been exploited. He has little understanding of the costly process of applying the idea commercially and thinks that he gets too little of the revenue. This is a tricky question. The situation can be compared with that of artists in many countries. The 'real' value of the creation of the concept in relation to that of the realization and distribution of the product is in itself a matter of societal values but prices are set depending on the relative strength of the actors in each part of the chain. If the society thinks that revenue is not fairly distributed it will have to create transfer mechanisms. This is quite frequently done with artists' work in many countries and, to a much lesser extent, through grants for inventors.

The inventor's communication network is often weak and he is afraid of communicating his idea with others. This is a disadvantage not only for development of the technical idea but even more so for development of the business idea. The inventor doesn't trust the entrepreneur or 'business creator' whom he regards as an unnecessary person in the realization of his idea.

In one case, an attempt was made by a local authority to match individuals with technical ideas with commercially oriented individuals with business ideas. However, it was of course very rarely that these interests matched. In a few cases they did match and combination seemed to be very strong but contained many conflicts. It is important that such combinations are created at a very early stage so that all parties feel involved in the idea development and are regarded as equal partners both in idea development and risk taking.

The capabilities needed to be a good entrepreneur are very different from those required to be a good inventor. Only in a very few are these characteristics combined in one person. For one thing the inventor is often the lonely genius while the entrepreneur is aware of how to achieve objectives with the help of his business relations and different resources.

The need for a project champion

It is necessary to have somebody who can push through the whole process of setting up a business and who has the power to carry through the process even when everything looks very difficult. That is a characteristic which is expected from the entrepreneur but unfortunately not often found with the inventor. There are also different competences needed at different times. Sometimes the technologist is the most suitable man, but at other times it will be the businessman.

A very attractive possibility that was found in a few very successful cases is that of changing project leadership over time while maintaining the same group of people. It typically started with the technical inventor as the pusher, was then explored under the leadership of a marketing man, realized under the management of a production man and planned for introduction and growth under a business administration person. All of them participated in the process all the time but project leadership was changed due to the change of focus of the project.

Transformation to private businessman

A gradual start during the old employment is advantageous as it permits business ideas to mature. An organized transformation process can be very advantageous both for the employer and the employee/entrepreneur.

The most successful cases are often found when the new firm is in the same industry as that of the former employer. Of course such a background for the entrepreneur will mean that he can rely on enormous market knowledge as well as technological knowledge. In most cases, the single entrepreneur will go for a small market segment the large organization has found not big enough to approach or too costly to specialize in. In many cases there can be a healthy collaboration and if the new business shows a very big potential it is sometimes 'bought back' later. However, it must be stated that, in many cases, there was a very negative attitude from the former employer and many big firms are literally a threat to new entrepreneurship. With the help of all kinds of contracts with employees large firms can hinder them from starting their own business in related areas.

Letting in other bigger owners

It is fairly common that succesful start-ups do not lead to any remarkable growth. This is because autonomy is often regarded as more attractive than expansion. A good profit is certainly hoped for but a very high rate of profit means having less than total control and the possibility to try out your own ideas.

Selling the idea or business

Selling an idea in an early stage is not very attractive since the financial reward is small and the inventor wants to see to it that his idea is realized. Selling later is not attractive for reasons mentioned above.

It is sad to see how often single inventors get relatively little out of their patents from ideas which have been exploited on a very large scale. Again this can probably be explained by the relative power of the actors. Inventions today should in many cases probably be made in large organizations and sold to other large organizations if there is to be a decent reward.

Business factors

We now discuss hindering and supporting factors from the enterprize point of view. While we focused earlier on the perspective of the individual, we will now focus on the creation and organization of resources.

Complementing knowledge

The successful companies have managed to put together knowledge from areas in a complementing way so that the complete area of business, technology, and management has been covered in the managing team. It is very clear that such a team has much higher success possibilities than the single entrepreneur, no matter how entrepreneurial he is.

Knowledge provided from outside the company is of less value although better than none when the need is not understood. A consultant cannot be of the same help as a stable organization. Here the decision makers are in close psychological contact and many decisions must be taken with intuition as the last resort.

Market development

Market development takes generally much more time and resources than expected. This situation is amplified by the fact that we deal with technology based activities and inventors. A similar product might not even exist in the market and the new firm might face the necessity of establishing new understanding and sometimes even new industrial standards. Unfortunately the inventor quite often does not foresee this till he is ready to start distribution of his first produced products. Then he is not prepared financially to survive long market development periods.

We met many inventors who were so enthusiastic about their own ideas that it was impossible for them to understand the difficulties for others in seeing the advantages of their idea. They also find it frustrating to have to explain the potential of their idea time after time to different parties such as public authorities, banks, partners, manufacturing and marketing organizations.

Financing

Arranging the financing takes time and effort that many did not foresee. Financial planning is often not thought of and considered less interesting than many other tasks. One of the effects of inadequate financial planning at an early stage is that efforts might have to be made later to raise additional capital. This is, however, sometimes more difficult than raising the whole amount at the start.

The incapability of internal financing of rapid growth comes as a shock to many. In general it is often found that raising capital for expansion is just as difficult as raising the initial capital. This is especially true for fast-growing high tech firms.

It is of great help to the firm to have contacts with a representative from a financing institution who can be of professional help with a combination of financial advice and industry insight. The understanding of the dynamics of the economy in the industry is rarely present within the firm.

The same thing is of course true for a possible partner in an investment or venture capitalist firm. It is normally required that he has some technical knowledge to understand the process of technical development and the commercialization of entirely new products.

Growth strategies

Strategies for growth often become difficult at a very early stage for these kind of businesses. One reason is, they will have in the

98

early phase itself a considerable export share. The company will then need an established service organization to create international credibility within a narrow segment.

In the early period of growth there are several steps of particular difficulty which can be observed. The very first step to get over is to change focus from the lonely inventor to the more complete enterprise. Hopefully this change of focus is done in the inventor's mind already before he establishes the firm. The next really big step is to move from the small local business activity to a still comparatively small but well-built and managed organization split up into different functional areas. A third extremely difficult step seems to be to gear the organization to rapid growth with constant change instead of being a 'hobby'.

Managing the process

The length of the start-up process tends almost always to be more extended than anticipated by the inventor. Development time is very often underestimated. Another and often much more severe problem we observed is that market development seldom starts till the product development is completed.

The area in which the start-up is taking place has also a major impact on start-up time and possibilities for success. Successful start-ups are usually in areas related to earlier activities. Product development means a lot but market knowledge gained earlier means even more. A regional relation is also important, i.e. acting in an industry that is strong in the region or where the region has natural competitive advantages.

Institutional factors

Here we will consider the public as well as private organizations which the technology based entrepreneur might contact, get support from, or choose to collaborate with.

Sectoral support

Organizations created to support these kind of firms are often limited to technical development or export planning and are seldom focused on business development. One effect of this is that the entrepreneur will have to spend a lot of effort on transferring his ideas from one organization and its bureaucrats to another. In many cases he will have to start his argumentation from the very beginning each time. There is also a big risk that basic assessments will change from one organization to another.

How to deal with changing assessment is a politically difficult question. It is of course a desired effect that public servants with different functional specialities contribute to different aspects of an assessment. For example, there will be mainly technological assessment when the inventor is applying for financial support for technical development, market potential assessment when he is applying for export support, etc. To create a better overall assessment national agencies for support of technical development have tried to include more and more of a market potential evaluation at an early stage. This can help the entrepreneur to get better permanence in his contacts with these organizations. On the other hand early market assessment of new product ideas might tend to discourage radical innovation. The balance in policy and behaviour here is difficult to optimize, but whatever is decided must be made very clear to the inventor/potential entrepreneur at a very early stage.

Difficulties in getting an overview

Because there are many institutions involved the first-time entre-preneur often has difficulties in getting an overview and in understanding the different roles. For example, it can be difficult to know what is support, advice, and 'friendly advice' which in reality has to be followed to get support. The entrepreneurs who manage best are those who have started one or several times before. This can also be expressed as 'you should have experience from these contacts already when you start the first time!' It is not as impossible as it might sound. One measure that has been taken is to organize local experience exchange groups.

Slow service

The civil servants deal with the files of the proposed new business as they are supposed to while the entrepreneur needs revenues to survive. This is to say that there is a fundamental difference in perspective between these two groups. In many cases the com-plaint heard from the entrepreneur is that public handling takes too long. In most cases any time at all will mean a delay in the business development. However, the situations concerning a single entrepreneur must be dealt with with extra care since they cannot take as much delay as a large organization.

Areas lacking support

Functional areas like technical development, prototype produc-tion and financial planning, are often well covered while assistance in general business planning is more rare. Another very interesting observation is that investments in public support seem to carry some of the same malfocus that individual technology based entrepreneurs suffer from. The inventor may not foresee that market development typically costs ten times more than technical development, but public support is often available only for technical development.

Insufficient competence in institutions

Unfortunately the institutions do not attract employees with wide experience in entrepreneurship and managing start-ups. At the most some of them have made studies of it.

This is a social issue that depends on culture and can be differently dealt with only in the long run. An example of successful interchange between public administration of business matters and industry is the Japanese experience. It seems that individuals can easily move between organizations like MITI (Ministry of International Trade and Industry) and private firms.

Attitude to risk

Private banks tend to be more willing to take risks than the special development funds created by government to financially support new high risk firms. This was one finding from the earlier mentioned study in Sweden. The same observation has been reported from some other countries. Why should it be so?

This is not as strange as it first sounds. Again it has to do with the very different perspectives of people in public service organizations and those in day-to-day business situations. There is some evidence that the best risk takers in these categories might be the local bank branch managers with a profit centre responsibility.

Difficult formal communication

The communication style of many institutions seems to suit large corporations better than the individual entrepreneur. This is quite natural considering their organization principles, procedures, and manning. They will also work with projects offered by large organizations and many bureaucrats will find the large firms easier to work with than the entrepreneurs.

The untouchables

There is a risk that clerks in the institutions can act as they want without constraint and the individual entrepreneur cannot take time to fight the formality. If he is trying to argue, there is often no formal way of doing it anyway. In the empirical studies the author has come across there were some cases where 'untouchable power' has led to total disaster for the entrepreneur.

Of course public authorities must be able to and should delegate power over allocation decisions. However, here one can apply knowledge of idea handling in large organizations. One important method of giving new ideas a decent chance is known as multiple channelling. In a large organization new ideas are given more ways of communication than the formal organization hierarchy. In public administration there could be parallel ways also.

Patents

Patents are often taken too early and turn out to be a hindering factor later. This is to say that the inventor is frequently hindering himself from getting a better protection at a later stage.

One conclusion which follows from this observation is that there is a need for protection also in the idea stage. The need for an 'idea patent' has been mentioned earlier. The legal aspects of such a concept are complicated but it might be worth considering a system of a temporary idea patent that can be followed by a patent application within a certain time frame.

Influence from big companies

Innovative big companies with a defined new venture strategy are a stimulation to regional start-ups. This is a well-known phenomenon but unfortunately it works in both directions. As we could see clearly in our study in Sweden a big company which does not want closely related spin-offs in its region can also prevent such start-ups.

New venture firms

A rapid development of new venture and venture capital firms, often after American models, has given the inventor more alternatives for finding powerful and experienced partners. As has been discussed already, the inventor is often reluctant to share his idea with that kind of organization. Although such firms can be helpful there are always cases with a less serious approach in a rapidly developing industry and as a result of some unhappy experiences, inventors easily become even more reluctant. On the other hand we have seen cases of advisory firms run by very well-known and succesful inventors and they are very highly respected by individual inventors.

Society and culture

Attitude to private enterprise

The attitude to private enterprise has an important influence on the individual's willingness to try. General changes can clearly be observed like the comparatively negative attitudes to private enterprise during the late 1960s and early 1970s in some countries as compared with the favourable attitudes of today to innovation and industrial development.

Nowadays much effort is made in different countries to stimulate technology based entrepreneurship both for large companies and by individual entrepreneurs. However, there is one phase which should be given more attention and that is the expansion after the first successful start-up. That process can often be accelerated tremendously by the right kind of assistance.

Education and training

There is some evidence that the national education system in a society will influence the basis for entrepreneurship in that society. One obviously good base for becoming an entrepreneur is to get through a practically oriented high school education preparing for engineering work or possibly in business administration. In our study in Sweden we found a gap in the supply of such individuals since specialized education at the high school level had been replaced by more general programmes.

Entrepreneurial infrastructure

It is known from different studies and experiments that it is of great help to entrepreneurs to have other entrepreneurs to serve as a model and as discussion partners. That is one reason why entrepreneurship is often locally concentrated in areas such as the well-known Silicon Valley and along Route 128, and also places like the Gnosjö area in Sweden. Developing the infrastructure regarding exchange of experience and other communication between entrepreneurs in the region is possible on a local government level.

Revenues for inventors and entrepreneurs

In many countries today there is a debate concerning the need for more ideas for technical and industrial development. Much could probably be gained if that debate focused on the prerequisites for exploiting already existing ideas. In our study in Sweden, just as in several other studies, it has been found that there was no lack of ideas but the obstacles for exploiting them were often regarded as overwhelming.

Many societies could probably gain from an analysis of how to allocate a fair revenue to the 'technological artist' in comparison with business organizations. The high rewards for 'financial artistry' in many countries are pulling people to resource reallocation activities instead of resource creation activities.

103

The reward system in a society for inventors and entrepreneurs should be dealt with from two different perspectives. One is as a prime mover to start and run your own business, the other is as a driving force for growth and expansion. The revenues for growth are often too small. It might even create tax problems if your firm is growing too quickly and you will definitely have to share control of the firm.

In one spectacular case the founder, owner and managing director of a company carefully managed it so it did not grow any more. If it did, he would have to sell a part each year to pay property taxes! All attempts by local authorities to assist him in a growth process (in order to create more jobs locally) were skilfully avoided.

Conclusions

The most important conclusions can be summarized in three major areas and some minor points. Since these conclusions are of course based on the described results, the presentation of conclusions will be brief.

Cross-functional competence

A management team of 2–5 persons where the individuals together cover all areas of management is of critical importance. The problem is not at all limited to the engineer who lacks market knowledge but is much wider. The single entrepreneur is often a fictional character.

Financing growth and expansion

A main obstacle is a lack of equity. Loans are often more easily available but it is more difficult to get risk capital/equity or, in some cases, the inventor does not want to let it in anyway.

The time aspect

The processes very often take too long a time and the resources run out. In many cases this can be avoided if complete general management knowledge is available and used.

Other conclusions

The most important other conclusions can be summarized in the following points:

– Autonomy dominates as driving force
– Revenue for the individual is low

- Institutions are difficult to communicate with
- Attitude in society to enterprise is negative
- The starting position is of paramount importance
- Market investments are often very heavy and made too late.

Policy implications

There can of course be many different policies conducive to achieving a certain goal. This limited study can only identify some possible routes in creating an environment that will be fertile to the growth of new technology based companies. Hence, the following presentation should be seen more as a discussion of possibilities than strict recommendations.

Major areas for support

The most important conclusions in the study cover:

- cross-functional competence
- financing and growth
- the time aspect.

In general terms one can say that what is needed is external capital and external knowledge. We have earlier concluded that the capital needed for market development is much bigger than that for product development. We have also noticed that the support available is more directed to technical development than to market development.

A first policy implication should as a consequence be that support for market development similar to support for technical development be considered. It is clear that market development is often started too late and that the size of the investment required comes as a surprise to the owner. It is possible that the heart of the problem is not clear to the politicians either.

A second important policy area is that of contacts between the inventor and venture capital. It is surprising that the Small Business Investment Company (SBIC) model as developed in the USA has not been tried more in Europe. That kind of capital organization is probably much more attractive to the individual inventor and entrepreneur than the private venture capitalist.

A third policy implication relates to an idea as to how to channel funds. Public funds to support technology based potential entrepreneurs could be managed by commercial banks. They have many branches so they will be more easy to reach. The assessment of business ideas can be more 'pluralistic', i.e. there is more than one channel to pursue the idea and these channels bring you into contact with people with different values.

A fourth policy implication is the need to create cross-functional support in addition to, or as a substitute to, some functionally specialized institutions. The concept of business development could be the relevant focus.

But supportive functions should not only be created as public institutions but with more directly involved individuals. A common method is to stimulate contacts between entrepreneurs in a region by, for example, experience exchange meetings and controlled location of new units to entrepreneurship-intensive environments. But more active measures can be used. One possibility is to create a system where experienced entrepreneurs can be of more direct help to the new entrepreneurs. For example, some experienced entrepreneurs can act as recommended and publicly supported consultants.

Additional areas for support

The discussion of policy implications follows the points listed under conclusions.

Autonomy dominates as driving force

The willingness to become independent can be influenced by information campaigns. Special get-together programme activities have been one efficient method of stimulation. Such activities can include entrepreneurship tests, consultations with experts, and talks with experienced entrepreneurs as well as special entrepreneurship courses which provide advice on how to start your own firm.

It is also important to direct information not only to those who are looking for it but also to those who can be interested if they are supplied with knowledge of the possibilities. One kind of information with a high potential is 'information on the whole thing and how to get specialized information'. That can also help the potential entrepreneurs who find it difficult to imagine the whole expected process from its early beginnings.

Revenue for the individual is too low

It has earlier been stated that many societies should gain from an analysis of how to allocate a fair revenue to the 'technological artist' in comparison with the business organizations. The high rewards for 'financial artistry' in many countries are pulling people to resource reallocation activities instead of resource creation activities.

106

Inventors can of course be treated in the same way as artists. If the economic reward structure does not allocate the way society wants it to, then politicians introduce reallocation processes. Just like artists can get grants from public funds, inventors can get the same kind of support for creating their art. Such systems already exist. Of course, one has to take the drawbacks of central planning optimization. The other alternative is to make the invention function a stronger negotiator. That can take place partly through the creation of 'inventor houses'.

It was also stated earlier that the revenue system in a society for inventors and entrepreneurs should be dealt with as a problem in two stages. One as a prime mover to start and run your own business, the other as a driving force for growth and expansion. The revenues for growth are of a different kind compared to those of becoming independent. The driving forces for growth are control power and building up of personal wealth. But for many technology based entrepreneurs that is only interesting if they can keep control over the activities. However, this appears to be difficult in many cases. It might even create tax problems if the firm grows too much and the creator will definitely have to share control of the firm. For such reasons it is very important for a society to create mechanisms which help or at least do not hinder expansion of small private businesses. One thing which has to be considered is how property tax systems are designed. Another is the income tax system and possibilities for the individual to spread patent incomes over several years for example.

Institutions are too difficult to communicate with

A core reason for this problem is the tremendous difference between entrepreneurs and bureaucrats. A direct policy solution to that is to let institutions hire external entrepreneurs as consultants to new entrepreneurs instead of trying the almost hopeless task of getting an entrepreneurial attitude in the institutions. But changes can also be brought about in the public organization in the field.

One thing is to create a more consistent value system between institutions handling the same project. Of course the conclusions can be different depending on the stage of the project but it is preferable if the entrepreneur can recognize the evaluation patterns through the project.

It must also be possible to develop the officials' attitudes and decision basis. What is needed in this area is not more conceptual knowledge but a confrontation with actual cases and situations in the field.

A quite serious recommendation is to let the banks manage the public funds instead of letting them be managed by special public agencies.

Universities – a badly utilized potential

Universities are a kind of institution which is often mentioned as having great potential for stimulating, initiating, and assisting local technology based entrepreneurship. Stanford, MIT and others have been referred to. But there are also many cases which are not so successful.

One risk is that these matters are dealt with on too high a level. University presidents and professors get in contact with representatives of local industry. Liaison functions are created. But the single entrepreneur is not able to take part in them. He only wants to know how to talk with whom in what department and without an expensive formal contract. The contacts must be made easy and immediate. Sometimes it takes longer to create a contract than to get the comprehensive research knowledge.

Attitude in society to enterprise is too negative

It is important to influence public opinion to private enterprise if entrepreneurship is wanted. Critical journalism tends to report more on problems than successes and on industry more as a polluting problem than as a creator of wealth. This must be dealt with by publishing positive results on employment by start-up firms.

The important base for potential entrepreneurs that is created by practical job-preparing high school education has also been mentioned. It seems advantageous to create and maintain such, usually engineering, high school education rather than replacing it with more general education programmes.

The start position is of paramount importance

The most successful start-ups were said to be when the new firm is in the same industry as that of the former employer of the new entrepreneur. On the other hand we could expect negative attitudes and even hindering actions taken by the large corporation. It is therefore important to teach large corporations the potential advantages of having former employees starting their own businesses and how to deal with the problem of creating good potential partners instead of bitter memories. Here the lessons of Silicon Valley can really be of help rather than as cases of building huge entrepreneurial areas. In general there might be little a society can do to influence the attitude of large firms other than in a very long perspective. But there is at least one possibility that should be pointed out. Large OEM firms tend to be less and less vertically integrated to achieve higher flexibility. This means that they also rely more and more on an efficient network of suppliers located as close as possible to their own plant. So large complex firms depend more and more on efficient small suppliers and this can make teams react more positively to local, related entrepreneurship. This opens a number of policy options for local administration like creating adequate industrial areas, industrial parks, etc.

Market investments are often very heavy and made too late

This can mainly be dealt with in two ways. First of all there should be market development support just like product development support. This is to deal with the unexpected level of investments which risk killing the project when it is already technically successful.

The fact that market investments are often made or started too late is usually caused by the inventors' simple lack of knowledge. Compulsory business planning, maybe with free help to create the plan, should accompany a project proposal before it is given any support even if only for technical development.

References

Eisenhardt, K. and Forbes, N. (1984) 'Technical entrepreneurship: an international perspective', *Columbia Journal of World Business* Winter: 31–8.

Gallagher, K. (1986) *Reference Report*, Department of Industrial Management, Newcastle University.

Karlsson, C. and Gadde, L-E. (1983) *Villkor för teknikbaserat nyföretagande i Västsverige*, Institute for Management of Innovation and Technology, Göteborg.

Chapter six

Competitiveness and the management of strategic change processes

Andrew Pettigrew, Richard Whipp and Robert Rosenfeld

Introduction

This chapter represents an early attempt to present the research framework, study questions and preliminary findings from a project seeking to link the relative competitive performance of British firms to the capability of those firms to adjust and adapt to major changes in their environment. The research is being carried out at the Centre for Corporate Strategy and Change, University of Warwick in collaboration with Coopers & Lybrand Associates.

The unfolding of economic events during the 1970s and early 1980s has drawn further attention to the relative decline of the British economy and the continuing loss of competitiveness of large sectors of British industry. In the search for explanations of Britain's declining competitiveness a multiplicity of factors has surfaced. Pollard (1982) has emphasized the short-term focus of British economic policy making and our failure as a nation to invest in the modernization of capital equipment. Researchers at the Science Policy Research Unit at Sussex University also dwell on the relationship between technical innovation and British economic performance, pointing to shortcomings in the way certain sectors of British industry develop and improve products and production processes (Pavitt 1980). Meanwhile economists such as Caves (1980) and Blume (1980) identify the poorer productivity of certain UK industries compared with their US equivalents, and how the UK's financial structures and institutions inhibit our ability to direct savings into appropriate investment channels. The problem of explaining Britain's economic decline has also attracted scholars interested in taking a very long-term view. Wiener (1981) digs into the culture and class system in British society, arguing that there has been a systematic misdirection of talent in Britain into public sector administration, the City, and the universities and away from industry and engineering.

Lazonick (1983), on the other hand, argues that the decline in Britain's economy during the twentieth century is due to structural rigidities in its economic institutions that developed in the nineteenth-century era of relatively free competition.

But is Britain's declining competitiveness to be explained exclusively by national economic policies, macroeconomic variables, the deep-rooted social and cultural biases of UK society, the peculiarities of our financial institutions and our tax system, and the patterns of trade union activity and industrial relations? We think not. Given the substantial changes in the economic, political, and business environment of large firms over the past two decades, a critical factor affecting the relative competitive position of British firms must be the capability of firms to adjust and adapt to major changes in their environments and thereby improve their competitive performance. The importance of these adjustment and adaptation processes suggests that the nature of management itself is a crucial aspect of the competitiveness issue. Part of the management task is to identify and assess changing economic, business, and political conditions, and develop and then implement new strategies to improve the firm's competitive performance.

Accordingly, a central proposition of this research is that the way large organizations assess the changing economic, business, and political environment around them, and formulate and implement strategic and operational changes is an important input in the equation leading to the maintenance and improvement of competitive performance. Furthermore, these managerial processes of strategic assessment, choice, and change are not just questions of the economic calculation of strategic opportunity carried out by men and women driven by rational imperatives. The process of perceiving and then assessing environmental change and its implications for new strategies, structures, technologies, and cultures in the firm is an immensely complex human and organizational process in which differential perception, quests for efficiency and power, visionary leadership skills, the vagaries of chance, and subtle processes of additively building up a momentum of support for change and then vigorously implementing change, all play their part.

Thus the objective of this research is to describe and analyse processes of decision making in selected firms as those firms attempt to manage strategic and operational changes. Strategic decisions and changes are viewed as streams of activity involving individuals and groups which occur mainly but not solely as a consequence of environmental change, and which can lead to alterations in the core purpose, product market focus, structure, technology, and culture of the host organization. Strategic is just a description of magnitude of alteration in, for example, market focus and structure, recognizing the second-order effects, or multiple consequences of any such changes.

Given the pragmatic requirement for strategic changes to be vigorously and operationally implemented through to the factory or unit level this research is concerned to identify the processes by which both strategic and more operational changes are made. However, the fact that strategic changes have to be operationally implemented does not have to imply that 'implementation' is a discrete activity which follows the formulation of strategy. Part of the empirical and theoretical focus of this research will be to build on recent work by Mintzberg (1978), Quinn (1980), and Pettigrew (1985a) which treats the formulation and implementation of strategy as a continuous and iterative process in which additive accumulations of managerial decisions combined with the triggering effects of environmental disturbances can produce major transformations in the firm.

The research focuses on the transformation processes of firms in mature industry and service sectors. Choice and change processes are being examined in organizations faced with the dilemma of survival and regeneration. This allows the analysis of the what, why, and how of firms surviving with mature products in over-crowded markets whilst at the same time providing an external and an internal environment, possibly new products, new structures, new systems, new cultures, and a new managerial capability to regenerate the firm for the future.

Empirically the research examines processes of decision making and change in a pair of firms in each product market. Using the kind of package of criteria of success adopted by, for example, Lawrence and Lorsch (1967) and Peters and Waterman (1982), one firm is deemed a higher performer for the product market and the other relatively speaking a lesser performer. The chosen firms must also be large for their sector and each pair must either be both unionized or both non-unionized. A further objective in choosing the sample from mature sectors is to look at two sectors with a history of growth and two with a history of contraction or slow growth. Thus, for example, automobiles and publishing could represent maturity with contraction, and insurance and merchant banking could represent maturity with a history of growth. The research thus includes a 'higher performing' and a 'lesser performing' firm in each of four sectors, automobiles, publishing, insurance, and merchant banking, eight cases in all. High level and high quality access has been negotiated in eight organizations. Fieldwork has begun in the automobiles and merchant banking sectors and these sectors will be used to illustrate our argument for a research framework throughout.

The research takes the perspective and methods of the business historian, business strategist, and organization theorist. The intention is to collect longitudinal data gathered in semi-structured tape recorded interviews, through short periods of observation in each firm, and by the analysis of archival material. Each of the case studies requires the collection of retrospective and real time data. The project studies change as a continuous process in context, and thus avoids the methodological trap of trying to understand either strategic or operational changes as discrete episodes divorced from the antecedents in the firm, and the ongoing development of the social, political, economic, and organizational context which is influencing and influenced by particular change events (Pettigrew 1985b).

Management and competitiveness

There are a number of issues which arise naturally at the beginning of a programme of research into the management of strategic and operational change and its relation to competitive performance. It is worthwhile to consider why the 1970s and 1980s in Britain form a particularly appropriate period of study. Given that recent experience in the UK provides clear evidence of the transformation processes within firms as they attempt to survive and compete, it then becomes necessary to address two central problems before embarking on detailed research. First, one must examine the possible relationships between competitiveness and the nature of strategic change. Second, a research framework is required which can capture those relationships and at the same time attempt to extend existing insights into the question of the competitiveness of British industry.

Over the past two decades successive changes in the political, economic and business environment have caused many organizations to rethink their business strategies. The most visible evidence of such changes is seen in the structural alterations within firms which have led to reduced numbers of employees. Among the more well-known examples of the reductions in numbers employed between 1977 and 1981 were British Steel 47 per cent, Peugeot-Talbot 56 per cent, BL 40 per cent, Courtaulds 31 per cent and GKN 30 per cent (Centre for Corporate Strategy and Change 1985). Much of this activity has been done, and continues to be done, in the name of business survival. However, there is a growing awareness in some firms that the key strategic dilemma over the next 10–15 years will be the extent to which they can ensure the survival and regeneration of their organization. This need for learning and the management of change to continue through the 1980s assumes a capability on the part of firms to assess changing market conditions as well as the ability to make the appropriate adjustments to improve competitive performance.

The mature industries of the UK would seem suitable locations for research into the management of change and competitiveness for two main reasons. In the first place, the continued poor performance of traditional British industries remains a problematic and live issue for industrialists and academic commentators alike. Yet, thus far, longitudinal studies of the process of managing strategic and operational change have not figured largely in the many debates around British industrial performance (Williams *et al.* 1983). Recent reports have remarked yet again on the persistently low comparative performance of UK industry. The National Economic Development Council (NEDC 1985) published figures in September 1985 which revealed the severity of Britain's industrial decline over the past 10 years. The NEDC showed that in the basic non-oil manufacturing sector, whether measured by annual growth rates in investment, share in total employment or the yearly rise in value added, the key manufacturing sectors of metal products, engineering and other manufacturing have shown far worse figures than in West Germany, Italy or France. In the 'metals', 'minerals and chemicals', 'metal products, engineering and vehicles' and 'other manufacturing' categories Britain is the only country to have sustained decreases in value added.

This continued poor performance makes one duly critical of past explanations which appear to be tied closely to the contemporary circumstances which they attempted to explain. There is an apparent need not only for research into the relationship of competitiveness and strategic management but most especially for studies which try to understand the long term and more proximate determinants of that link. The House of Lords Select Committee (House of Lords 1985) on the causes and effects of Britain's deteriorating balance of trade in manufactured goods is sympathetic to this perspective. The committee's report outlines a range of long-, medium-, and short-term factors. In the long run it sees poor rates of investment and a variety of cultural factors as important; in the medium term it focuses on demand considerations; and in the short term it highlights the impact of North Sea oil and government financial and exchange policies. Whilst the Select Committee is sensitive to the range of historical and more immediate aspects of the UK's balance of trade and competitive performance it approaches them almost entirely at the macro level. The varying experience of individual firms within these circumstances is not addressed. It is these attempts by companies to formulate and implement competitive strategies within these circumstances which therefore forms the centrepiece of our research.

If the depth and continuity of the problem of UK competitiveness makes the need to understand it more urgent then the singular conditions of the 1980s add a second imperative. It is now widely recognized that the intersection of a new generation of technology with radically novel market structures has produced a turbulent environment for business. This is especially true in the mature industries of the advanced economies who now face entirely different forms of competition than hitherto. Abernathy drew attention (Abernathy *et al.* 1981, 1983) to the profound impact of Japanese business practices, especially in manufacturing technique and process systems, on US companies. Others have suggested (Kaplinsky 1984) that the development of information technology based on micro-electronics has thrown previous assumptions about market operations into turmoil. On the one hand computer based technology has provided the opportunity for corporations to operate on a truly global scale, to seek scale economies on a much broader base of operations, and to effect product and production changes at a greater speed than ever before. On the other hand, the new technology has enabled certain companies to alter fundamentally the nature of competition within given sectors. The shift often involves the shortening of traditional product cycles or project lead times with the emphasis now placed on flexible responses within increasingly crowded markets (Sabel 1981, Piore and Sabel 1984).

These major shifts in technology and market conditions raise questions about the capacity of firms to identify such changes and their ability to become flexibly responsive to the apparent increased speed of change. In the present therefore the problems of conceiving and operationalizing strategic changes have become particularly acute. Modern firms, faced with the dilemma of survival and regeneration, are required to go through several transformation processes in sequence and/or in parallel. Detailed study of a small number of UK firms as they attempt to adjust and manage their way through an era of survival and regeneration could be of some use. By virtue of the scale and intensity of the transformation processes required such firms could provide a setting where research of theoretical and practical substance on the management of change and competitiveness could develop.

Unit of analysis

A first basic task is to identify the unit of analysis for the research agenda and more importantly the preliminary understanding of the connections between management and competitiveness which it embodies.

In the broadest terms this research focuses on the process(es) of managing strategic and operational changes in organization in mature industry/service sectors and the relationship between those processes and relative competitive performance (see Introduction). In short, the unit of analysis is the process of decision making in selected firms as they seek to manage strategic changes. Yet, as will become clear below, this research will try to describe and analyse these processes as they operate at the level of the firm but within their appropriate contexts both inside and outside the organization. Our arguments for a contextual and processual approach to the study of change have been set out in detail elsewhere (Pettigrew 1985a, 1985b, Whipp and Clark 1986). However, the need for such an approach is increased by the evidence from the established literature on Britain's performance (ESRC 1983) and more recent reports (NEDC 1985, House of Lords 1985). All the writers involved indicate the deeply embedded economic, social and political characteristics of the UK compared to other countries and hence they imply the need to examine business within this distinctive national setting.

Before examining a research framework which can be used to explore the competitive performance of firms in a processual and contextual way, the relationship between strategic change and competitiveness requires closer attention. Our existing understanding of strategic change contains two main features which link strategic management and competitiveness conceptually. First, competitive performance and strategic change would, *a priori*, appear to be intimately linked if one accepts K. R. Andrews' (Andrews 1970) view of strategy. Competition becomes for him the essence of business strategy: competition is one of the key targets for any business strategy. Or, in Andrews' words, strategy 'can be seen as rivalry amongst peers, for prizes in a defined and shared game'.

Second, some recent writers on management have rejected the long-accepted 'rational-analytic' models of strategic change

116

(Quinn 1980, Evered 1983). Instead strategic change is regarded as a process which assumes a variety of patterns. These may contain long periods of continuity, learning and incremental adjustment interspersed with hiatuses or revolutions featuring abnormally high levels of change activity (Pettigrew 1985a). Moreover, far from strategic change being a straightforward rational process it is best considered as a jointly analytical and political process (Pettigrew 1985a, Whipp, Rosenfeld and Pettigrew 1987).

At the heart of these analytical and political processes of strategic change are those dominating ideas and frames of thought which provide systems of meaning and interpretation which in turn filter both intra-organizational and environmental signals. There-fore, the way in which businesses perceive their competitive position, and the decisions they take to adjust their competitive position, must perforce be inextricably linked to those dominating frames of thought which inform an organization's analytical and political processes of strategic change. We are especially con-cerned with the combined relevance of those rational/objective and political/subjective aspects of strategic change processes to competitive performance.

In order to extend this understanding of the link between competitiveness and strategic change the subject of competitive-ness itself deserves further attention. There are useful distinctions to be made between the levels at which competitiveness may be understood and their dynamic nature across time. There are three major levels involved: the firm, sector and national/international levels.

Many researchers in the UK have defined competitive perfor-mance according to the ability (usually of a single firm) to win orders and achieve market share (Cable and Doyle in Francis 1985). In practice, market share has been a well-used yardstick for enterprises. The 80-page *Financial and General Fact Book* of the Chrysler Corporation of 1973 (Chrysler 1973) is quite clear that competitiveness is revealed by market share. The volume has large appendices which display 'The Competitive History of the Automobile Industry as shown by Percentage Shares of New Passenger Car Registrations' from 1923 to 1973.

Yet to view the competitiveness of a firm simply in terms of market share/penetration is really only to deal with an outcome of the process which lies behind it. What concerns our research is the range of possible bases on which a company may compete in order to achieve a given market share. Whilst some are more difficult to quantify than price competitiveness, other bases such as competi-tiveness in quality of design and process, and the competitive edge derived from selling and marketing are becoming increasingly recognized as relevant (Lorenz 1986). The remarkable turnaround of Jaguar cars between 1979 and 1984 is a good example. Much attention has been given to the improvement in the quality and reliability of Jaguar's product as the main reason for the company's progress from virtual extinction to spectacular profit. However, the role of sales and marketing has been crucial. The company is quite clear on this point. Rebuilding the image of the car in customers' minds was vital to the specialist car producer's success. In 1979 a dealer described Jaguar's franchise network as 'an embarrassment ... There was no service back-up, no parts, no customer care, no interest'. Under a new managerial regime from April 1980 and via what the chairman describes as an 'holistic approach' to strategic change, dealers were tightly linked to the changes introduced within the factory. In the words of the UK Sales Director:

> What is not so well known is how closely the dealers were involved, and kept informed about progress, and how much the dealer network helped to influence attitudes inside the factory and vice versa. A positive feedback loop was set up between factory and franchise to help people think about the whole of Jaguar, not just their little bit.

A rationalization of the dealer network from 290 in 1980 to 114 in October 1986 and a 10-point plan ranging from a Franchise Development Fund to a continuous dealer research programme has been the expression of what the chairman told the dealers in 1981: to extend 'our pursuit of perfection into your offices, showrooms and workshops'. The result is that customer satisfaction levels on new car delivery leaped from 20 per cent in 1980 to 90 per cent in 1985 in the all-important US market, a figure only Mercedes Benz can match (Collier 1986).

Within the merchant banking sector, the increasing level of competitiveness within the last 5–6 years has focused attention upon the marketing and distribution end of the firms' activities. Up until the late 1970s, the British merchant banks competed very much among themselves within a well-defined market, namely domestic UK corporations. By the 1980s, the other members of the UK financial services industry began to encroach upon the traditional areas of livelihood of the merchant banks: the major clearing banks, stockbrokers, and insurance companies widened their range of services to areas like corporate finance, commercial lending, venture capital, and investment management. In addition, the relaxation of foreign exchange controls in 1979 signalled the arrival of the giant US, Japanese, and west European securities firms.

The increased number of competitors for a relatively static market of clients in the UK began to alter radically the nature of conducting business. Previously, much time and effort was placed upon the maintenance of a strong relationship between the merchant banker and the client. This was generally viewed as a long-term 'partnership' – if the client required financial advice or financial service, he or she would call upon his contact at the bank and they would arrange what could be done. In general, the bank-client interface was 'relationship-oriented'. The interface began to change with the increase in competitors. The US investment banks began contacting the established clientele of the merchant banks offering improved or innovative services, and cheaper transaction costs. From the point of view of these new competitors, they were simply buying market share. A more fundamental change was also occurring. The relationship between client and bank began to shift from 'relationship-oriented' to 'transaction oriented'. Though price competition became more critical, non-price factors began to play a much larger role. In particular, the merchant bank's reputation in a particular area such as corporate finance served to attract clients. This reputation grew on the back of successful work undertaken in areas such as mergers and acquisitions, equity underwriting, and debt flotations. It became increasingly important for merchant bankers to provide new ideas to established clients as well as spend a larger proportion of their time contacting potential new clients with new ideas for their approval.

Of course firms compete first and foremost within sectors which display differing business and market features according to the stage they have reached within their sector life cycle (Abernathy 1978). Competition in the auto industry of the 1980s is apparently dominated by the ability of firms to meet basic productivity and scale economy standards as well as methods of work organization set by a diminishing set of market leaders. As in the early stages of the auto sector life cycle, collaboration between certain firms has once more become commonplace in order to meet these competitive standards (Sinclair 1983, cf. Shearman and Burrell 1987). The way a firm aligns itself within the dominant design hierarchy of the sector has also been stressed as a key contributory aspect of competitive performance (Whipp and Clark 1986). It is worth pointing out, though, that following market/domination models as a guide to competitive position has been challenged by analysts (Jones 1986). Jones has drawn attention to those firms who employ a viable strategy of limited market share based on, inter alia, competing on product exclusivity, high quality and price, rather than low cost, mass production policies.

As Francis points out (Francis 1985) one effective measure of competitiveness relates to the national, and by implication, international level. In common with the National Institute of Economic and Social Research, he favours a measure according to GNP per head or exports per employee as compared with other advanced countries. He rightly argues that measures of competitiveness based on market share take little account of movements in the volume of world trade. It has long been recognized that national, macroeconomic factors can effect general competitiveness and specific measures. The Select Committee Report (House of Lords 1985) concludes that 'improvements in (UK) competitiveness have therefore been obtained largely through the exchange rate'. When the effective sterling exchange rate was low during the mid-1970s Britain's competitiveness rose; when the exchange rate moved upwards from 1978 to 1981, 'the effect on competitiveness was catastrophic'. Given the violent exchange rate fluctuations of the mid-1980s money market experts consider (Fay and Knightly 1986) that a UK exporting company:

> can do all that a good capitalist should – modernise, cut labour costs, improve production methods, shave profit margins – and still show a catastrophic loss at the end of the year because it came out on the wrong side of a sharp currency fluctuation.

The considerations of competitiveness which operate at the national or international level can only grow in importance as British companies are forced to come to terms with the so-called 'new era of global competition' (Stopford and Turner 1985).

It is insufficient though to approach competitiveness according to a fixed hierarchy. Rather, as implied in the foregoing outline, the bases of competition at each level and hence the rules for competing are not stable or constant; on the contrary, they change over time and seemingly in the 1980s with increasing speed. In the nineteenth century, a single industry, as in the case of ceramics and other staple industries, contained sub-sections which operated according to quite contrasting rules of competition (Whipp 1984). The same was true of the UK auto industry between 1896 and 1930. By the 1960s competition rested mainly on price. Yet it was the ability of foreign car manufacturers in the 1970s to develop a further competitive advantage on quality, reliability, delivery and after-sales service which transformed the basis of competition (Jones 1981). Or, in other words, competitive advantage by the 1970s derived from both price and non-price factors. More spectacularly perhaps it was the way in which foreign car makers were able to supply the fuel-efficient sub-compact cars to the US market following the twin oil price shocks of 1974 and 1978–9, and thereby respond to new patterns of demand, which led to the marked decline in competitiveness of the so-called 'Big Three' domestic producers.

The US example returns us naturally to the linkages between competitiveness and the management of strategic change. It would be reasonable to maintain that following this hierarchical and dynamic understanding of competitiveness the ability of an enterprise to compete at any given moment and within whatever prevailing market configuration relies on: one, the capacity of that organization to identify and understand the nature of competition and how it changes; and two, the potential of a business to mobilize and manage the resources necessary for whatever response is chosen. Irrespective of the decision that is made, the capacity to carry out the changes it implies depends on the critical ability to manage that process of change. Furthermore, adopting a contextual and processual approach to the management of strategic and operational change enables our research to embrace both the vertical and horizontal axes of competition. The contextualist mode of inquiry addresses the competitive forces which operate at the firm, sector or national/international levels. The processual mode captures the changing bases of competition at each level and across time.

A research framework

In order to elaborate the relevance of a contextual and processual approach to the relationship between the management of strategic change and competitive performance it is necessary to outline what a possible research framework might look like. The elements of that framework are itemized in note form in the appendix. If management's general task is to: assess changing economic, business and political conditions; and identify and implement new strategies which improve the firm's competitive performance, this implies that management's especial responsibility becomes the management of three related areas. This involves the management of not only the content of a chosen strategy but also the management of the process of change, and third the contexts in which it occurs (Pettigrew 1985a). Each of these three areas contains a collection of research themes and issues.

There are four groups of issues which arise in relation to the content of a specific strategy. These include the dominating frames of thought within the organization; the strategy's central objectives; the source of the strategy; and the extent to which the strategy anticipates the means of implementation. At the outset one must discover the nature of previous competitive strategies used by the firm during its emergent, developing or mature phases: reconstructing past policies and actions down to the present should enable the leadership style, background and competence to emerge. More importantly this should in turn reveal the dominating frames of thought within the company which determine the way it perceives its environment and its competitive position in relation to other firms. The main recipes, formulae and dominant logics of the firm are also of interest. As Pettigrew shows (Pettigrew 1985a) the experience of ICI in the 1960s and 1970s is a fitting example of the importance of such mental constructs. Along with the rest of the petrochemical industry, ICI in the 1960s chose to increase capacity by building ever larger plants. Capital expenditure on new plant became almost a corporate measure of a manager's success. As all the major companies adopted a similar policy a crisis of overcapacity resulted. ICI was hit harder than most precisely because top management was unable to abandon the policy of plant expansion. Their dominant frames of thought prevented them from making the necessary shifts. The dominant logics of these executives helped to filter out the 'bad news' of the falling away of growth rates in heavy chemicals and the corporation faced a major period of crisis from 1979.

Second and somewhat obviously the components of a strategy should be inspected. This inventory should include the contribution made by each function of the company and their individual relevance to its competitive performance. Such an account is particularly appropriate when the National Institute's research (ESRC 1983) has identified a number of weaknesses in, for example, non-competitive practices in labour markets or the underdevelopment of training. The extent to which these components provide a cohesive knowledge base and tactical repertoire for the business as a whole are also of concern. The built-in, seldom articulated assumptions which underlie the formal objectives should also be distinguished.

Third, and decisively, the origins and sources of the company's chosen competitive stance must be traced. This task is given greater urgency since Francis (Francis 1985) observes that: 'British businessmen are relatively lacking in knowledge about what to do' regarding improving competitive performance, and that 'the knowledge we have about how to do things, coming as most of it does from North America, West Germany, and particularly,

Japanese experience, is not immediately transferable to British conditions'. The turbulent course of the successive Rootes, Chrysler UK and Peugeot-Talbot companies in Britain is an apt example. From the outside there would appear to have been three distinct phases and sets of policies: Rootes down to 1964, Chrysler between 1964 and 1978 and Peugeot's increasingly from 1978–9. On closer inspection a far more complex picture emerges. Elements of Rootes-based thinking continued in various forms through to the present in parallel with Detroit-inspired strategies which in turn became subtly and more directly refashioned by a complex mix of British and European political and market configurations (Whipp 1986).

The role of specialist advisors in forming competitive attitudes should also be accounted for. In the past bankers, stockbrokers and consultants have offered solutions to what were perceived to be the key problems of the era: advocacy of the 'PIMS' model, or measured daywork systems in the 1970s are cases in point. A large part of the long-term pattern of company organization in the UK car industry can be attributed to the influential advice of banks and stockbroker analysts. The experience of the Rover Company and Lloyds in 1930, or the tangled web of mergers during the 1960s, are notable examples (Whipp and Clark 1986). Fourth, it is vital to find out if and how alternative competitive stances are evaluated and once a strategy is chosen how far the manner of implementation is conceived as an integral part of the strategy formulation.

The second main area of the research framework relates to the contexts in which any strategic change occurs. There are two contextual levels: the inner and the outer contexts of the firm. The inner context consists largely of the structure, culture and politics of an organization. Structure here refers not only to the formal framework of relationships within a company but also to the multiple structures produced by the composite actions of individuals within an organization. The culture of an organization includes the beliefs, meanings and rationales used to legitimate action together with the languages, codes and rules which inform those actions. The politics of an enterprise relate both to the internal distribution of power and to the plurality of contenders involved. Each has a direct or indirect bearing on competitive performance by the way it shapes company strategies in either their mode of creation or execution.

It is, for example, important to discover the extent to which successful companies in competitive terms are characterized by integrative and therefore facilitating decision-making frameworks; or, as in the case of ICI in the 1970s (Pettigrew 1985a), are less successful strategies associated with segmental and retardant patterns? In the case of the two automobile producers currently under research, Jaguar and the Peugeot-Talbot company (previously owned by Rootes and Chrysler) the differences are stark. The problems of its main aim of competing head-on with Ford in Britain apart, Chrysler UK between 1967 and 1978 adopted a decision-making framework which increased its difficulties. Chrysler management rejected the Rootes Group's holding company structure for a US based model based on three divisions: Overseas, Passenger Cars and Commercial Vehicles. After three attempts an organizational structure emerged of a board, administrative committee, and a variety of policy committees. Although a logical move given the relative lack of financial planning, accounting procedures and product planning models under Rootes the new structure was inappropriate to the rapidly changing circumstances in which the company operated (Whipp, Rosenfeld and Pettigrew 1987). All levels of management agreed that imposition of a twelve volume Organizational Manual to govern all modes of board, administrative and departmental decision making was unwieldy. One director summed up the position as 'stultifying . . . if it wasn't covered by the manual then it didn't exist'. Consequently, important operational decisions over, for example, scheduling took months not days. Rather than make decision making more formal and controlled it resulted in managers resorting to informal networks to subvert and bypass the official structure. In Jaguar, it has been the rejection of such 'top heavy' structures and their replacement by a system which builds on such unofficial problem-solving networks which stands out. The formidable achievements in product innovation and speed of implementation of new manufacturing technology are directly attributed to the organization of engineeering and planning around not disciplinary specialisms but problems or project-based groups (Whipp 1986). The culture of a company interests us in so far as it is open to outside influence and above all in the extent to which that culture either constrains choices of competitive policies or is used by those involved to effect change.

One of the sharpest instances of using a company culture to effect change and enhance competitive performance is Jaguar Cars. Indeed a great deal of the company's performance from 1980 to the present rests on a major shift in the core beliefs and assumptions of the Jaguar management and work-force. The new senior management team from 1980 have not only introduced 500 new engineers, totally recast the existing management, created new purchasing, finance, sales and marketing, and communications

124

departments, and brought out a completely new saloon model, but they have also given coherence to these differing activities by creating, or more properly reviving, a common culture. In essence this has meant recovering and developing the commitment to engineering excellence and quality which had flourished under the Lyons regime in the relatively easier market conditions of the 1945–72 years. This commitment had all but disappeared during Jaguar's existence as simply a component in British Leyland's cars division. It would have been inconceivable for Jaguar to have accomplished such a wide-ranging set of performance changes (e.g. in quality, inventory turnaround, project timing) which are internationally acknowledged without a complementary alteration of attitude from all levels in the company. In short a 'culture of excellence' has been engendered by a continuous programme of action which includes: a major commitment to training (costing 2 per cent of turnover compared to the UK industry average of 0.15 per cent), quality circles, direct dealer/shopfloor meetings over quality issues reinforced by symbolic monthly awards, and backed up by high profile national awards to supplier companies, and perhaps most important of all an extensive 'hearts and minds' scheme which involves employees in a range of company sponsored non-work activities (Beasley 1984).

Within the merchant banking sector, the culture within many of the merchant banks defined the strategic options which were feasible. In Robert Fleming, there is a strong belief that the successful expansion into new lines of activity is most likely through the use of a joint venture with another firm. There are widely-held beliefs among top management at Flemings regarding what constitutes an 'ideal' partner: non-participation in the particular target market, bringing in skill and knowledge that is not available within Flemings, and above all, a feeling that the potential partner shares the same sort of family values and emphasizes the importance of good human relationships.

Since the announcement by the London Stock Exchange of deregulation in 1984, many of the merchant banks have purchased stockbroking firms and stockjobbers (marketmakers). The approach taken by the merchant banks was to a large degree influenced by the cultural constraints of the organization. At Hill Samuel, top management within Hill Samuel & Co. (the banking arm of Hill Samuel Group) recognized the need to acquire a top stockbroking firm. However, at the Group level, there was much resistance from the investment management side. The argument against the purchase of a stockbroker was that it would create a conflict of interest if the investment managers were forced to channel all (or even a larger proportion) of their equity purchase and selling activities through an in-house firm. These investment managers felt they would lose many valuable clients who felt this would be improper. The proposal to purchase a stockbroker was raised a number of times at the Group level, and was rejected consistently. As it happened, the favoured broker used by Hill Samuel Investment Management was Wood Mackenzie (accounting for 25 per cent of UK equity transactions). Top executives at Wood Mackenzie called up their contacts at Hill Samuel Investment Management and told them that it was likely that Wood Mackenzie would agree to be acquired by a merchant bank or a foreign bank and felt that it was only fair to warn Hill Samuel Investment Management executives that this would inevitably occur. Faced with the possibility of having to pay commissions to the stockbroking arm of a competitor, Hill Samuel Investment Management abruptly changed their mind and recommended the purchase of Wood Mackenzie.

The impact of internal politics on business strategies is well rehearsed (Pettigrew 1973). Our research is especially interested in internal politics which are conceived as the management of meaning. This requires an exploration of the way eventual strategies and competitive stances are the outcome of often highly subjective interests and decision-making processes and their reliance on tacit knowledge and private codes.

The outer context of strategic change processes comes closer to the macro and national scale approaches to competitive performance; it may be conveniently divided into four areas: the economic, business, political and societal formations in which firms must operate. The relevance of the economic environment has been indicated (pp. 116–21) and its treatment of macroeconomic understandings of competitiveness. However, in the business environment a number of features demand separate scrutiny. It is clearly worthwhile to connect the behaviour of firms to the market structures and their position *vis-à-vis* the 'best-practice' firms of the industry who set the tone for leading strategies and their operating concepts. The extent to which a company's attempts at strategic changes are facilitated or constrained by its ensemble of relations with financial institutions, suppliers, contractors, manufacturers' associations and so on, is of vital interest. The experience of many UK and European enterprises during the past two decades has made the political environment a major consideration in competitive performance. The impact has extended from the general policy implications of governments through to the detailed intervention of the state into individual sectors, of which the car industry is a classic example

(Dunnett 1980). Nowhere was this more evident than in the case of the Rootes, Chrysler and Peugeot-Talbot operations. Rootes were forced to locate their new production facility in 1960 not at their Coventry base but in Linwood in Scotland. The government's attempt to use the industry as a tool of regional development cost the company dearly in terms of dispersed production and the transport of engines and trim from Coventry to Linwood (Whipp, Rosenfeld and Pettigrew, 1987). Moreover, the broader use of the auto sector as a means of economic management by successive administrations resulted in 24 major changes in policy on the industry. In an embattled organization such as Chrysler UK, already reeling from profound alterations in the car market with the increase of foreign competition and the effects of world oil price rises of 1974, the fluctuations in government policy were disastrous. The Chrysler board reports of 15 January 1975 concluded therefore that such changes made forecasting, and therefore planning, 'difficult to the point of being practically impossible'. This is not to argue that government policy causes poor performance in firms but that the actions of successive administrations have increased the difficulties which strategically weak companies already face.

The UK merchant banks are overseen by the Bank of England, which has direct, regular contact with the banks as well as through the Accepting Houses Committee. Membership to the Accepting Houses Committee is the indication that a merchant bank has achieved a particularly high status within the City as a reputable commercial banking organization, One of the responsibilities of membership is to come to the aid of any fellow firm which gets into financial trouble, at the request of the Bank of England. A recent example of this was the failure of Johnson Matthey Bank in late September 1984. Due to a series of questionable loans, rumours began to spread around the financial world that the Johnson Matthey Bank would collapse. If such an event was to occur, the thinking was that it would inspire a lack of confidence in the British banking regulatory system (the Bank of England) and lead to a flight of capital to other financial centres. Given the worsening of this crisis, by the end of September, the Bank of England stepped in and 'asked' 25 of London's leading banks (including the Accepting Houses Committee members) to make available 250 million pounds in standby loans to safeguard Johnson Matthey depositors. The 'lifeboat' was launched without the conviction of many of the banks asked to participate. Indeed, among the merchant banks there was much grumbling about the size of the risk and the lack of any sort of 'reward' for participation.

Nevertheless, solidarity was maintained and the loans were provided.

As a tool of regulation and control, the Bank of England prefers informal meetings among its various constituents rather than overt control mechanisms. All the reputable financial institutions in the City share the Bank of England's preference for discreet control as it maintains the high reputation which is critical for success as a financial centre.

The related social formations within societies may leave a number of imprints on the efforts of businesses to formulate and implement new strategies. It has been argued that there are distinctive assumptions and values within societies which can either enable or obstruct certain types of commercial activity (Crozier 1974). More recently geographers have alerted us to the way these social features may operate differentially between regions and other localities; areas which become of greater relevance as the spatial division of labour within organizations grows (Massey 1984).

The third, final, and perhaps most critical, yet most elusive area of the research framework concerns the processual dimension of strategic change. It is through this dimension that research can capture the dynamic aspects of strategic assessment, choice and change as well as competitive performance. In essence, we are interested in the long-term pattern of events by which strategies are conceived and their competitive purposes put into operation. One needs to ascertain therefore: who champions and manages new strategies, what decision arenas and processes do they emerge from, what models of change govern the conception and implementation, and how appropriate are they to the contexts in which the firm operates (Pettigrew 1985a, Whipp 1986). Of equal relevance is the way in which progress is measured and evaluated and the extent to which 'organizational learning' is recognized as a possibility (Jelinek 1979). It would appear that competitive businesses find ways of recording and storing for future reference their more successful strategies and the processes associated with them. The question naturally arises as to whether there is technology available (either in-house or bought-in) which can lend greater coherence and deliver enhanced control over the strategic and operational change process. Examples are provided by GM's Project Saturn or Austin Rover Group's use of computer aided engineering (CAE).

As much of the foregoing implies, contextual research into competitiveness at the level of the firm hinges on the relationship between managerial perception, action and the contexts in which management operates. The analytical challenge is to connect up the content, contexts and process of strategic change with competitive performance. We have suggested a range of possible linkages in this chapter. Perhaps the most critical connection for our research is the way managers mobilize the contexts around them (Pettigrew 1985a, 1987) and in so doing provide legitimacy for change. The contexts in which management operate are not inert or objective entities. Just as managers perceive and construct their own versions of those contexts so do they subjectively select their own versions of the competitive environment together with their personal visions of how to re-order their business to meet those perceived challenges.

Given that companies exist in a plurality of time frames any account of the management of strategic change must pay attention to the wealth of temporal features involved (Whipp 1987). The way time is socially constructed by people and the way such active perceptions of time may transform the detailed course of projects and their processes is a vital concern. Indeed, it is via the rich possibilities of human thought and action, which the process of change contains, that both the contextual pressures and intended content of named strategies are transformed. Our approach to strategic and operational change leads us to suspect at this stage that it may be in this process where the competitive performances of companies are either made or broken.

Conclusion

The adoption of a contextual and processual approach to strategic change, allied to a dynamic understanding of the different levels of competitiveness has clear implications for our research method (Centre for Corporate Strategy and Change, 1985). Data collection methods have been devised which can embrace the spread of activities and processes identified in this chapter. Documentary and oral evidence are combined. Examination of the content, contexts and processes of strategic change and their relevance to the mix of competitive measures and issues raised here require inspection of, not only the range of relevant secondary material (related to the society, sector or company), but also of the variety of forms which the primary material generated within an enterprise assumes. Historical and real time interviews are needed to span the processes involved. The quality of access becomes of paramount importance. The preliminary understanding of competitiveness and strategic change outlined above leads to the collection of necessarily disparate categories of evidence in order to reconstruct a process which touches on so many aspects of a firm's existence. Above all, the research framework demands both the craft skills associated with social and historical reconstruction together with the critical process of triangulation between the personal testimony of those involved, appropriate documentary evidence and the researchers' developing understanding of competitiveness and strategic change.

In essence this research hopes to extend our comprehension of that relationship by maximizing the use of an integrated conception of the problem combined with a flexible approach and methodology. Put briefly the research employs a synthesis of contextualist and processual orientation to strategic change in order to discover how managing that change relates to the different levels of competition. Such a synthesis raises the possibility of moving beyond those accounts of competitiveness which focus solely on the firm, or the sector or the societal unit of analysis (cf. Francis 1985). More especially, a research agenda which takes such a conceptual starting point would hope to highlight both the subjective bases, and the more objective definitions, of competitiveness: it would also expect to reveal the way these conceptions change interactively with the essentially human process of managerial assessment, choice and change.

References

Abernathy, W. (1978) *The Productivity Dilemma: Roadblock to Innovation in the Auto Industry*, Chicago: Johns Hopkins University Press.

Abernathy, W., Clark, K. B. and Kantrow, A. (1981) 'The new industrial competition', *Harvard Business Review*, September/October: 69–81.

Abernathy, W., Clark, K. B. and Kantrow, A. (1983) *Industrial Renaissance*, New York: Basic Books.

Andrews, K. R. (1970) *The Concept of Corporate Strategy*, Homewood, Illinois: Irwin.

Beasley, M. (1984) 'Participation at Jaguar Cars', *Industrial Participation*, Autumn: 18–21.

Blume, M. E. (1980) 'The financial markets', in R. E. Caves and L. B. Krause (eds) *Britain's Economic Performance*, Washington DC: The Brookings Institute.

Caves, R. E. (1980) 'Productivity differences amongst industries', in R.E. Caves and L.B. Krause (eds) *Britain's Economic Performance*, Washington DC: The Brookings Institute.

Centre for Corporate Strategy and Change (1985) 'The management of strategic & operational change', Research Outline, Warwick University, October.

Chrysler, Corporation (1973) *Financial and General Fact Book of the Chrysler Corporation*, Detroit.

Collier, R. (1986) 'Building the franchise image', Mimeo, UK Sales Department, Jaguar Cars Ltd.

Crozier, M. (1974) *The Stalled Society*, New York: Viking.

Dunnett, P. (1980) *The Decline of the British Motor Industry*, London: Croom Helm.

ESRC (1983) Papers presented to Economic and Social Research Council, Workshop on Competitiveness, November.

Evered, R. (1983) 'So what is strategy?' *Long Range Planning*, vol. 16, no. 3: 57–72.

Fay, S. and Knightly, P. (1986) 'The pit and the pandemonium', *Observer*, 12 January.

Francis, A. (1985) 'The competitiveness of British industry: concepts, issues and research questions', paper presented to ESRC Competitiveness Research Groups Meeting, Manchester, October.

House of Lords Select Committee on Overseas Trade (1985) London: HMSO, October.

Jelinek, M. (1979) *Institutionalising Innovation. A Study of Organisational Learning Systems*, New York: Praeger.

Jones, D. (1981) *Maturity and Crisis in the European Car Industry. Structural Change and Public Policy*, Brighton: Sussex University, Science Policy Research Unit.

Jones, D. (1986) 'Ford Talks', *Financial Times*, 11 February.

Kaplinsky, R. (1984) *Automation: The Technology and Society*, London: Allen & Unwin.

Lawrence, P. R. and Lorsch, J. W. (1967) *Organization and Environment*, Boston: Harvard University Press.

Lazonick, W. (1983) 'The dynamics of industrial development: a research agenda for contemplating Britain's economic future', paper presented to ESRC Workshop on Competitiveness, November.

Lorenz, C. (1986) *The Design Dimension*, Oxford: Blackwell.

Massey, D. (1984) *Spatial Divisions of Labour*, London: Macmillan.

Mintzberg, H. (1978) 'Patterns in strategy formation', *Management Science* 24(a): 934–48.

NEDC (1985) *British Industrial Performance. A Comparative Survey over Recent Years*, London: National Economic Development Office.

Pavitt, K. (ed.) (1980) *Technical Change and Britain's Economic Performance*, London: Macmillan.

Peters, T. J. K. and Waterman, R. H. (1982) *In Search of Excellence: Lessons from America's Best Run Companies*, New York: Harper & Row.

Pettigrew, A. M. (1973) *The Politics of Organizational Decision Making*, London: Tavistock.

Pettigrew, A. M. (1985a) *The Awakening Giant: Continuity and Change in Imperial Chemical Industries*, Oxford: Blackwell.

Pettigrew, A. M. (1985b) 'Contextualist research: a natural way to link theory and practice', in E. Lawler *et al.* (1985) *Doing Research that is Useful in Theory and Practice*, San Francisco: Jossey-Bass.

Pettigrew, A. M. (1987) 'Theoretical, methodological and empirical issues in studying change: a response to Starkey', *Journal of Management Studies*, vol. 24, no. 4: 64–8.

Piore, M. J. and Sabel, C. (1984) *The Second Industrial Divide: Possibilities for Prosperity*, New York: Free Press.

Pollard, S. (1982) *The Wasting of the British Economy: British Economic Policy 1945 to the Present*, London: Croom Helm.

Quinn, J. B. (1980) *Strategies for Change: Logical Incrementalism*, Homewood, Illinois; Irwin.

Sabel, C. (1981) *Work and Politics*, Cambridge: Cambridge University Press.

Shearman, C. and Burrell, G. (1985) 'The structures of industrial development', ESRC Competitiveness Research Group at Lancaster Working Paper no. 1.

Sinclair, S. (1983) *The World Car: The Future of the Automobile Industry*, London: Euromonitor.

Stopford, J. and Turner, L. (1985) *Britain and the Multi-nationals*, Chichester: Wiley.

Whipp, R. (1984) 'The art of good management: management control of work in the British pottery industry 1900–1925', *International Review of Social History*, vol. xxix, no. 3: 359–85.

Whipp, R. (1986) 'The dimensions of strategic change in Rootes, Chrysler and Peugeot Talbot', Mimeo, Warwick University, December.

Whipp, R. (1987) 'To every time a purpose: an essay on time and work', in P. Joyce (ed.) (1987) *Historical Meanings of Work*, Cambridge: Cambridge University Press.

Whipp, R. and Clark, P. (1986) *Innovation and the Auto Industry. Product, Process and Work Organization*, London: Francis Pinter.

Whipp, R., Rosenfeld, R. and Pettigrew, A. M. (1987) 'Understanding strategic change processes: some preliminary British findings', in A. M. Pettigrew (ed.) (1987) *The Management of Strategic Change*, Oxford: Blackwell, 14–55.

Wiener, M. (1981) *English Culture and the Decline of the Industrial Spirit. 1850–1980*. Cambridge: Cambridge University Press.

Williams, K., Williams J. and Thomas, D. (1983) *Why Are the British Bad at Manufacturing?*, London: Routledge & Kegan Paul.

Appendix: Content, contexts and processes in the management of strategic and operational change and competitiveness

The following is a checklist of research questions and issues. The format minimizes the interrelationships between content, contexts and process dealt with in the chapter although certain key linkages are indicated.

Content

1. The firm's competitive strategy when it was part of an industry which was emerging, maturing, declining but also rejuvenated/reformed.
2. Strategy components:
    - financial
    - technological
    - marketing
    - human
    - governance

    knowledge base by department and collectively

How related, synthesized and cohesive is the knowledge base and how is it used? Major link to process.
3. Key objectives in:
    - general/grand strategy sense of long term
    - more immediate (annual?) goals
    - pro-active/re-active
    - social construction of goals
4. Built-in assumptions and expectations and their formal versus implicit expression. What contributions does the strategy intend to make (in Andrews' sense) to shareholders, customers, employees, communities, others.
5. Sources:
    - pressure from below – imposed from top
    - impact of competitor practice versus in-house
    - internally driven or externally pushed
    - specialist advisors (stockbrokers?)
    - consultant role?
    - How are alternatives assessed? Scenario writing?
6. Methods of evaluation, assessment built into strategy. What measurements, rules envisaged?

Contexts

A. Inner

1. Antecedent conditions. Company history. Thought sets and their degree of past-embeddedness. Pattern of crises 'transforming events'/critical dramas. Course of past successful, unsuccessful strategies. Impact, duration, ramifications.
2. Structure:
    - facilitating/integrative v. segmentalist, retardant
    - division of labour at all levels of organization
    - structural repertoire

- structuration. Social structures made up of composite actions which both constrain and assist individuals
3. Leadership style, background, competence.
4. 'Dominating frames of thought' in the organization with regard to strategy. Values, assumptions of powerful groups who control the firm. Major link of internal context and the broader values and group assumptions to content.

   Related to: 'bodies of thought'; recipes; formulae and 'dominant logics' of firm or specialist functions.
5. Culture:
   - beliefs, meanings, rationales and languages of the organization. Expression in metaphors, myths but also
   - 'game rules' which consciously and indirectly inform action and the way they are interpreted by players, groups
   - openness of culture to outside influence, e.g. community, professional associations
   - to what extent does company culture constrain action or conversely is it used by actors?
6. Politics:
   - distribution of power
   - politics as the management of meaning expressed in acknowledged language, codes
   - plurality of contenders (management) labour; intra-management (or labour) and the range of means available in exerting power

B. Outer
1. Economic environment:
   - competitive status of other companies in the market but also, competitive position of the industry as a whole (e.g. degree of foreign penetration)
   - competitive status at the macro level, e.g. exports, output per head, bases of competition (price, quality, etc.) and their changing from across time within given sector
2. Business environment:
   - market structure including price leaders, 'best practice' firms
   - manufacturers' associations
   - suppliers/contractors/consultants as information brokers
   - dominant strategy models and operating concepts
   - speed of market change compared to industry life course
3. Political environment:
   - general pattern of state intervention in given sector
   - specific policy actions of separate administrations (economic policy regulators, regional policy, social engineering)

4. Social and economic trends relevant to company's fortunes and policies as enabling or constraining conditions, e.g. 1950s 'easy profits/sellers' market', 1970s rampant inflation, 1980s 'New Realism' and how company is influenced by or seeks to use them:
   - structuration in sense of not only distinctive practices/ assumptions of a society but also at the town or regional level, e.g. recruitment practices, career expectations in W. Midlands versus South East
   - related to 'spatial division of labour' within UK

C. Process
   1. Starting point – when/why was change need sensed?
   2. Managerial perceptions, process and actions. How has management managed/attempted to manage the context and process (e.g. by signalling new areas for concern, anchoring signals in issues for attention, mobilizing energy and commitment, ensuring problem areas and solutions gain sufficient legitimacy and power)?
   3. Who are change managers/groups? Dependent on a few people or coalitions (product, idea champions).
   4. Decision arenas – formal and informal decision making.
   5. Pattern – long periods of continuity, learning and incremental adjustment interspersed with hiatuses or revolutions featuring abnormally high levels of change activity.
   6. What objective/subjective models of change exist? Project centred or goal centred?
      - how does this compare with process in reality?
      - are there multiple sub-processes?
      - how is progress conceived, measured, evaluated? What are human, economic, technological, market indicators? Monitoring.
   7. Implementation covered in strategy formulation. Major link with process/content.
      - imposed/negotiated style? Prior construction with signals
      - communication elements? Briefing groups, rehearsals, training opportunities
      - single plant islands to spread pattern
      - to what extent are contingencies covered? How flexible?
      - is problem of organizational learning recognised?
      - methods, procedures, mechanisms for learning
      - information stored, retrieved, re-activated
   8. Is there a technology available/used for greater coherence? Control of strategic and operational change process.

9. Internal/external consultants used to advise, manage, change:
   – background, tools, length of stay, work organization
10. Language/discourse of the process. Image and reality of change.
11. Time: Given that companies live in a plurality of time frames, what are the time frames of the change process derived from in/outside company? E.g. calibrated in years, financial years/ reporting periods/career paths/product cycles/technological generations.
    – 'objective' time frames
    – socially constructed time frames and interaction with the more 'objective'
    – how is past subjectively ordered to legitimate action in process in present?

Chapter seven

Social approaches to the competitive process

L. Araujo, G. Burrell, G. Easton,
R. Rothschild, S. Rothschild, C. Shearman

Introduction

The approach which forms the basis of this chapter emphasizes the social aspects of the competitive process. In this respect, its focus is different from that of other work in the literature on the theory of competition. We shall argue here that while strictly economic elements of the competitive process are of essential importance, attention must be given to those aspects of competition which are grounded in the experiences, values and 'world views' of the managers through whom the process is enacted and given an organizational shape. We shall present evidence which suggests that competition among firms can be characterized in such social terms. In particular, we shall argue that industries may usefully be seen as social networks which emerge, develop and mature over time. This view has led to the construction of a social model of industrial development. The model provides the framework for what follows as well as an initial and partial test of it.

Competitiveness is conventionally taken to be synonymous with 'performance', but the actual means of processes whereby firms achieve satisfactory performance levels are ill-understood. Conventional models of competition tend to depict clearly defined firms competing for the attention of rational consumers in well-delineated markets. Such a depiction is based upon a set of simplified assumptions which frequently obscures the complex nature of the process of competition. Existing models of this process and of the path of development of industries involved in it are typically based upon the assumption that the reactions of managers to externally generated 'stimuli' are predictable. Decision makers are seen as being driven variously by the logic of profit maximization (Waterson 1984) or the imperative of innovation (Rothwell and Zegveld 1981, 1982) or the need to discover and occupy an 'environmental niche' which will permit corporate survival (Astley 1985a). The theoretical and empirical justification for these approaches is rarely addressed.

Like others concerned with the social dimensions of organizations (Huff 1982, Mintzberg and Waters 1985), we see industry broadly in terms of shared and interlocking world-views leading to similar perceptions of environmental conditions and strategic behaviour. Shared experiences, whether in terms of educational or working backgrounds, reinforce the tendency for individuals to view problems in the same way and to legitimize and sanction similar policies, procedures and structures (Di Maggio and Powell 1983).

Our concern with the social aspects of the competitive process encourages an emphasis on managerial perceptions and the nature and variety of the relationships which exist among organizations and key individuals within given industries. In particular, our research investigates the similarities and differences in management's responses to the problems facing firms in a competitive industrial setting. We address the ways in which individual managers and organizations perceive and evaluate their competition (actual and potential), the channels through which information affecting these perceptions is acquired and the extent to which such perceptions affect policy and strategy. In particular we are concerned to understand how these factors differ at different stages in the social development of industries.

A social model of industrial development

While much of the analysis of Britain's industrial performance tends to focus on either the macro level of nation state or economy or the micro level of individual firms, much less attention is given to the notion of an 'industry' itself. Since economies are made up of different mixes of industry (Ingham 1974) and since firms engaged in competition tend to identify themselves with particular industries, it is our view that a meso level approach provides an important insight into the forces shaping and constraining industrial development and consequently the competitive process itself. With this in mind we have developed what might be termed a 'social' model of industrial development.

Outlined in more detail elsewhere (Shearman and Burrell 1987), our social model depicts the process of industrial development as typically involving four 'stages'. Our approach has been to focus on the actual process of competition, or inter-firm interaction, within an industry and the way in which this might shape industrial development. Conventional definitions of 'industry' in terms of, for example, the British Standard Industrial Classification, have

138

been replaced by a view of 'industry' as those constellations of entities perceived by the core membership to belong to a given industry, irrespective of whether or not they may be matched precisely in more objective terms of their technological, product, market or other similarities. Similarly, 'competition' is seen to extend beyond the stereotype of individual firms, clearly demarcated one from the other, engaged in cut-throat competition. Close, co-operative modes of action can and do co-exist with competitive interactions.

The focus on the social aspects of inter-organizational relationships clearly differentiates this model from other approaches to industrial development. Firms are seen as part of a set of interlinked relationships with other entities within any given industry, and the number and density of these relationships differ as the industry develops. Moreover, sets of interrelationships arise not only among organizations but also among individuals whose actions, particularly during the early stages of an industry's life cycle, may constitute a major dynamic force for development.

Initially ideas for the model emerged from the network analysis literature. Here the notion of 'network' as a metaphor for social relationships is combined with a device to measure quantifiable bonds and transactions (Mattson 1984, Hammarkvist 1983, Rogers and Kincaid 1981) but the emphasis lies more on the form and content (i.e. technological, legal, economic or social) of a relationship at a given point of time than on its dynamics and context. It is in the social nature of inter-organizational relationships and their inter-temporal dynamics, however, that the key to understanding industrial development at this level lies. Industries, and consequently the social relationships within them, evolve over time. For this reason our model combines a focus on the primacy of social relationships with the notion of industrial life cycles. This is not to deny the relevance of economic, technological, legal or other relationships within an industry but to suggest that social and psychological features are ever-present and have a crucial impact upon inter-organizational relationships and such interactive processes as competition. Four ideal-typical stageposts are taken to mark the process of industrial evolution. These are:

1. the community;
2. the informal network(s);
3. the formal network;
4. the club.

The community phase represents the early stage of an industry's development where there is little recognition of the nature of the 'industry', 'product' or 'market'. Companies on the whole are newly established, small in employment terms and possibly spin-offs from firms in other industries seeking to exploit the potential of technological convergence. Loyalty to the 'organizations' tends to be low. Entrepreneurs set up small 'companies' as problem-solving forums, often closing them down so as to allow them to emerge as different legal entities. Company name changes are frequent and, faced with this instability, individuals tend to identify more with the wider community as a whole. Products are at the prototype stage but knowledge of the technology is wide-spread and communally shared. Little specialization of function within companies is evident and most are involved in identical problem-solving activities. Organizational structures and flexible and social relationships within the industry are dynamic and multi-faceted. Thus the early stage of an industry's development resembles a *gemeinschaft* in which individuals, firms and groups interact in a fluid set of complex and varied relationships.

Eventually the sense of community and the community itself gives rise, through internally generated forces, to the informal network(s). These represent the processes by which some order arises out of the fluid and ad hoc relationships which characterize the early community. The industry begins to acquire some sense of its own existence and identity. Its products and technologies differentiate it clearly from other industries and its market bound-aries become discernible. Firms typically graduate from the small to the medium sized and an individual's loyalty to the firm grows. While social interactions remain frequent and multi-faceted, a widening geographical location and declining sense of communal values reduces their complexity and richness. Certain channels of communications are openly preferred. Relationships have not yet crystallized as they would in the later stages of an industry's development, but the elite groups of key individuals and organiza-tions which are in the process of emerging provide a focus for their direction and management. Links with other companies and individuals are increasingly perceived in terms of economic costs, and knowledge within and about the industry becomes organized until relationships begin to evolve into the formal network.

This stage represents many if not most industries at the height of their development. Numerically there are fewer companies present than in the earlier stages and market shares are well established. Elite groupings of key individuals and organizations have solidified into the core of the network and shape the industry's general direction and perceptions. Firms are differentiated by their status levels, corporate cultures, product ranges and market responses. Communication channels between individuals and organizations are relatively formalized, emanating from and ending with the core of the network. The formal network stage may last for decades until a crisis gives rise to the club.

Here major threats to technology and/or markets engender high levels of uncertainty about the industry's survival. As knowledge of the 'crisis' permeates the network, the core 'implodes' to form a small defensive 'club' with a well-defined sense of external threat, self-interest and industrial loyalty. Membership is by invitation only and legally binding. Trust between members is not very high. Less rigid in some respects than the formal network, the club stage may enrich the range of cross-organizational relationships but the measure is essentially transient, pragmatic and purposive.

Primarily social in nature then, these four metaphors – community, informal networks, formal network and clubs – characterize the dynamics of power and inter-firm relationships. A number of mechanisms drive this evolution from communities to clubs. The concept of cyclical bursts of innovative activity which give rise to industrial development is reminiscent of the work of Kondratieff, Mandel and others. Essentially spontaneous and unpredictable in their initial stages, these bursts are preceded by widespread industrial and economic stagnation (Mensch 1979, Clark, Freeman and Soete 1981). Certain factors do, however, facilitate the development of a 'community'. Robson and Rothwell (1985) have identified what might be termed the symbiosis or 'dynamic complementarities' that can exist between large and small companies. Undoubtedly, this plays an important role, as do certain spatial advantages (Oakey 1984 and Astley 1985a). Cumulative benefits associated with geographical proximity and infrastructural resources and support reinforce the already disproportionate advantages enjoyed by some regions at the expense of others. Convergence of technologies may be a further facilitating factor.

Movement from the community stage of industrial development to that of informal networks and, ultimately, the formal network is driven by the dynamics of organizational growth. The movement from organic towards mechanistic forms of organizational structures (Burns and Stalker 1961, Hage 1965) which characterizes this process reflects Astley's (1985b) idea that evolutionary development entails structural metamorphosis. By the time an industry reaches the formal network stage of its evolution, companies within it are specialized, structured, formalized and centralized. Organizational growth in turn is facilitated by opportunistic choice (Astley 1985a). This declines as an industry stabilizes. Competitive relationships are initally absent, emerging only as demands begin to exceed available resources. Pressure of congestion eliminates the weakest. Choices diminish as an industry approaches its optimal size, with members locked into ossified relationships.

Astley (1985a) suggests that this stability is relatively fragile and that industries are destined to collapse eventually. The process of decline can be attributed to various factors ranging from product obsolescence and insufficient R&D investment to the failure to acquire knowledge of appropriate peripheral technologies (Richardson 1985).

A more important feature of the progress from the formal network stage of industrial development to that of the club can be described as a state of perceptual inertia. Suffering from the ossifying effects of accumulated experience (Boswell 1973, Senker 1979) and problems induced by horizontal and vertical integration (Harrigan 1983), declining industries are frequently not aware of the problems which they face. Realization, when and if it occurs, is invariably too late, and the only means of dealing with external threats to survival appears to lie in that mode of behaviour characteristic of clubs. The lack of flexibility manifested by industries at this stage provides a major incentive for 'spin-offs' (Shapero 1980) which may prove conducive to successful innovation (Von Hippel 1977, Roberts 1977) if suitably embedded in a community context.

The development of the research programme

The motivation for our research is the identification of managerial perceptions in the competitive process. We have chosen to evaluate the perceptions of management across as wide an industrial spectrum as possible. The approach is based on the assumption that the subtleties of different managerial perspectives are unlikely to reveal themselves through large-scale surveys or questionnaires. The intention is to analyse in detail a small number of cases in order to identify and explain sets of perceptions within management groups.

The selection of the case industries

Our study focuses on the manufacturing sector. This restriction enables us to avoid some of the problems which arise when products are sold by retailers and in this way are subject to choices made by those who are not final consumers. The relationships between manufacturer and retailer, it should be noted, are frequently bilateral in nature and consequently constitute elements of market imperfection which we wish to avoid. The central importance of the manufacturing sector for the UK economy is itself a justification for our particular attention. Within this sector there can be found a variety of institutional and market arrangements, and our concern has been to consider only those industries which are free of substantial monopolistic or monopsonistic elements. The requirement that there be a large number of sellers and buyers naturally constrains the choice. An additional consideration of importance from our point of view is that the industries chosen should show evidence of a wide variety of perceptions of the competitive environment, and we have taken the view that this will only be the case when the composition of the industry is heterogeneous. Perhaps the most important of the distinguishing features of the industries which we have selected are:

(a) the extent of import penetration, and
(b) their position in the 'industry life cycle'.

The need to consider these features has substantially reduced the number of industries which we consider appropriate cases for investigation. On the one hand, we are interested in those industries which have managed to succeed, despite their relatively embryonic nature, in the face of competition; on the other hand, we are interested in those instances in which industries, despite their long-established character, have seen their domestic market seriously eroded by competition from abroad.

There are, of course, a number of industries which meet our initial requirements. Several of these would have been appropriate cases for study and many were explored. Most were rejected on the grounds of difficulties involved in obtaining adequate data or background information, or problems of definition or access. After some protracted consideration, the following three industries were selected: commercial vehicles, temperature controllers and medical lasers.

We describe each of these below. It will be apparent that these industries differ from one another in crucial respects: the extent of import penetration, the heterogeneity (in terms of size and competitive behaviour) of their constituent units, and their position in their respective life cycles. In this way we have set about linking some of the themes arising from our empirical results with the notion of industrial maturity as represented in the conceptual approach. Medical applications of fibre optics in the field of endoscopy involve the marriage of a number of technologies – lasers, chemical sensors and advanced optoelectronics – at the current technological forefront. As technological advances increase the variety of potential applications and products, an 'embryonic' market segment is beginning to emerge. By contrast the temperature control industry represents a relatively well-established, though not fully mature, market, while commercial vehicles can be characterized as a mature and potentially declining sector.

The case industries

The UK commercial vehicle industry forms a part of the total UK vehicle manufacturing industry. Although the term 'commercial vehicles' is generally used to include all vehicles other than cars and car-derived vans, we shall use it in the more specific sense of those trucks in the medium to heavy range. We do not include coaches, buses, light 4×4 utilities nor any specialist vehicles.

The fate of the commercial vehicle industry is clearly relevant to British industry. Its history is dominated by two trends: the trend towards the merging of companies and the movement of the mass producers up the weight range (Bhaskar 1979).

In the 1950s the UK boasted 40 separate commercial vehicle producers but by 1978 only 10 remained. Today, in the area we study, ERF stands as the sole surviving UK independent (Chairman's statement 1984). Leyland Vehicles survives though it seems to be searching for yet another identity while Foden is controlled by Paccar of the USA and Seddon Atkinson by Enasa of Spain.

In the post-war period manufacturers divided up into the mass producers and the specialists. As the former saw profitable opportunities at the top end of the weight range and moved gradually towards it, the specialists found their territory invaded. This was a period when the demand for trucks outstripped supply and the profit potential remained rich enough to encourage the Europeans to export to the UK market. In the late 1960s Swedish trucks were first seen on British roads and this flow increased in the 1970s. Today the Germans, French, Dutch and Italians are all represented in significant numbers. As the influence of the Europeans has increased, that of the Americans has decreased and recently there has taken place the withdrawal of Bedford from the heavy commercial vehicle sector, and the merger of Ford with Iveco. The full impact of these events has yet to permeate the market.

At the present time the commercial vehicle industry is suffering from forty per cent over-capacity (Rhys 1986). The problem of the 1950s and 1960s has been turned around completely. Whereas the problem then was to satisfy growing waiting lists, now the scramble is for orders. Not surprisingly this has resulted in price-cutting which was at its worst in 1984 after the oil price falls of 1983.

Our study focuses on a subset of the commercial vehicle industry. Because of the industry-accepted classification of market segments, it is possible to concentrate on the medium to heavy truck industry. We consider not only the local manufacturers and assemblers, but the importers of vehicles. There are 11 participants at present who dominate the UK market. The commercial vehicle industry is essentially a mature one.

The temperature control industry can be considered as a subset of the process control instrumentation industry which in turn can be defined as comprising firms manufacturing and/or rendering services in the area of instrumentation measuring, controlling and recording process parameters. Its identity is derived from the rather specialized nature of measuring and controlling temperature, one of the main process parameters.

In the 1960s the development of the plastics industry in the UK gave rise to a market for dedicated temperature controllers, temperature being the main process variable in extrusion and injection moulding plastics. A single machine could take as many as six controllers and the rate of usage combined with harsh conditions generated a large replacement and retrofit market. The same instrumentation could also be applied successfully to the control of a number of other temperature processes, cutting across a wide range of industries. Whenever there is electrical heating being used there is a market for dedicated temperature controllers.

More recently, the demise of the British plastics industry – basically at the original equipment manufacturer level – and the development of specialized control systems for plastics extrusion and injection moulding machinery has greatly diminished the importance of this market segment. This development coupled with the introduction of microprocessor based controllers has led to a redefinition of markets, and boundaries are being blurred amongst different subsets of the overall industry. Eventually, with increasing miniaturization and cheaper memory circuits as well as advances in software techniques, it will be possible to cover the whole range of temperature control problems with one controller – on a single chip. The instrument will be limited only by the physical limitation of space available at the front end of the instrument for control buttons and display.

At present there are around 15 major manufacturers and importers of temperature control equipment, of the type defined above, in the UK and an unknown number of small local assemblers. The doubt about the precise number of major manufacturers springs from the difficulty experienced by the participants themselves of defining the product/market boundaries. The result is a lack of market data, particularly market shares. It is clear which firms make products in this category. It is even obvious which firms are the market leaders. It is, however, not clear at the tail of the distribution which firms can be said to be major manufacturers. The bulk of the firms concerned are either medium-sized independent organizations or medium-sized subsidiaries or divisions of larger firms. Heterogeneity of market conditions does not encourage mass production or major scale economies. The industry is maturing but not yet mature.

In contrast, the case of the medical laser 'industry' represents the very earliest stages of industrial development. Indeed, it is only possible to use the term 'industry' because certain features are just becoming apparent. Within the last five years, key individuals who are widely recognized as important figures have formed new companies to manufacture and assemble lasers with such medical uses as surgical excision or photocoagulation of blood vessels. These companies are exceptionally small, often consisting of two or three individuals with very little division of labour amongst them. The researchers face tremendous problems, with an absence of production engineering, finance and marketing skills being perceived as their major difficulty. Often, the R&D work has been carried out within university departments (particularly where optoelectronic physics is a strength) and it is academics who, in attempting to capitalize upon their technical expertise by producing safe and reliable lasers for a wide variety of medical uses, predominate in these tiny enterprises. One department of physics in a Scottish university has a staff who have set up, independently, a research unit dedicated to medical lasers, and two new commercial firms, each of which has developed a medical laser product. Clearly these three entities are likely to be interrelated but the two companies are by no means fully co-operating with each other.

The entry of a large firm into the field further underlines the process of industrial crystallization. The company concerned has been formed by the reorganization of parts of a well-established major firm in the defence industry which had experience with military lasers, and sees a considerable market for medical lasers developing in the next decade. There is still scope, however, for 'personality clashes' within the industry to have major repercussions in terms of a new company formation. The arena in which these differences are aired is now composed of the British Medical

Laser Association and its annual conference as well as the continental equivalent – the European Medical Laser Association. Both organizations have come into existence in the last three years.

Typically, researchers have a less than flattering opinion of the level of expertise possessed by the end-user of medical lasers – the hospital consultant. Frequently, the laser designers believe that the quality of the medical research papers produced by hospital specialists is very low in terms of their analysis of the laser equipment. Their day-to-day handling of the equipment is also seen as ill-informed and, in some cases, even dangerous. The industry, then, is characterized by an experimental approach to product design and assembly on the one hand and to product utilization and modification on the other.

The financial institutions recognize this fact and venture capital is only just becoming available. Expenditure on R&D consumes a very high proportion of company budgets but long-term corporate strategies in terms of marketing and product development are conspicuous by their absence. Companies tend to accept any contract, almost irrespective of its impact on medium-term development. There is a very high level of agreement on the nature of the technological problems faced by the industry, although preferred solutions do, of course, differ.

Methodology

The methods which are being used in the analysis of these case studies to produce data of relevance to our overall objective are the following. First, we are concerned to identify the 'market sector' or industry's focal organizations. We wish to include as many as possible of the firms in the industry in the interviewing process. Whilst 'complete' coverage of an industry is likely to prove impossible (since our definition is a subjective, managerial one with the boundaries of the industry being defined by the participants rather than by ourselves), we aim for as much breadth of coverage as possible. Access has not proved to be a problem in any of the three industries.

Second, having identified the 'focal' competitors, we are interviewing several of the key managers in different functions in each of the industry's major competitors on the basis of a semi-structured interview schedule. A small sample of the customers attached to each of these industries will also be interviewed so that their perceptions can be compared with those of their actual or potential suppliers.

The interview attempts to elicit the perceptions of each of the individual managers, irrespective of their function, concerning markets, customers, competitors, marketing strategies and the ways in which these strategies affect processes within the firm. Each interview is taped with the permission of the interviewee and usually lasts between one and two hours. Perceptions are being compared among departments within the same firm and among participants in the market, including customers, consultants, trade bodies, etc. This yields evidence as to how perceptions are formed and how they affect, and are affected by, market behaviour. These managerial perceptions and the way they link with actions in the firm and in the market provide a major focus for the research.

Third, in addition to these perceptual variables, market structure data for the commercial vehicles industry have been obtained. It is a measure of the maturity of this industry that such data are readily available. Boundary problems in the temperature control industry and the turbulence in the medical laser industry render any market data suspect.

The extent to which the three industries conform to our model of industrial development will be made clear in the next section. However, the limitations of the model should be admitted before this is done. The model tells us little of why, at the micro level, certain firms consistently outperform others. Nor does it illuminate intra-firm strategy or formulation within the context of a given industry. Concentrating as it does on changes in industries over time it cannot account for similarities which emerged between and among industries and which were perceived as vitally important issues by participants. Two of these themes, configurability of products and pre- and post-sale service, are the subjects of forthcoming publications.

Research themes

In this section we present some preliminary findings from the research organized around three main themes – perceptions of competitors, the nature of competition and patterns of co-operation. However, a number of qualifications should be noted. The results described here are the output of a continuing research process and should be regarded as tentative. Nor is it true that the themes discussed here exhaust all the possibilities. They are simply those that appear at present most salient and interesting. The qualitative form of the research does not readily lend itself to quantitative analyses though some work of this kind has actually been carried out. The results described here derive from a content or thematic analysis which uses individual interviews as the basic unit.

What is being attempted cannot be described as, in any sense, a test of the model. The model itself is not specified clearly enough to enable us to do this, and in any case provides only a partial view of the issues. The data, as indicated earlier, do not make possible a formal test of the model. We are therefore in the familiar position of social scientists engaged in an iterative process lying between empirical analysis on the one hand, and theory on the other. What follows reflects this position.

Perceptions of competitors

In the commercial vehicle industry the nature of the product makes industry definition a very simple matter, and enables the participants to establish a universal consensus about the composition of the industry, its history, its current state and its future prospects. The fact that commercial vehicle manufacture is a highly capital intensive industry requiring a minimum efficient scale of production means that the composition of the industry will tend to be stable over very long periods. Consequently the issue of a possible conflict between what might be termed 'concentrators' and 'dabblers' cannot arise: firms are either committed for very long periods or will not participate at all. There is one exception to this generalization. Where a manufacturer is located outside of the UK, it may withdraw after an unsuccessful attempt to establish a product or a product line in the UK market. One of the Japanese manufacturers has attempted to establish itself in the UK market from a base in the Republic of Ireland but has so far failed to make an impact. The fact that such a firm may move into and out of a market in a short space of time might in some sense qualify it as a 'dabbler', but it is clear that in all other aspects the firm cannot be seen in this light. The number of firms which are deemed to belong to the commercial vehicle manufacturing community is a matter of both subjective and objective agreement. Not only is definition at this level of aggregation straightforward and beyond dispute, but there also exists a clear view in the minds of all participants about the characteristics of the product in general and about the variety and specifications manufactured by each firm within the industry. The precise nature of the perceptions on these matters is informed and enhanced by the availability of a large number of trade journals, by opportunities for regular contact (about which more below) amongst the representatives of the firms, and of course by the highly accurate data provided by the SMMT.

There is a virtual consensus within the temperature control industry as to who the key players are. There is much less agreement about who can be considered to be taking the minor roles. Thus the industry is perceived to have a solid core but a rather amorphous and vague periphery. This is partly a function of lack of information and partly of competitor categorization. Companies which do not specialize in temperature controllers are regarded by some individuals as, de facto, not of the industry. Others include them simply by virtue of the fact that they manufacture the product in question. Competitors are perceived to fall among a number of categories. The core competitors compete only in this industry and dominate the industry across the board. A small number of niche competitors also specialize in the industry but in only one sector. A group of companies 'dabble' in the industry either because they regard it as only a sector of the process control market on which they concentrate or because they make temperature controllers as ancillary to another, highly specialized, product line. Importers are regarded as a 'race apart' in this low import penetration market.

As one might expect in an emerging industry, there is very little consensus in the case of medical lasers as to who are the major corporate players. Indeed, events are moving so rapidly with regard to the formulation of new companies, the takeover or merger of more established firms in the field and the changing of names of others that managers find it difficult to keep themselves informed about who is in the 'game' or how they are to be labelled. Even bearing this in mind and allowing for some usage of 'dated' nomenclature there is very little agreement on who is in the industry. Distinctions between 'serious' players and 'dabblers' or between 'professional' and 'unprofessional' outfits are made but little agreement is found on how particular companies fit into the different categories. There is, interestingly, more consensus on named individuals and their reputations but because of the dynamic organizational flux surrounding these key actors the competition is not given a coherent corporate identity. Compared to temperature controllers, let alone commercial vehicles, the picture is far from clear. The data seem to accord well with the model. As industries mature their boundaries become clearer to the participants, the roles that individual companies play become differentiated and companies rather than individuals are the focus for competition.

The nature of competition

The most important of the variables in the competitive process in the commercial vehicle industry is perceived to be the technical specification of the product. The manufacturers of commercial vehicles are required by both the demands of their market and legislation to produce products which conform to a number of clearly defined requirements. On the technical side, commercial vehicles within any given weight range must be capable of offering tractive power and carrying capacity, a combination which itself imposes constraints upon the freedom of action of the manufacturer. In addition to this, manufacturers are required to satisfy a number of legal requirements as they relate to weight, speed and so on. Their capacity to compete is therefore heavily constrained by engineering convention and the prevailing legislation. However, within this context, a firm may be able to gain a competitive advantage in several ways. The first is through the medium of materials or combinations of components. In an obvious sense the quality of the materials used or their appropriateness to the tasks to which the vehicles will be put by their operators, will be an instrumental variable in the competitive process, and manufacturers will be anxious to show themselves to be as technically advanced and as sensitive to customer requirements as possible.

The latter objective gives rise also to a second form of competition via specification. The problems of satisfying diverse requirements emanating from a single customer source can be addressed in essentially two ways. The first is through the provision of a product range which enables a customer whose requirements go beyond those which can be readily satisfied by a single variant, to acquire all of his vehicles from a single manufacturer. The virtue of such an arrangement from the customer's point of view lies in the economies of servicing and maintenance and in the leverage which he will subsequently enjoy in dealings with the firm or its dealers. The virtue of the arrangement from the point of view of the firm is that the long-term commitment of the customer is secured.

The second way in which the problem of satisfying diverse consumer requirements can be addressed is by means of a configurable product. In the context of commercial vehicle manufacture configurability may characterize the product at two levels. Commercial vehicle manufacture is increasingly taking the form of assembly of components purchased from other manufacturers, e.g. gearboxes, engines, chassis, etc. One of the advantages which this development offers is that the customer is well placed to specify the particular combination of drivelines etc., which will satisfy his particular requirements. Consequently, a manufacturer's ability to 'configure' at this level must be deemed to be an advantage. The issue to be decided then concerns the manufacturer's choice of sources from which to acquire his components, and this is clearly an element in the competitive process. The second level at which configurability plays a role is that of the performance of the product itself. The capacity of a commercial vehicle to perform a multitude of tasks in a range of operating environments without modification, or with relatively inexpensive modification, is an important concern at the design stage and from the point of view of marketing.

Subject to the product range offered by manufacturers, there are two other principal forms of competition. The first is through price. The opportunities for price shading in this industry are many and varied. The most obvious manifestation arises where fleet purchases are involved, but other less easily identified practices include generous buy-back arrangements, trade-ins and so on. It is to be noted that the importance of price as a competitive variable may be diminished in the long run by the expansion in commercial vehicle leasing, a phenomenon to which we shall not refer here but which must be deemed to be one of the major recent developments in commercial vehicle marketing and distribution.

The second form of competition is one which is now of crucial importance, and is likely to remain so in the future. The manufacturer's capacity, either directly or through its network of distributors, to provide service and back-up to customers is universally regarded as being the key to commercial success. The fact that users of commercial vehicles depend upon them to satisfy their own customers makes reliability an overriding concern in the selection of the product. It is no exaggeration to say that the success of some companies can be attributed almost entirely to their reputation for service, and since technical developments have meant that all commercial vehicles are likely to be similar in all crucial respects, the failure of some firms to retain market share must be attributed to their relatively poor reputation for service or back-up. The natural corollary of this fact is that the size, location, and quality of a manufacturer's distribution network are crucial factors in the determination of its overall success.

Technology can be and is used as an important competitive weapon, e.g. better fuel economy and thus cost reduction is a distinct advantage. The new technology which involves computer aided design and manufacture had permeated the industry. It had resulted in the use of new lightweight, high-strength materials and has led to improved safety features and quieter vehicles. Further improvements are being sought: in gearboxes which are now semi-automated and in fault diagnosis and condition monitoring systems. If vehicles are not to be condemned as 'out of date' such improvements must be researched and implemented. However, most of the technological developments under discussion will take place in the production process rather than in the product itself. They are likely to produce economies of scope rather than economies of scale.

In summary, in the commercial vehicle industry competition occurs on all fronts. While respondents distinguish among attributes of products, differences are deemed to be relatively insignificant.

The nature of the competition in temperature controllers is seen by industry sectors to be at the level of the product, within each distinctive technological category, e.g. microprocessor based single loop controllers or multisegment programme controllers. Competition is seen to be about features offered per pound of instrument. The (somewhat tortured) catchphrase within the industry to describe this process is 'leapfrogging each other in small steps, upwards in the features offered and downwards in price'. Comparison of individual products is difficult, given the fragmentation of demand and the increasing microsegmentation that suppliers are forced to employ in order to retain distinctive advantages in particular segments. Distribution is assuming increasing importance as a differentiating variable – as the cost of sales increase, prices fall, and suppliers look for ways of decreasing transaction costs, e.g. concentrating direct sales calls on major accounts and relegating marginal and idiosyncratic purchases to distributors or agents. Pre- and post-sales services provide a separate area for competition. Executives employed by the market leader claim that these added benefits provide their key competitive edge, but this perception is not shared by competitors. Nevertheless, it is universally agreed that a minimum level of service is required and that the low level of imports is directly attributable to the failure of importing agencies to provide even this much.

The fragmented market and the ability and willingness of competitors to provide almost tailor-made instrumentation results in marketing strategies which can only be described as niche strategies. Competitors believe they have special competences and highly selected target markets and claim not to have any direct competitors in their own areas.

There is considerable agreement about the technological agenda within the temperature control industry. Disagreements occur only in relation to the timing and the ultimate point that it will prove economically worth while to reach. Technological development is incremental and to some extent predictable. Research and development drives the product development process and firms leapfrog one another in the race to provide more features at less cost.

In the longer term the effects of technology have to do with the redefinition of industry boundaries and of primary orientation amongst industry members. Whereas the market leader will probably continue to define its core skills and knowledge as being in the field of temperature control, other firms may look for opportunities to tackle emerging segments and allow themselves to be customer led in the definition of their primary orientation. For example, some might look for systems applications combining sequencing and continuous control in segments they know particularly well, while others might be more tempted to specialize in distributed control systems for biotechnology applications. Another avenue for diversification lies in the direction of tackling particular projects or development jobs that will enhance the firm's skills in the control of other process parameters or the combination of different forms of control within a single 'package'. Thus, technological innovation is likely to take place both within the 'product' and the manufacturing process.

Overall, in the temperature control industry there are perceived to be distinctly different strategies available to competitors (e.g. full market versus niche), different perceptions as to what might be the key elements of a firm's offering (value per feature versus service) and different visions of possible future development paths. In short the market is seen to have a high degree of fine grained structure with different competitors having the capacities to exploit it.

Within medical lasers competition operates on several fronts. It can take the form of competition within the discipline of the hospital specialist or consultant. Companies may seek to position themselves in the market for 'ophthalmic lasers' or 'gynaecological lasers', etc. and see their competition being other devices in this area which carry out a similar function. Thus, for example, lasers engage in competition with ultrasonic devices to dispel kidney stones. The nature of competition here is in consumers' acceptance or rejection not of a particular product or device but of a whole area of laser application. Competition may also take the form of technology differences within lasers themselves. CO_2 (carbon dioxide) lasers and Nd:Yag (Neodymium:Ytrium Argon Garnett) lasers in some areas of application possess similar properties and can therefore be considered as competitive technologies within the area of lasers. Competition exists among products in terms of the functions they perform. Put simply, certain lasers act as high technology knives for precise surgical excision; other lasers act as photocoagulant devices used for suturing wounds and broken blood vessels. Many managers see this division as being of central importance.

Thus, the nature of competition in medical lasers is not so much a matter of agreed principles of price or of product features as of a mélange of cross-cutting assumptions, few of which are shared. Indeed within the same company managers may well differ on the issue of the basis of competition. For some the question is the surgeon's speciality and the need to target gynaecology or ophthalmics, etc. Others will seek to develop the CO_2 laser market across all the specialities at the expense of the Nd:Yag technology. In another manufacturer of the same CO_2 technology, the key competitive concern is to offer photocoagulation facilities as well as those of surgical cutting within the same machine.

There is a marked absence of agreement about what would produce a competitive edge in the medical laser industry. Even the much sought after, but as yet unachieved, development of CO_2 laser delivery through fibre optics is not seen universally as the necessary next step in technical achievement. Some see the effort involved as not being worth while. At this stage there are many distinct sources of separate product and technical developments; there is no notion of 'best practice' in almost any area of production or marketing.

The importance of technological developments in the medical laser field cannot be exaggerated. Companies owe their existence for the most part to technological innovation and many of them see themselves as technical problem solvers rather than as product manufacturers. The absence of a design standard and the proliferation of technologies using differing laser tubes means that a wide variety of technical innovation is both possible and to be expected. Managers in these companies tend to say that the laser technology itself is 'old' (i.e. twenty years) and that the laws of physics preclude 'revolutionary' developments. Yet, incremental development may be of a sharp, significant kind. What is certain is that R&D on these technological problems is of tremendous significance to companies. The medical laser industry is primarily technologically driven, with the key area being problem solving and the development and/or improvement of essentially prototype products.

To summarize, in the earliest phase of industry development, as exemplified by medical lasers, firms can be characterized as being relatively unaware of direct competitors. If anything, they seem to be in competition with the other technologies. There is little consensus about market structures; indeed even the concept of market has relatively little meaning. The object is to overcome technological problems rather than to overwhelm competitors.

In the maturing temperature control industry market, product and competitor structures are often perceived with a surprising degree of unanimity, though with less agreement about what constitutes the key sources of success. Alternative structures are perceived as co-existing, and the view is that there may be a multiplicity of solutions to any given problem.

Commercial vehicle manufacture, representing as it does a mature industry, provides an instance of a more stable and generally accepted set of perceptions. The product offers less scope for substantive differentiation, and the fine distinctions which may be drawn by suppliers may not be held to be important by customers. There is broad agreement about the sources of success and little choice but to compete in terms of all of them.

Each of these descriptions is consistent with a view of the social maturation of an industry taking place in parallel with the evolution of technology and markets.

Formal and informal co-operation and communication

In this section we contrast the type and extent of co-operation among firms within each of our case industries. Because of the relatively small size and close-knit nature of the commercial vehicle industry, many opportunities exist for formal and informal meetings amongst the participants. At the formal level there are the various committees of the Society of Motor Manufacturers and Traders, while at the informal level there are numerous regular commercial vehicle exhibitions as well as opportunities for individuals to meet and to test-drive one another's products.

Information about the activities of individual companies is readily available from high-quality trade journals, distributors, components' suppliers, customers who either purchase from or who have experience of other manufacturers, and from employees who meet regularly or who move from company to company. This last category of employee is a particular feature of the industry, largely because the technical aspect of the product, and a traditional respect for it, encourages people to move from job to job only within the industry. In a small number of cases historical accident has meant that manufacturers are also in close physical proximity to one another, and in this case the natural inclination of individuals of like mind and similar background to be drawn together informally is enhanced. Against this must be set the fact that the universal nature of the product and its market makes geographical proximity a relatively unimportant element in the processes of co-operation and competition.

Although there exist opportunities for meetings amongst the individuals concerned, there is also evidence of more formal co-operation at the level of the firm. Where the product range of an individual company is incomplete, it may in certain circumstances act as agent for a competitor. Typically, the relationship is one in which the first firm agrees to sell, either under the original name or its own marque, certain varieties of its rival's range which do not overlap with its own. The benefits are twofold. The first firm enhances its appeal to its potential customers and consequently to its dealers; the second firm gains access to dealer networks which it might not otherwise enjoy. Co-operation may also take place at the R&D stage where companies may choose to pool resources and develop joint designs for cabs, e.g. the Club of Four in Europe. Co-operation at the R&D stage is also possible between manufacturer and component supplier.

There are three main channels of information and interaction among competitors in the temperature control field. The first comes from their interaction with customers in the field and, in particular, with end users. The second occurs because of job rotation in the industry while the third results from the direct interaction amongst individuals at industry exhibitions, Institute of Measurement and Control dinners and occasional social meetings. Published sources are regarded as unreliable and uninformed.

Interaction with customers is a primary source of information about competitors' activities, as customers use contacts with rival suppliers both to trade information and to check the power of currently favoured suppliers. This may be seen as a way of counteracting the supplier's dominance in the relationship, as far as technical knowledge is concerned. Very few customers have specialized personnel who can specify the nature of a problem, let alone discuss problem-solving strategies with suppliers.

Control problems, especially at the end-user level can seldom be defined in terms of temperature control. They usually include other parameters as well as measuring, transmitting, recording and data logging. Each supplier has developed a capability for panel building which often involves purchases of instrumentation from rival suppliers, usually at the customer's request.

The extent of social interaction is reinforced by both the history and geography of the industry. Most of the firms currently operating in temperature control are first-, second-, or even third-generation spin-offs from the original pair of companies upon which the industry was founded. These spin-offs are clustered geographically around the original sites and now comprise two distinct areas – the south coast around Brighton and an arc from North London to Cambridge. Such geographical proximity allows individuals to change firms easily and means that chance social meetings are far more likely.

The social network that results is heterogeneous in nature. There are local clusters of strong relationships embedded in a broader network of weak relationships. Communications are, in general, informal, unplanned and conform to unwritten rules. Certain items of information may be exchanged (e.g. third-party activities) while others may not (product development plans).

A few co-operative activities exist but these are centred largely around the Institute of Measurement and Control.

Distributors and systems houses – themselves actively involved in panel building and small project work – also play a key role as information brokers by maintaining bridges to several rival suppliers at the same time.

Job rotation within the industry is another source of socialization of individuals to the industry 'recipe' (Grinyer and Spender 1979) – i.e. shared perceptions of the ground rules according to which each player competes. It provides information, stories and legends about the mode of operation of each firm or of key individuals, which may persist long after the information is hopelessly outdated. 'Incestuous' is the commonly accepted metaphor for this process.

As indicated earlier, within the field of medical lasers two companies have been developed and spun off from, and a third one is closely associated with, a single university department of physics. From this shared institutional origin and historical consanguinity must come the basis for much formal and informal co-operation. Yet, of course, the existence of this plurality of companies might also suggest that conflicts of interest, opinion and product will be very likely. Nevertheless, the area of medical lasers is characterized by a small network of highly involved participants, whether they be medical consultants, university researchers, applied physicists, or medical sales people. They meet at a small number of conventions each year but correspond, interact and do business with each other on a regular basis. There is much talk of growth in the industry and so spin-offs and more particularly spin-outs are common. Key figures are well known even if their institutional bases are not and there is considerable movement of personnel. Links within the 'industry' between companies and hospital consultants are deliberately close, since the 'only' way to develop customer acceptance of a technology or a product is perceived to be through extensive trials in a surgical situation. In order to gain certification from the FDA (Federal Drugs Administration in the USA) clinical trials are essential. Consultants for their part gain access to 'free' machines and much advice for use in their surgical procedures and in experimental situations.

Thus it is relatively easy at this early stage in the development of medical lasers to trace out the careers and enterprise locations of the original prototype champions. As the technology develops, as products become more sophisticated and as old companies exit from the field it will become more difficult to identify formal and informal co-operation. At the moment, the latter is a key feature of the medical laser industry.

In the areas of co-operation and communication the fit of the model to the case study data is perhaps clearest. The community stage is well represented by the medical laser industry. Communication patterns are people- rather than organization-based. Co-operation occurs informally and across organizational lines and loyalty to the technology is as important as loyalty to the organization. Non-commercial organizations figure prominently. The informal network, identified with the temperature control industry, has more established patterns of communication. The geographical proximity of many of the competitors may, accidentally, have reinforced the strength of the network. The network is largely based on informal communication, and is by no means uniform in character. Mobile employees provide the network nodes and the content of communication is highly prescribed. Formal co-operation is limited.

By contrast, the formal network, as represented by the commercial vehicle industry, contains many examples of formal co-operation short of the mergers and acquisitions which are also common in the industry. Both formal and informal communication occurs, the channels for the former being clear, well understood and efficient. Common experiences and outside threats are just two of the forces driving competitors to manage, in a formal way, the industry of which they are members.

Summary of characteristics of the case industries

Table 7.1 summarizes some of the key characteristics of the industries under study, with emphasis on the contrasting elements. These characteristics are a mixture of the economic, the technological and the social. The interdependence of these characteristics is a phenomenon which needs to be emphasized once more. The development of the social aspects of an industry over time parallels

Table 7.1 Summary of industry characteristics

	Medical lasers	Temp. control	Comm. vehicles
Import penetration	Unstable	Stable, lowish	Increasing, high
Company description	Small (1–10)	Small – medium	Large
Perceptions of 'industry' boundaries	Not shared	Shared by those with 'primary orientation'	Shared
Perceptions of corporate membership	No shared views of companies, but of individuals	Shared view of core, but not periphery	Shared
Perceptions of market	Unclear	Segmented, fragmented, unstable but cushioned	Precise, segmented
Competitive process	By function, technology or discipline area, disparate	Price per product feature, service, niche strategies; separate	Price (given similar product features); service, head on
Product definition	Unclear	Wide variety of alternatives	Clearly by weight
Manufacturing	R&D prototypes	Some customer specification, small batch production	High standardization, large batch production
Type and level of uncertainty	Lack of experience and commercial knowledge	Low uncertainty, incremental exchange	Uncertainty due to global events
Perceived good management practice	Absence of sharp practice, nice stands, glossy brochure	Good service, high product reliability, long-term commitment	Close links with distributors and good pre- and post-sales service
Management problems	Everything – expertise is purely technical	Integration of heterogeneity caused by organizational looseness and product flexibility	Cost reduction, responses to competitors' initiatives
Technology	Emphasis on product innovation	Mixture of product and process innovation	Emphasis on process innovation
Patterns of communication/ co-operation	Informal, people based, includes research industries	Informal, heterogeneous communication patterns. Little formal co-operation	Formal communication networks. Many forms of co-operation

and interacts with those of an economic and technological nature. We are aware that the social model on its own provides an inadequate explanation of these interactions. Nevertheless the industries chosen to represent the community, informal and formal network stages of development appear to conform in crucial respects to those prescribed by the model. Those elements which remain unexplained will require further study, and the application of analytical techniques at both the empirical and theoretical levels.

Policy implications

Britain's future competitiveness depends on the creation and maintenance of a variety of industries to provide wealth, employment and taxable revenues. Such industries, located in the formal network stage, inevitably face the highest levels of international competition. Within the context of global economic recession, governments have sought to confront such pressures through a shift of structural emphasis from the older 'sunset' manufacturing bases now in decline to the so-called 'sunrise' new technology industries which, it is hoped, are the key to future long-term economic growth and prosperity. The social model outlined in this chapter, however, suggests that such analyses mis-specify the key elements in the process of industrial development. Confusion has arisen about the definition and nature of emerging industries. The so-called 'new' technologies, particularly in the information technology sector, tend to be automatically equated with embryonic industries. Not only does this fail to acknowledge the ever-increasing pace of technological development and maturation in general, but it also reflects the failure of a purely technological measure accurately to portray the extent of an industry's maturity. A closer examination of the nature of the social relationships involved in that industry provides a more useful insight. For example, far from being typical of the community, or even informal network, stage of development where the boundaries are less clearly defined and the social relationships more fluid, many of the 'sunrise' industries involved in the information technology sector and the British government's Alvey programme reflect those social structures and defensive postures so characteristic of the club phase. Similarly, regions characterized by a predominance of 'sunset' industries may in fact be fostering those very conditions in which truly embryonic industries seed and grow. In Scotland's 'Silicon Glen', for instance, there are signs that the region's current development and growth derives from the emergence of a community type of infrastructure reflected in the frequent and close links among individuals involved in the local universities, financial community and the Scottish Development Agency.

The social model suggests that these and many of the other assumptions implicit in government policy and academic arguments might need to be reassessed. For example, not only are the notions of industrial 'immaturity' and 'embryonic' industries sometimes misconstrued, but the context of industrial regeneration and reindustrialization is also confused. The possibilities suggested by much of the literature on new technology based firms, for example, depict industries with social relationships of a much more formalized and established nature than those characteristic of an emerging industry. Examples of the latter form of reindustrialization do exist but are few in number and qualitatively different in terms of their organizational structure, role and inter-organizational relationships from the larger (i.e. 15 people or more) high technology SMEs or 'NTBFs' (Rothwell and Zegveld 1985) which are to be found in industrial regeneration (Shearman and Burrell 1988).

As far as government policy is concerned, all four types of industrial structure need to be encouraged within a framework of national and regional industrial strategy, though changing political objectives may shift the balance among them. The emphasis lies not so much on 'industrial policy' as on 'policies for industry'. The potential of communities is great but they are inevitably difficult to develop. Governments might foster appropriate infrastructures but the employment generation will be low. Industries at the informal network stage tend to be more sustainable. Governmental or regional 'policies for industry' here might focus on promoting the crucially important transition from community to informal network of its domestic industries, while seeking to buy in the expertise of community-type industries globally. The formal network stage holds out the best prospects for employment. An industry's experience of this phase may be prolonged through industrial regeneration or 'reinvigoration' (Shearman and Burrell 1987). While the creation of clubs is essentially a defensive measure which implies that it may be too late effectively to promote the industry in the longer-term global competitive context, it nevertheless provides short-term employment and wealth and may under certain circumstances prove conducive to the growth of a new range of industries. As indicated earlier, the social model of industrial development is designed primarily for analysis at the meso rather than the macro or micro level. Little has been said about internal firm characteristics or of how the management of particular enterprises may resist, modify or distort the underlying dynamics of the industries to which they belong. It is, however, assumed that firms are not so malleable in their strategies and structures as to be able to circumvent the processes of industrial development entirely. What the model does provide is a framework or context for understanding managerial perceptions and informing policy. For it is not until a greater understanding is gained of the way in which managerial perceptions and industry behaviour are formulated and communicated that policies at the

European, national and regional levels can be more effectively tailored and implemented. A simple example might be R&D subsidies. As the model suggests and the experience of the case industries verifies, the mechanisms whereby such a subsidy might be effected are inherently different in the case of all four structures. The type of subsidy required and the capacity to deal with it in the case of the medical laser industry bears little resemblance to that found in the larger, more mature structures common to commercial vehicles. A failure to understand the dynamics and processes operating at the industry level therefore means that government interventions will continue to be somewhat crude and ineffective. The social model demonstrates that the key to this understanding lies in the fact that industries are socially organized and involve significant degrees of co-operation as well as competition, the nature and balance of which evolve and change as the industry matures.

References

Astley, W. Graham (1985a) 'The two ecologies: population and community perspectives on organisational evolution', *Administrative Science Quarterly* vol. 30.

Astley, W. Graham (1985b) 'Organisation size and bureaucratic structure', *Organization Studies* vol. 16, no. 3.

Bhaskar, K. (1979) *The Future of the UK Motor Industry*, London: Kogan Page.

Boswell, J. C. (1973) *The Rise and Decline of the Small Firm*, London: Allen & Unwin.

Burns, T. (1981) 'A comparative study of administrative structure and organisational processes in selected areas of the NHS', SSRC Report HRP 6725.

Burns, T. and Stalker, G. M. (1961) *The Management of Innovation* London: Tavistock.

Clark, J., Freeman, C. and Soete, L. (1981) 'Long waves, inventions and innovations', *Futures* 13.

Di Maggio, P. J. and Powell, W. W. (1983) 'The iron cage revisited: institutional isomorphism and collective rationality in organisational fields', *American Sociological Review* 48.

ERF (1984) Company Report.

Grinyer, P. H. and Spender, J. C. (1979) 'Recipes, crises and adaptations in mature businesses', *International Studies of Management and Organisation* vol. IX, no. 3.

Hage, J. (1965) 'An axiomatic theory of organisations', *Administrative Science Quarterly* 10.

Hammarkvist, K. O. (1983) 'Markets as networks', Marketing Education Group Conference Proceedings, Cranfield.

Harrigan, K. R. (1983) *Strategies for Vertical Integration*, Lexington, Mass: Lexington Books.

Huff, A. S. (1982) Industry influences on strategy reformulation', *Strategic Management Journal* 3.

Ingham, G. K. (1974) *Strikes and Industrial Conflict: Britain and Scandinavia*, London: Macmillan.

Mattson, L. G. (1984) 'An application of a network approach to marketing: defending and changng market position' in N. Dholakia and J. Arndt (eds) *Alternative Paradigms for Widening Market Theory*, Greenwich, CT: JAI Press.

Mensch, G. (1979) *Stalemate in Technology*, Cambridge, Mass: Ballinger.

Mintzberg, H. and Waters, J. A. (1985) 'Of strategies, deliberate and emergent', *Strategic Management Journal* 6.

Oakey, R. (1984) *High Technology Small Firms: Innovation and Regional Development in Britain and the United States*, London: Frances Pinter.

Rhys, G. (1986) 'Economics of the motor industry', *The Economic Review*, January.

Richardson, P. R. (1985) 'Managing R&D for results', *Journal of Product Innovation Management* 2.

Roberts, E. B. (1977) 'Generating effective corporate innovation', *Technology Review* vol. 80, no. 10

Robson, M. and Rothwell, R. (1985) 'What is the role of the small firm in innovation in the late 1980's?', paper presented to the 15th European Small Business Seminar, New Technological Developments: A challenge for small enterprises, Chester, October.

Rogers, E. M. and Kincaid, D. L. (1981) *Communication Network Analysis*, New York: Free Press.

Rothwell, R. and Zegveld, W. (1981), *Industrial Innovation and Public Policy: Preparing for the 1980's and the 1990's*, London: Frances Pinter.

Rothwell, R. and Zegveld, W. (1982) *Innovation and Small and Medium-sized Firms*, London: Frances Pinter.

Rothwell, R. and Zegveld, W. (1985) *Reindustrialisation and Technology*, London: Longman.

Senker, P. (1979) *Skilled Manpower in Small Engineering Firms: a Study of UK Precision Press Tool Manufacturers*, Brighton: Sussex University, Science Policy Research Unit.

Shapero, A. (1980) 'The entrepreneur, the small firm and possible policies', paper presented at six-counties programme workshop in entrepreneurship, Limerick, Ireland.

Shearman, C. and Burrell, G. (1987) 'The social structures of industrial development', *Journal of Management Studies*, July.

Shearman, C. and Burrell, G. (1988) 'Changes to new technology based firms and new industries: employment implications', *New Technology, Work and Employment* vol. 3, no.2: 87–99.

Tonnies, F. (1963) *Community and Society*, Translated and edited by C. P. Loomis, New York: Harper & Row.

Von Hippel, E. (1977) 'Successful and failed co-operative ventures: an empirical analysis', *Industrial Marketing Management* 6.

Waterson, M. (1984) *Economic Theory of Industry*, Cambridge: Cambridge University Press.

Chapter eight

Competition and the momentum of technical change

Tim Ray, Janet Evans, Mark Boden, J. Stanley Metcalfe, Michael Gibbons

Introduction

This chapter aims to promote technology as the central pier in a bridge between dynamic aspects of competitive behaviour exhibited by innovating firms, and wider patterns of economic change which arise as new, up-and-coming technologies displace less advantageous ways of doing things. We begin with an outline of our conceptual framework. This represents an attempt to capture the essence of the dynamic processes by which individual firms orchestrate programmes of competitive innovation amidst turbulent technological and market environments. Case studies are then presented which reflect selected aspects of our empirical investigation of competitive innovation in the manufacture of carbonless copy paper, home computers and optical fibre communications systems.

Competition, firm and environment

Some introductory remarks about the nature of competitive innovation will help to establish the context of our discussion. Few would dissent from the proposition that organizational and technological innovation has been the mainspring of economic growth in the advanced industrial world. Without continuous technological transformations and their correlated organizational developments, we simply would not have experienced the continued increases in per capita GDP which distinguish the modern age. In turn, these transformations are intimately linked to the process of competition and the market mechanisms which function to generate new technological knowledge and apply it to the production system in a continual stream of product and process innovations.

Competition has a number of interpretations within the literature. In broad terms one has a dichotomy between competition as an efficient state of resource allocation and competition as a process generating economic change. In this study our concern is with the latter, to understand how organizations (firms) develop technology to improve their long-term competition position, and to understand the mechanisms which translate technological change into economic progress. Of course, one is also concerned with national economic performance, and what is important here is that domestic firms gain a share of the world income streams associated with the development and exploitation of new technologies. Whether these shares are gained through domestic production and exports or through direct foreign investment, including collaboration ventures, or through technology licensing does not in the first instance matter. This is not, of course to argue that, from a national viewpoint, one can be indifferent to which of these routes are followed, but simply to assert the primacy of the issue of how a capacity to articulate a technology is developed. In each of our case studies we find a rich structure of trade, investment and licensing arrangements: ranging from the simple collaboration in the exploitation of a foreign licence in the carbonless copy industry, to the complex networks of foreign investment and licensing which are found in automotive batteries and the cardio-vascular drugs industry.

To understand the links between competition and progress it is necessary to comprehend the working of two complex mechanisms, viz. those which generate technological variety, and those which select between different varieties to determine how their economic importance changes over time. Without variety, and this choice of alternatives, there can be no competition, without selection there can be no economic progress. Difference is the basis of rivalry, and the best available technology is of no economic significance unless it can come to displace inferior technological forms. Of course, many differences between firms impinge upon this competitive process but none of them can override the dominant long-run importance of differences in product quality and process efficiency. Such differences are the basis from which investment and market-ing strategy can be deployed to gain permanent competitive advantage. In this study we find it useful to analyse technology along two separate dimensions, those of revealed performance – defined in terms of performance characteristics embodied in products and processes – and of the knowledge bases which are necessary to stimulate performance in a given context. By identify-ing a knowledge base with a technological regime we can then classify different product and process designs in terms of particular configurations of the knowledge base. Technological competition

166

is then of two kinds, competition between regimes (e.g. between carbon paper technology and carbonless copy paper technology, or between optical fibre or copper coaxial cable technologies in telecommunications) and competition within regimes, but between different design configurations (e.g. multi-mode and single-mode optical fibre cables). In short, we are interested in competition between technologies simply because it is the development of technological variety and its subsequent integration into the economy which determines the rate of increase of resource productivity in its broadest sense, taking account of improvements in product quality as well as in input productivity.

However, technological competition does not occur of itself. Rather it is contingent upon the particular institutional forms of market capitalism, in which organizations compete by acquiring knowledge bases and transforming this knowledge into improved products and processes of production. Thus attention has to be focused upon firms and their strategic actions to engage in rivalrous competition. Our investigations of technological competition are thus premised upon a number of propositions, the principal ones being as follows:

1. The modern firm is a complex organization often, if not typically, producing a wide range of products, using processes from different design configurations. Hence it is vital to identify the operating sub-units which are articulating the technology under investigation. Rarely are these coterminous with the firm whose boundaries are conventionally defined in terms of control over units of capital. A primary research task is always to identify the relevant organization sub-units responsible for competing via a particular technology.

2. Traditionally, organizational theorists have found it useful to define the firm in terms of an implicit boundary between the firm and its environment. From the viewpoint of technological competition two aspects of the environment are crucial: the market environment assessed in terms of the rate of growth of demand for the valuations placed on performance characteristics, and the degree of segmentation into specific sub-markets; and the technological environment, assessed in terms of its richness for generating competing varieties, its dependence upon scientific as distinct from experimental knowledge, its division between codifiable and tacit forms of knowledge, and the costs of advancing technology. In all of our case studies these environments have changed significantly as technology is developed and diffused, so changing the focus of competitive advantage and requiring corresponding changes in strategic response if competitive positions are to be maintained.

3. The appropriate measure of the economic significance of any given product or process is its market share, appropriately defined, and the competitive mechanism is working properly if it results in an increasing market share being commanded by superior technological forms. Notice that market share of a particular technology is not the same statistic as the market share of any given firm although the two are obviously, if sometimes loosely, related. Notice also, that market share is only one of many performance indicators of a given firm. Moreover, it is the strategic, competitive actions of firms which determine how the market shares of competing technologies evolve over time. Within our framework changes in market share of a particular technology are related to three dimensions of firm performance: the efficiency with which the firm translates its knowledge base into revealed performance; the effectiveness with which it allocates profits to expanding the output of its existing products and processes through investment and marketing expenditures; and, fundamentally, its creativity in changing revealed performance in a competitive way through R&D, learning activity, or other mechanisms such as a joint R&D venture. For our purpose it is the long-run creativity of firms which determines the long-run significance of different configurations and regimes, whether those firms survive, and if so what market share they command for their products and related processes.

Summarizing a complex argument, we argue that the market environment evaluates current efficiency to determine current profitability, which in turn provides the resources for growth and creativity. It is easily shown, for example, that a firm can only increase the long-run market share of its technology if that technology is consistently of above average practice in terms of its performance characteristics.

4. Finally, we stress the vital role of creativity, as the element which generates variety through innovations in revealed performance. At root it is inter-firm differences in creativity which drive the competition process and continually enhance resource productivity. Within our framework creativity is linked directly to the acquisition of a knowledge base. Once acquired such a base can create not only opportunities and an agenda for change but substantial barriers should the organization seek to alter its design configuration, or more radically its technological regimes. A conventional way of performing is acquired, with built-in conceptual and strategic inertia should the operating sub-unit seek to change direction.

With this as background, we can now develop the perspective on technological change which shapes our view of competition.

The technological dimension

The central theme of our argument is that technology is a system-on-the-move. This system centres on a dynamic interrelationship between the evolution of new technologies and parallel changes in what the users of particular technologies require. Thus static equilibrium models of competition, which centre on passive responses to changes in price, are rendered inappropriate to the disequilibrium that follows from successful innovation.[1] This disequilibrium centres on differences that arise between competing firms who are in the process of striving to translate technological advances into an improved share of the market. These competitive advantages are, however, usually of a transitory nature because, over time, competitors will respond with further technological advances which are designed to ensure that they recapture an acceptable market share. Moreover, the competitive responses of rival firms are not usually slavish copies of the original technological advance, but an intelligent attempt to better what went before, and so leap ahead of the original innovator by meeting prevailing user requirements more effectively. Thus, as will be explained later, competitive innovation is like a race between unequals, in which competing firms vie with each other to push technology towards the evolving requirements of its users and potential users.

With the increasing levels of complexity that have accompanied the development of industrial technology, it has become more apparent that fully-developed innovations are not realized in an instant by a given individual or organization. That is to say, complex innovations are not normally somewhat momentous, discrete events but rather the products of gradual evolution. They represent a cumulative synthesis of what went before, as technology builds on technology: albeit with an occasional input from some externally generated source of knowledge such as university science.

A sequence of related innovations will normally occur as the result of a sustained attempt to improve a particular way of doing things. These improvements push forward the prevailing levels of best practice technology in that particular regime of technological development.[2] Thus, new regimes of technological development, like a poor hand in poker, normally offer scope for improvement. In the first instance, these improvements are likely to be concerned with nursing the technology through its infant stages of development and towards commercial viability. Further improvements might then be a prominent feature of the diffusion of the technology into economic activity.[3] In this context, the initial nurturing of an infant technology and its subsequent commercial development, may be seen as a process which has momentum. With this observation in mind, the present chapter sets out to relate the momentum of technological change to the anatomy of innovative activity undertaken by individual firms.

Technological change and the arena of competition

The evolution of new technological regimes can provide new ways of doing things that undermine markets for more traditional technologies. In consequence, the innovating firm not only has to reckon with firms that operate within the same regime but it also has to take account of firms that produce products that compete for that regime (in the way, for example, that coach services compete with rail transport). It is therefore important to have a dynamic conception of what defines the innovating firm's competitive environment. To this purpose, we take the view that user requirements define the arena for competition in which rival products and technologies vie with each other to provide features which users perceive to be desirable.

The competitive arena is defined by user requirements for, what we have elected to call, product performance characteristics. This concept of performance characteristics is related to the idea that users do not usually want a piece of technology for its intrinsic qualities but rather they require a product that exhibits a number of desirable properties, or performance characteristics. These performance characteristics may be supplied by a number of different design configurations, which may well draw on widely different technologies. For example, as one of our case studies shows, the performance characteristics associated with telecommunications transmission systems could be provided by electrical signals in copper wires or by light waves in optical fibres. That is to say, both technologies exist in the same arena of competition (i.e. both technologies meet similar sets of user requirements). It therefore follows that there is a clear distinction between performance characteristics (which meet a user demand), and technological parameters which simply describe the technology that is used to provide the characteristics.

As user requirements change, so the dimensions of the competitive arena will change. Over time, these dimensions will map out a 'corridor' of user requirements. The lower limits of the users' corridor represent the point where product performance characteristics fall short of user requirements (for example, the pen that does not write), while the upper limit of the corridor is represented by performance characteristics which are superfluous to user requirements.[4] Thus, a practical objective for firms is to maintain a trajectory of product development which stays within the users' corridor of requirements.

A user will normally be prepared to pay a given price for an overall package of characteristics. In theory, if not in practice, it is possible to break down a product's price into the price paid for each constituent characteristic. Thus the concept of a 'price per unit characteristic' could be used to rank the constituent characteristics of a product in a league table of desirability. At the top of the league are strong characteristics which represent major selling points, while at the bottom of the league are weak properties which either cost a huge amount to produce or, are the unwanted consequence of an overall technological package (such as the side effects of some drugs).[5]

The idea of a league table of characteristics, associated with a given product, might be useful when it comes to producing rules of thumb for practising managers. For example, if managers are able to form a conception of the relative ranking of characteristics associated with their products, they can give some emphasis to promoting strong characteristics and minimizing or removing weak characteristics.

The competitive arena and its role in an evolutionary framework for assessing technological change

The central theme of an evolutionary perspective on technological change is the set of processes by which different forms of technology are generated, and then acquire weight within the economic system. In this context the competitive arena may be seen as the forum within which the economic selection mechanism operates.

Economic growth, brought about by technological change, is not a balanced process. The rise of new technologies, at the expense of more established ways of doing things, will create disequilibrium and imbalance as the structure of the economy changes to accommodate these new technologies. Thus technological change reflects Schumpeter's famous concept of 'creative destruction', which related to dynamic patterns of industrial development:

> industrial change is never harmonious advance with all elements of the system moving or tending to move in step. At any given time, some industries move on and others stay behind; and the discrepancies arising from this are an essential element in the situations that develop.[6]

171

The restructuring of the economy around up-and-coming industries and technologies bears some similarity with biological evolution. In the same way that new species, that better fit the biological environment, will flourish at the expense of less well adapted species, so new technologies that meet prevailing user requirements effectively will flourish at the expense of what users perceive to be less satisfactory technologies, although it should be stressed that, while the biological analogy is a useful heuristic device for illustrating patterns of technological change, it does not have any power to explain the processes involved.

A new technology will define a long period niche in the economic system which is related to the degree to which it is better than other technologies. The corollary to this is that user requirements and constant patterns of demand for different products and services comprise the mechanism for determining the extent to which one product is better than another. However, it should be stressed that user requirements are not fixed but instead change over time. It seems to us that five dimensions of change are particularly important.[7]

1. *A 'push me pull you' relationship with the technology in question*. Unlike random mutations in biology, suppliers of a technology interact with users and are able to orient their technological development effort towards enhancing and creating product performance characteristics which they anticipate will be in tune with evolving user requirements. Rival suppliers will continually bid up the currency of best practice technology to enhance their competitive position and, in the process, raise user expectations.

2. *Advances in competing technologies*. Competing technologies can provide new or enhanced performance characteristics which have the effect of raising user expectations.

3. *Changes in complementary technologies*. Technologies do not normally exist in isolation but instead form part of a network of interdependent relationships with other technologies. In consequence, advances in one technology might cause an imbalance between the performance characteristics of that technology, and the performance of interdependent technologies, thereby redefining the pattern of user requirements associated with the related technologies.

4. *Changes in the legislative or regulatory environment*. New laws, rules or standards may have a profound effect on users' relative preference for different product performance characteristics.

5. *Changes in relative prices*. Exogenous changes in relative prices (i.e. exogenous to the technology in question) may redefine

user requirements by altering the price paid for various product performance characteristics.

The long period niche for a technology could be filled by one firm's development of an innovation or technology but it is more often the case that a number of firms develop a technology. This may arise from simultaneous invention by firms with similar backgrounds and commercial postures.[8]

Alternatively, firms might be attracted towards the technology because they perceive that its development by a rival firm could give that firm an unacceptable competitive advantage.

Once firms have entered the long period niche they are likely to push forward best practice technology through a process of Schumpeterian[9] competition. This type of competition may be represented by the metaphor of a race, in which firms vie with each other to develop the technology embodied in products and/or production processes. The winning posts in this race are determined by the point at which it is no longer profitable to engage in further technological development. As this point is approached, the scope for commercially viable improvements to the technology will diminish and the pace of technological change will tend to slacken off as the technology becomes mature. With the onset of maturity, leading firms in the development of the technology will have 'run out of road' and, in consequence, less advanced firms (followers) may be able to catch up with the best practice design configurations pioneered by the leaders. Thus, technological maturity is often accompanied by the emergence of a dominant design configuration, although, as a caveat, it should be stressed that maturity is not fixed and can shift as a result of changes in user requirements, arising from competing technologies, complementary technologies, legislation or changes in relative prices. That is to say, the dimensions of the long period niche can be redefined in such a way that the scope for technological development is either lengthened or shortened.

The anatomy of innovative activity

In order to assess the dynamics of the processes that are associated with inducement, advance and diffusion in the race to technological maturity, it is necessary to look inside the 'black box' and consider the internal operation of the firm. In this context, we have found it instructive to focus our analysis on the technological knowledge base of the firm. It is co-ordinated by the firm's organizational structure, which shapes information flows and delineates particular areas of responsibility for organizational processes.

173

If technology is treated as a knowledge system, rather than simply as a collection of artefacts, then it is possible to view the firm as the custodian of a bundle of technological knowledge. This knowledge can then be marshalled to meet the changing sets of constraints and opportunities that are generated by a changing operating environment. It is the repeated application of an evolving knowledge base to a particular problem that produces a trajectory of related innovations, as firms seek to improve a product and/or production process.

Knowledge does not come out of thin air, but rather it has to be acquired and assimilated by the firm. In consequence innovation may be seen as a learning process in which the firm comes to terms with uncertainty. This learning may centre on internal activities such as R&D or on the acquisition of externally generated knowledge through imitation of rival products, purchase of know-how through technology licence agreements, research agencies, joint ventures, mergers, take-overs, scientific discoveries, and so on. It would therefore appear that key themes in understanding differences between competing firms arise from questions relating to: the ways in which firms acquire technological knowledge; the efficiency with which firms acquire technological knowledge; the efficiency with which they put that knowledge into practice; and the extent to which that practical application of knowledge is appropriate to evolving user requirements.

From our empirical work it has become clear that it is not possible to identify the knowledge base of individual firms in any precise way. Difficulties arise because the relevant knowledge is embodied in the minds of the employees of the firms in question, and each firm is fragmented according to the dictates of the internal division of labour. In consequence the knowledge base of a firm is not a homogeneous commodity but rather a complex amalgamation of sub-knowledge bases, each of which is associated with various constituent elements of overall innovative activity. Nevertheless, if these caveats are borne in mind, we believe that the concept of an accumulated technological knowledge base at firm level provides a valuable insight into the complexity of innovative activity.

In the case studies which follow, we attempt to illustrate the basis of our ideas about the users' corridor of requirements and the dimensions of the long-period niche, in three contrasting technologies: carbonless copy paper, home computers and optical fibre communications systems. These studies represent a first cut at charting the processes of competitive innovation and, for the most part, focus on the dynamics of inter-firm competition.

On the basis of information which we are currently acquiring from our programmes of industrial visits, it would appear that our concept of an intra-firm knowledge base is entirely compatible with our inter-firm perspective on competition. It is this intra-firm activity that assimilates, generates and articulates technological knowledge, which enables the firm to produce technological hardware in the form of products and production processes. The flow of knowledge between firms may then be seen as crucial to the dynamic diffusion process by which the long period niche for a technology is filled.

Patterns of technological competition

In the following section we will illustrate some of the above principles by drawing selectively on our case study work. We will use the development of carbonless copy paper and home computers to illustrate technological variety and the establishment of trajectories of technological improvement. These same concepts are illustrated in the study of optical fibre communications systems, which also demonstrates how the factors which shape the market environment may be applied in a particular example of technological development.

The case studies provide the opportunity to identify both common and different features of competitive activity in industrial sectors characterized by significant technical change.

Carbonless copy paper

Introduction

When a new technology is first introduced it is embodied in an innovative set of design configurations which present a rich agenda for post-innovation improvements. These improvements, while applicable and directed at both product and process performance, are of two main kinds. The first are those that are developed within the original set of design configurations and the second those that arise from attempts to produce improved performance characteristics from a different set of design configurations. This case study illustrates both kinds but its main feature is the dominance of the original set of design configurations and the effect this had on the competitive environment.

175

Original innovation

Carbonless copy paper was first introduced in 1954 after approximately fifteen years of research by National Cash Register (NCR) of Dayton Ohio in the USA. NCR was not a paper manufacturer but a business machinery company and the research was initiated in its own R&D department, as a result of pressure from business forms producers for a replacement for one-time carbon paper and re-usable carbon paper. (One-time carbon paper (OTC) has a thinner layer of carbon than re-usable carbon paper and it is all transferred during copying from the very light-weight base paper on which it has been deposited.) Many attempts had been made to produce such a pressure sensitive paper but with little success. Two basic innovations were necessary. One was that of micro-encapsulation, the second, the production of a colourless dye or former which on interaction with other chemicals resulted in a coloured material. The first carbonless papers appeared in the USA in 1954 and shortly after this Wiggins Teape, the leading fine paper company in the UK, signed a licence agreement with NCR for exclusive production and sales rights in Europe. It was only after the expiration of the key NCR patents in 1970 that a significant number of new producers entered the market. The microcapsule system accounts for more than 95 per cent of the world's need in chemical carbonless copy paper.

Carbonless copy paper was developed to be used for multipart business forms as a replacement for bond paper interleaved with one-time carbon (OTC). To become acceptable and offer an alternative to one-time carbon, carbonless copy paper systems had to exhibit certain performance characteristics. These included the production of a clear legible copy durable over many years and able to be handled without excessive smudging or degradation. Copies had to be suitable for photocopying and microfilming, provide some element of security against forgery, and be hygienic and environmentally acceptable. A subsequent requirement of machine readability was very much more difficult to achieve. Furthermore, the paper had to be acceptable to the printers of business forms in terms of its performance through the printing presses.

Technology of carbonless copy paper

The two main systems of the design configuration of carbonless copy paper are the two layers of materials that are coated on the back (CB) and on the front (CF) of the sheets of paper in a multipart set. Each has seen improvements over time.

CB coating: the CB coating is an emulsion containing the microcapsules and binders and spacers. These latter two materials are essential for efficient coating and give some protection to the microcapsules themselves during the coating process. The microcapsules, typically only microns in diameter, contain colourless dyes called formers, and a complex mixture of solvents. The manufacturing process, complex coacervation, as well as the materials used were the key elements of the technological innovation and were heavily and effectively protected by patents, as were many of the post-innovation improvements.

CF coating: the CF coating, the coreactant, contains the colour developer which reacts with the colourless dyes (formers) in the microcapsules when these are ruptured.

The quality of the copy depends on many factors including the colour formers and coreactants, the size and uniformity of the microcapsules, and the thickness and uniformity of the coatings.

Technical improvements and the variety of end products were achieved by different choices of chemicals employed in the sub-systems and in the production processes. Since the original processes and materials were heavily protected by patents much of this variety arose from the necessity to avoid patent infringement while wishing to exploit new market opportunities.

Pattern of post-innovation improvement

It is convenient to divide the technological development into a number of separate phases.

1950–60

In this first phase the technology was developed entirely by NCR. The first chemical carbonless copy paper NCR put on the market in 1954 produced royal blue copy, the colour formers being crystal violet lactone CVL (patented by NCR in the 1940s) and benzoyl leuco methylene blue, BLMB. The microcapsules were made of gelatine, the dye solvent was a polychlorinated biphenol and the coreactant was attapulgous clay. CVL reacted very quickly giving a billiant blue which after a few hours of exposure to daylight turned greenish. BLMB, however, reacted more slowly but is lightfast. Therefore original mixtures were mainly 50–66 parts of CVL and 3–50 parts of BLMB. Within this design configuration the agenda for improvement was considerable, particularly for product innovations which improved copy quality.

Gelatine capsules varied in size, permeability, grade and content. The original attapulgous clay was abrasive, contained impurities and reacted in different ways depending on the binders used in the paper manufacture. The base paper which NCR acquired from a number of different sources varied in its properties producing problems in consistency, and new coating techniques for pressure sensitive coatings had to be developed. NCR was very active in developing and patenting the technologies of microencapsulation, dyestuffs and coreactants but left the coating improvements to its subcontractors who purchased the coatings, in slurry form, coated the paper and sold the finished NCR paper back to the NCR company for sale in the USA. An unanticipated improvement was necessary when polychlorinated biphenols, although providing the necessary solvent characteristics, became environmentally unacceptable and were later completely replaced.

1960–70

This phase is dominated by the influence of the original innovator, NCR, in the USA and Europe. The technology was developed by NCR and its licensee in Europe, Wiggins Teape, and also Jujo, Fuji and Kanzaki, Japanese companies using new sub-systems within the dominant set of design configurations. NCR strengthened their competitive position by exploiting their competence in capsule technology by direct foreign investment in microcapsule manufacturing plants in the UK and Germany and by licence agreements with Jujo in Japan. NCR patents had not been taken out in Japan, and four companies began production in the early 1960s. Jujo Paper developed their own technology involving microencapsulation though later negotiated an NCR licence to utilize its colour formers. Mitsubishi started operation under licence to NCR while Kanzaki Paper and Fuji Photo Film developed independent technologies using microencapsulation which they later licensed to other European and overseas companies (Zanders, Feinpapiere Sincarbon, Sarrio, and DRG). Fuji were particularly active and successful in the development and patenting of colour formers.

Japanese carbonless copy paper, first appearing in Europe in 1968, was of a particularly high standard and reactivity, in part because of the requirement for a large number of handwritten business forms and the difficulty of mechanical reproduction of Japanese script. The base paper was superb, the copy quality excellent in blue and black and lighter weight sheets so large numbers of copies could be supplied.

Different design configurations

During the 1960s the production of 'conventional' carbonless copy paper using microencapsulation was effectively blocked to new

178

entrants in Europe and the USA by the key patents held by NCR. The strength of these patents meant that in order to enter the market new entrants had to develop completely new design configurations. A few manufacturers did develop such alternative systems. 3M's system used a metallic salt as developer and di-thio-oxamide dyestuff in capsules added to the paper. Pelikan in Germany used a spirodipyran colour former. Nashua (USA) developed a honeycomb structured CB coating. The relative lack of success of these different design configurations and the fact that most potential manufacturers waited for the expiration of the key NCR patents indicates the extent to which the NCR process was accepted as the dominant design configuration.

NCR continued to develop its technology and in particular patented phenolic resins (1964) to replace the activated clays that had been developed as an improvement on attapulgous clay for coreactants. These resins were first used in the USA and then in Japan, and although investigated by Wiggins Teape, were not used by them. Many are still patent protected. The resins of the phenolic derivative types could be applied at much lower coat weights and were not so moisture sensitive. An added advantage was that phenolic resins could be coated 'on line' as part of the paper manufacturing process thus obviating the need for a separate CF coating facility. The clay coatings could not match this advantage until the mid 1970s. Improved acid activated clays were introduced which gave quicker colour development and better image intensity but under certain conditions still showed fading under ultraviolet, temporary discolouration and poorer colour tone.

1970–80

The expiration of the key NCR patents resulted in a large increase in the early 1970s in the number of European manufacturers (see Table 8.1). Some companies licensed technology from Japan, the USA and Germany while others started independent manufacture. Almost all opted for the dominant design configuration of microencapsulation: Feldmühle in Germany with BASF capsules, Binda in Italy, Pelikan and Koehler in Germany. Wiggins Teape in the UK and Belgium, already supplying the majority of the European market, also launched their own product.

Product innovations

Synthetic microcapsules were also developed offering an alternative to the gelatine/gum arabic or carboxymethyl cellulose cell wall

Table 8.1 Developments in carbonless copy paper technology

| Major licensing agreements | | | | |
Licensor	Country	Licensee	Country	Date
NCR	USA	Wiggins Teape	UK	1955
		Mitsubishi	Japan	1962
		Jujo Paper	Japan	1967
Molineus	Germany	Carrs	UK	1973
		Ahlstrom	Finland	1973
		Hauffe	Germany	1973
Nashua	USA	Reed	UK	1974
		Aero	Yugoslavia	1975
		Loreto	Mexico	1975
		Seghal	India	1975
Renker	W. Germany	Detto	Venezuela	1978
		Papercote	S. Africa	1980
Fuji Photo Film	Japan	Sarrio	Spain	1970
		DRG	UK	1971
		Adamus	Argentina	1980
		Massuh		
Kanzaki	Japan	Zanders	W. Germany	1980
		Sincarbon	Brazil	1980
Nashua	USA	Voiron	France	1980
		Boisse Cascade	USA	
Bartsch	W. Germany	Copigraph	France	1980
		Lijnco	Netherlands	1980
Nashua	USA	Milani Fibriano	Italy	1981

| Other methods of manufacture | |
Company	Country
Koehler/Pelikan	W. Germany
Feldmühle (BASF)	W. Germany
Binda	Italy
Technopapel	Mexico
Moores Business Forms	USA/France
Mead/Fuji	USA
3M	USA

produced by complex coacervation. New wall materials, acrylates, polyamides, polyurethanes, UF/MF resins were used in new techniques based on interfacial polymerization to produce smaller more evenly sized capsules having higher solid contents, 30–50 per cent. However, such capsules were usually more costly. Europe especially used and still uses a great deal of gelatine capsule and this highlights the very important significance of compatibility and consistency. A change in one element of the carbonless copy paper system, such as new capsule wall materials, may be difficult to integrate into the system as a whole and it is often preferable to improve the individual elements of an existing system than introduce new ones.

An even higher performance coreactant, zinc salicylate, was introduced and patented by Kanzaki and Fuji during the 1970s for both domestic and European consumers.

During the early 1970s new colour formers were required to allow copies to be xeroxed or copied by electrophotographic means to a higher quality. Black copy was also becoming more popular. Relatively few chemical companies were actively engaged in innovative research and those were principally Fuji, BASF, Bayer, Monsanto and Ciba-Geigy. Families of colour formers were produced, indolyl red, phthalide reds, phthalide violet, spirodipyran-dyestuffs and, most important, the fluorans (Fuji 1969, NCR 1969 patents). Chemical companies worked in close co-operation with manufacturers whose individual recipes for the microcapsule contents would depend on many technical parameters as well as such factors as cost, compatibility, availability and characteristic of the market.

Capsule oils not only act as solvents for colour formers but also play a part in the efficient transfer to the active part of the coreactant layer. The early solvents have been replaced by hydrocarbons, mostly alkylated aromatics, or by chlorinated paraffins or by mixtures such as hydrogenated diphenyls or terphenyls in combination with kerosene or plasticizers. The respective properties of the constituents were carefully balanced to give the most cost effective mix for maximum print intensity, colour former solubility and print speed.

Process innovation

Coating technology also changed. The introduction of synthetic microcapsules enabled coat weight to be reduced, quality more readily controlled, and faster coating speeds attained. Special airknife units were developed to meter the thickness of the CB coating and air foils for drying were redesigned. Sophisticated inspection systems made quality control more consistent and in some plants blade and roll coaters were installed which had considerable potential for increased line speed. Cost reduction through more efficient manufacture became increasingly important.

Other microencapsulation technologies were established in protected environments. Moore Business Forms in the USA, the leading business forms printer worldwide, developed its own in-house system during 1972–5 for its own business forms. This used a single component dyestuff requiring special solvents and special capsule techniques but the carbonless copy paper was never traded on the open market. The second biggest producer of conventional carbonless paper in the USA, Mead, started production in the late 1970s of a new second product with capsules applied in hot melts, which could be used for spot printing and applied by printers.

Different design configurations

Some alternative configurations, non-capsular solvent systems, were developed in which the colour formers, dissolved in solvents, were applied as the CF coating together with binders, ureas and white pigments. The back coating contained reactive metal salts such as zinc chloride applied from melted waxes and paraffins (Frye/USA, Kores/Switzerland).

By the 1980s technological development was no longer focused on the problems of improving performance characteristics but was directed more to those of cost reduction and increased production and efficiency, consistency and quality control.

To summarize, we see in this technology the importance of post-innovation performance and the development of technological variety. It illustrates the point that when technologies are first introduced they appear in an immature form. In this example NCR proved particularly adept at following trajectories of post-innovation improvements and protecting itself with patents. The logical consequence was that any UK presence had to be obtained through licence agreements. It is clear that the nature of the licence agreements and their method of operation had a marked effect on the technological strategy of the major UK licensee, Wiggins Teape.

Home computers

Introduction

The case of the home computer provides a good illustration of three of the theoretical themes of this chapter. First, it is an example of the introduction of a radically new technology into specific niches. Unlike carbonless copy paper, for which there already existed a market, users of home computers were required to engage in substantial learning. Second, there is a continuous sequence of post-innovation improvements along clear trajectories, in particular those of increasing memory size, of lowering cost, and of increasing ease of use. Third, developments in home computer technology depended critically on integrated circuit

182

technology, illustrating the overwhelming importance of external technological development. Technological development in the design and manufacture of integrated circuits, in particular microprocessors, enabled the production of computers both small enough and cheap enough for domestic use. Indeed, home computers are generally defined as microcomputers sold for less than £500. As well as their low cost, it is their small physical size, their relative ease of use, their entertainment value and the vagaries of fashion which also define this domestic market.

Prototechnology

The first microprocessor chips were launched in 1971 while the following year Intel launched the 8008, the first microprocessor suitable for microcomputer construction. This led to the development of videogames and hand-held electronic calculators, which can be seen as technological antecedents to the home computer, and were part of a range of technologies performing a variety of functions. The development of the home computer market can be seen as primarily attributable to technology push, as there was no pre-existing technology to be displaced. It can, however, also be seen as partially substituting for this range of technological antecedents and also for manual ways of doing things. This process of partial substitution influenced the niches it came to occupy.

Arcade-type microprocessor-controlled videogames were the forerunners of home computers in terms of the latter's widespread use as game-playing machines, and can be seen as very basic computers. It is not surprising that makers of such games moved into the home computer market. Most notable are the American firms Atari, Mattel and Coleco. These games, like most home computers, used the domestic TV set for their visual display. Over the course of the 1970s calculator technology improved quite rapidly and prices dropped accordingly. With the advent of sophisticated programmable calculators it is easy to see their close ancestral relation to the home computer, indeed the design of the first crude Sinclair micro, the MK 14 kit, was originally based on the calculator microchips. Commodore and Texas Instruments are also among the firms which moved into the production of home computers from the calculator market. The technological development of home computers can be seen as proceeding upwards from calculators and videogames and downward from larger computers. Computer technology in general had improved quite rapidly. The memory storage available on a Random Access Memory (RAM) chip in a home computer in 1980 would have needed technology that occupied a large room less than thirty years before. The home computer was in this respect a product of steady evolutionary development in computer technology. The first microcomputer appeared in the USA in 1975. The Altair 8800 kit had 256 bytes of memory and cost $395. It was in kit form as were many of the early micros, and this is indicative of the fact that they were primarily aimed at hobbyists, who enjoyed the challenges of assembling and programming these machines. Slightly more upmarket assembled micros aimed at wider markets began to appear in the US from Tandy (TRS-80 Model 1 with 4K RAM – $599), Apple (Apple 11, 4K – $1298), and Commodore (Pet 4K and monitor – $599). These machines subsequently appeared on the UK market. The first UK firms to produce micros entered the hobbyist market with kits, Sinclair (at the time 'Science of Cambridge') in 1978 with the MK14 (£39.95) and Acorn in 1979 with the Acorn System 75 (£65). They were both very basic machines confined to the enthusiast market. The MK14 had only a numeric keypad and programming was carried out in a hexi-decimal code while the System 75 did have a full keyboard. These machines had very small memories. A wider market was opened up in the UK in 1980, when Sinclair launched the ZX80 (£80 in kit form, £100 assembled) a 1K RAM but expandable home computer with a touch sensitive keyboard which had to be connected to a domestic TV set. Acorn followed a few months later with their 2K Atom (£120 kit, £150 assembled), a precursor to the BBC machine with a full-size typewriter keyboard. Behind the development of these machines lies performance developments in computer language, particularly 'BASIC', which made home computers easy to use.

However, as home computers diffused more widely with the introduction of the ZX80 and particularly its successor the ZX81 with 16K (£50 kit, £70 assembled) their ease of use became increasingly important. This depended to a large extent on the language and keyboard quality, as did their reliability which depended upon design and size of memory, and power and speed of operation. This in turn depended on developments in RAM and Central Processor Unit (CPU) technology.

The trajectories of technological development

Home computers, even relatively early in their history, can be seen to possess a set of technical characteristics with which it is possible to differentiate machines and to look at their technical sophistication relative to each other. It is also possible to follow their paths of technological development and to see the shifts in the relative importance of these characteristics.

Improvements in the technical characteristics of home computers have occurred both continuously and discretely. Many of these, particularly the continuous development, derive from improvements in integrated circuit technology. One of the obvious outward signs of such continuous development, the following of a trajectory, has been the steady increase in the RAM size, roughly doubling each year in terms of the ratio of memory size to price. In contrast, the CPUs changed relatively little: most home computers continued to use 8-bit microprocessors but improved their utilization of the CPU's power through development in both software and hardware design. 16–bit CPUs did not appear in micros in the sub £500 price range until 1986 with the launch of Amstrad's PC1512. Sinclair, however, did introduce 32-bit technology into the home market – the unsuccessful 'QL' machine – although in a limited fashion (quadruply multiplexed).

While increases in memory size and the speed and power of operation represented one trajectory of development, another was in ease of use of home computers. BASIC and its various dialects (Beginner's All Purpose Instruction Code), the language used in most home computers, also improved incrementally in terms of its speed and power. In 1983 Cantab introduced the Jupiter Ace (£80) which used the language Forth but this was not particularly successful.

Continuous improvements in characteristics such as graphics capabilities, the number of colours displayable, the number available and the text format all add to the sophistication of the machine while making it easier to use. These advances, however, also depend on developments in chip technology. The introduction of the first colour home computer, however, represents a discrete advance and came in the form of the Commodore VIC–20 in 1982, named after the Video Interface Chip.

Ease of use was enhanced by other discrete improvements. These included the incorporation of standard typewriter quality keyboards. In addition, Sinclair attempted to develop various other 'membrane' types of keyboards. Although these brought the cost of machines down, they were often more difficult to use. Keyboard quality and sophistication greatly influenced the users' valuation of the machine. The existence of a numeric keypad, separate from the main 'QWERTY' keyboard, and the inclusion of programmable keys for frequently used functions also added to the overall sophistication of the keyboard, and were valued by users in terms of the increased ease of use they offered.

Discrete improvements were also made in the expandability of machines, incorporating more 'ports' and 'interfaces' so that monitors, disk drives, printers, modems and other peripheral devices could be connected. However, like the addition of a standard typewriter keyboard, not all of these features in themselves represent significant new technological developments. It was their incorporation into a machine that generally enhanced its overall level of technological sophistication. Other such discrete developments included the incorporation of peripheral devices into the main body of hardware, as Amstrad did with their all-in low-price system in the CPC 464 (including monitor and cassette data recorder). This again did not represent technological development in terms of the separate components, but it illustrates something of the state of the market in 1984, and the effects of user needs on both the direction of technological development and the configuration of the technology in products.

The success of such a system demonstrates the relationship between the development of the home computer and its complementary technologies. The availability of software and peripheral devices have been important determinants of success and are not easily quantifiable. A large software catalogue may help in the maintenance of market share. The availability of compatible printers, disk drives, cassette players, etc., is essential if a machine's potential for expandability to a larger system is to become a marketable commodity. This availability can be enhanced with the incorporation of standard interfaces. 'Bundling' has been a common retail ploy, offering the hardware complete with software and possibly peripheral devices.

From the rate and direction of development of these characteristics during the home computer's short history, a general move can be seen from the production of cheap, relatively unsophisticated novelty games machines towards more sophisticated, more seriously used machines. This illustrates a change in the balance of user needs and their valuations of characteristics. Competition and technological development in microcomputers has now led to the situation where what was available in 'business machines' costing well in excess of £1,000 five years ago is now available for less than £500.

Technological variety

A way of looking at technological variety in home computers is via the construction of hedonic relationships between product characteristics and product prices. Figure 8.1 illustrates the regression of the RAM size (M) onto the price (P) for a range of home computers available on the market in 1984. The line has the equation:

$$R = \alpha M + \beta$$

where α and β are estimated constants. With these observations $\alpha = 2$, $\beta = 103$, and this relationship explains 34 per cent of the variance in price.

Figure 8.1   Price versus RAM size in home computers

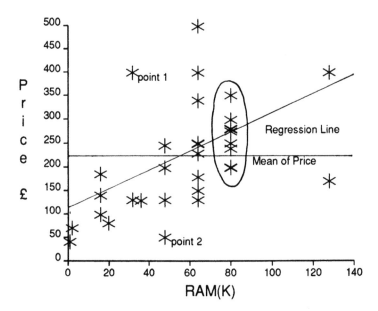

Adding further technical characteristics, including dummy variables to account for discrete characteristics, produces an equation of the form:

$$R = a_0 + a_1C_1 + a_2C_2...+ a_nC_n$$

where $\alpha_0,...\alpha_n$ are estimated constants and $C_1,...C_n$ are technical characteristics.

These additional characteristics include the keyboard quality (typewriter quality or otherwise, number of functional keys and availability of a separate numeric keypad). The inclusion of seventeen characteristics explains 80 per cent of the variance in price, showing that technological sophistication and the variety can be related to price differentials.

Returning to the simpler case of price versus RAM size, points on the graph correspond to models which experienced remarkably different market fortunes, illustrating that high performance to price ratio does not always ensure success. Acorn's BBC–B (point 1) was among one of the most successful machines in the market yet is furthest from the line. In contrast machines like the Oric Atmos (point 2), despite being well below the line, did not achieve any substantial market penetration.

The early years of the home computer generated a large amount of technological variety with very little compatibility between machines. An attempt at standardization with the introduction of the Japanese 'MSX' machines has been largely unsuccessful. This has been attributed to too low a technical level of standardization and too late an introduction to the market despite the MSX machines being close to the regression line in Figure 8.1 (cluster 3).

Technological survival and failure

It soon becomes clear that technological sophistication alone has not been a guarantee of success, as for example, Dragon came to discover despite launching the first machines with a 32K RAM for under £200 in 1982. Inability to offer machines above an increasing threshold of sophistication and with an acceptable performance to price ratio can be the cause of failure. The poor sales performance of the Acorn Electron may be in part attributed to its having a £199 price tag and only 32K of RAM at a time when many 64K machines were cheaper. As a 'scaled down' version of the success-ful BBC–B it showed that user valuation of the characteristics of the latter meant that they would rather pay the extra money for the extra performance and the better known machine.

Few firms have survived from the 'boom' years (1982–4) of the home computer market, and with the exception of Amstrad, the survivors entered the market at a relatively early stage. These older firms have generally maintained a level of compatibility as their product range has developed and have by and large introduced successively improved machines along the trajectories described earlier.

Technology alone has not been at the root of their success, nor can failure be attributable to the lack of an appropriate technology knowledge base. The BBC's choice of Acorn to supply the machine for its television computer literacy series has been a major force behind the 'BBC Model B's' market success, as has the government's programme for computer literacy in schools, which also promoted the machine. Retail, production, marketing and organizational arrangements have all had their influence, as have changes in user sophistication and awareness which have changed the user valuations of different characteristics. Amstrad's success can be attributed in no small way to their perception of changes in user valuations.

There are still a few 'Home' computers currently remaining in the market and these tend to be enhanced versions of earlier successful machines. They include the Amstrad CPC 6128 (CPC 464), the Acorn BBC Master 128 (BBC–B), the Commodore 128 (Commodore 64) with larger memories, greater expandability and other improved features still following the established trajectories. They aspire to compete at the lower end of the business market and illustrate the upward move of home computer technology towards this niche. The original definition of home computers as microcomputers costing less than £500 has also changed as technology has developed, with sophisticated business micros moving below this barrier.

Optical fibre communications

Introduction

The case of optical fibre communications systems may be used to illustrate some of the processes by which a technological regime evolves to the point where it is capable of competing 'head-on' with other, more established, ways of doing things. Optical fibre communications emerged from the confluence of a number of previously separate strands (or 'trajectories') of technological development. These constituent technologies embrace a wide diversity of approaches to producing the various components that, when configured into an appropriate system, provide the core performance characteristic that defines the users' 'corridor' of communications requirements: namely the ability to send information from one point to another.

Distinguishing features of the optical fibre communications regime centre on the use of light waves to transmit information in a dielectric waveguide, which takes the form of an optical fibre. Over the last twenty years, this regime has progressed from being a theoretical possibility to the point where it is capable of outpacing well-established communications systems. This progression has arisen from advances in two key areas of technology: optoelectronic sources (in the form of semiconductor laser diodes and light-emitting diodes) and the materials technology necessary to produce suitable optical fibres. Moreover, a number of relatively mature technologies, associated with electronics, applied optics and general engineering, have had to be tailored and modified in order to provide the components that are necessary to configure an optical communications system. (These components include such things as optical detectors, devices for joining fibres together, termination of fibre-ends and test instrumentation.)

The discussion which follows reviews aspects of the development of optoelectronic sources and optical fibres in order to demonstrate ways in which the interrelationship between the performance of critical component technologies affect the overall performance of optical fibre communications systems. By matching state-of-the-art sources with appropriate fibres and ancilliary components it has been possible to move through a sequence of generations of light-wave systems in which greater volumes of information can be sent over increasing distances between transmitters and receivers (thereby reducing the need for repeaters).

The technological problem

Optical communications systems are by no means new. Semaphore systems, for example, send information by means of light waves. However, the main problem with 'traditional' optical communications lay in finding a suitably powerful light source. In consequence, the advent of the laser in 1960 rekindled interest in optical communications. However, even if suitable lasers could be developed for communications, it was realized that to send unguided light waves through the atmosphere would introduce a number of problems associated with the need for line-of-sight links (between transmitter and receiver) and difficulties caused by atmospheric disturbances (such as rain, dust, fog, snow, etc.). What was needed was some method of guiding the light waves in a 'light-pipe'.

Although the transmission of light via a dielectric waveguide structure was proposed and investigated at the beginning of the twentieth century, the state-of-the-art materials technology was not able to produce a waveguide that was suitable for telecommunications applications. These early waveguides, which took the form of a silicon glass rod, could not transmit light without excessive losses. The principal cause of these losses was light radiating from the waveguide to the surrounding air at points where there were imperfections (such as scratches) in the glass-air interface. Problems also arose because of the fragile nature of an unsupported glass rod.

While glass rod waveguides were not practical for use in telecommunications, there was some interest in developing the technology for possible applications involving the transfer of optical images. Bundles of glass or plastic fibres were developed that were able to carry light short distances – for example, to light an instrument panel or to see round corners. In particular, endoscopes, developed for medical applications, have proved to be valuable tools for inspecting such things as the interiors of stomachs. This interest in optical waveguides led to proposals, advanced in the mid-1950s, for a waveguide composed of a transparent core surrounded by a transparent cladding with a slightly lower refractive index. The cladding serves as a support mechanism, and also helps to keep the light waves within the waveguide structure. However, these early clad-waveguides did not come close to providing the level of transparency that would be required for optical communications systems.

The first serious proposals for information transmission via a transparent dielectric medium (i.e. an optical fibre) were advanced in 1966 by Kao and Hockham,[11] working at Standard Telephone Laboratories, Harlow. Even so, fibres available at that time still exhibited unacceptably high losses. (These losses were in excess of 1000 dB per kilometre when the maximum acceptable loss for a viable communications system was estimated to be of the order of 20 dB per kilometre. Nevertheless, it was apparent that, if the losses could be reduced, optical fibre communications systems had a number of potential advantages over the established technology of transmitting information using electrical signals in copper wires.

By the late 1960s, national telecommunications network operators in Europe, the USA and Japan had begun to develop optical fibre communications technology in collaboration with their principal suppliers of more traditional systems.[12] The early lead in the development of a low-loss optical fibre was taken in the USA by Corning Glass. This company's efforts culminated in the early 1970s with a breakthrough which resulted in a fibre with a loss that was lower than 20 dB per kilometre. In 1976 the first major trial of an optical fibre communications system (which used fibres produced by Corning Glass) was undertaken in Atlanta by the Bell Telephone Company. During the following year, Britain became the first country in Europe to carry public telephone traffic through optical fibres. The route covered 13 kilometres between Ipswich and British Telecom's Research Laboratories at Martlesham Heath.

While optical fibre communications systems, developed in the mid-1970s, were still at an experimental stage, it was abundantly clear that the optical regime had a number of potential advantages over traditional systems based on electrical signals and copper wires. These advantages which have since been exploited in commercial systems, are summarized below.

1. High transmission bandwidth with a massive potential for further development.
2. Small size and low weight. For a cable of given dimensions, the capacity of optical fibres is more than three times that of coaxial cable. This feature enables optical fibres to be slipped into existing ducts for conventional cable, giving higher capacity and low infrastructure costs.
3. Electrical isolation. The passage of light waves in an electrical insulator (i.e. the optical fibre) makes the optical regime ideal for communications in environments where electrical short circuits or sparks could be hazardous.
4. Immunity to interference and cross-talk. This means that fibres in a cable do not interfere with each other.
5. Signal security. Signals cannot be obtained from the fibre in a non-invasive manner (i.e. without drawing optical power from the fibre). Therefore any attempt to divert information from the fibre could, in theory, be detected.
6. Low transmission loss. Allows for communications links with long spacings between repeaters.
7. Reliability and low maintenance.

In order to realize the advantages of optical fibre communications systems, compatible optical sources and optical fibres, together with related technologies (associated with such things as detectors, joining the fibres together, termination of the fibre-ends and optical testing equipment), have to be configured into viable systems. Although fibre technology initially lagged behind the development of the semiconductor laser, by the mid-1970s the principal constraint on first generation communications systems was that imposed by the problems of producing optical sources which operated satisfactorily at the wavelengths which are most suitable for the efficient propagation of light waves in the fibre. These wavelengths represent 'windows' at which, by virtue of the physical structure of the fibre, light waves are able to be propagated with minimal losses. They occur at wavelengths in the region of 850 nanometres, 1,300 nanometres and 1,550 nanometres, with the higher-wavelength windows offering the lowest losses.

The problem with optical source development is that the semiconductor materials used to produce the light waves, have a natural propensity to emit light at wavelengths which are too short for efficient propagation at even the first window of suitable transmission wavelengths (i.e. 850 nanometres).

However, by producing sources from appropriate compounds of elements, it proved to be possible to increase the emission wavelengths to a point where sources could be produced that were capable of operating in that first window. In consequence, first-generation systems operated at 850 nanometres and used state-of-the-art fibres which were of the multi-mode type. Subsequent improvements in source technology enabled multi-mode fibre systems to be produced that operated in the second window (i.e. 1,300 nanometres). By 1983, a new type of fibre, known as single-mode fibre, had become widely available and, when used with the then recently developed single-mode sources, was capable of providing systems with a higher information carrying capacity. Further developments in sources have led to the commercialization of 1,550 nanometre single-mode systems. All of these developments are shown diagramatically in Figure 8.2.

The technical challenge of producing appropriate components for optical fibre systems has prompted the development of a wide diversity of design configurations and 'sub-trajectories' of development. In some instances, the diversity produces clear winners, in the sense that one component technology or design configuration is unambiguously better than the alternatives. However, the question of which type of component to use can depend on how the system is being configured (i.e. on technical parameters) and also on the type of application in which it would be used by the customer. For example, in the case of optical sources, progressive improvements in laser diode technology have been paralleled by the introduction and refinement of light-emitting diodes (LEDs) which are suitable for use in optical fibre communications. Although less powerful than lasers, LEDs are generally cheaper, more reliable and involve simpler drive circuitry. In some applications, LEDs are an appropriate choice, while in others (e.g. very long unrepeated links), lasers represent the only method of providing the required performance characteristics.

The long period niche for optical fibre communications systems

User requirements for communications systems are not static, rather they shift over time. A preliminary attempt will now be made to relate the five factors effecting shifts in user requirements, outlined earlier (pp. 172–3) to the example of optical fibre communication systems.

Figure 8.2   Improvements in repeater spacing and transmission bit rates for successive generations of optical fibres.

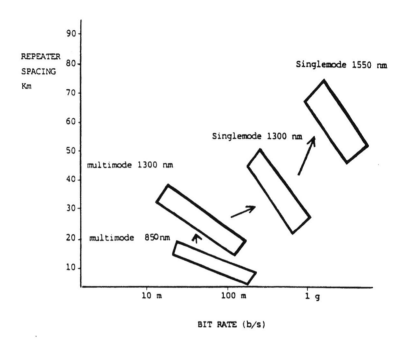

Original wavelengths for optical fibre transmissions were between 800nm and 900nm. With the development of better optical sources it was possible to exploit the superior transmission characteristics achieved at 1,300nm. Single-mode transmission at 1,300nm enhanced performance characteristics still further, and this trend could be extended by a move to 1,550nm.

Source:BICC

1. *The 'push me pull you' relationship.* In order to move from theoretical concept to commercial viability, optical fibre communications systems have been subjected to the influences of both 'technology push' and 'user need pull'. The exact weighting given to these influences at different points in time depends on the perspective of the observer. However, at a simplistic level, it could be noted that amid the historical evolution of the corridor associated with communications systems it was realized that the optical fibre regime had a potential for development. This potential was

194

realized following a period of 'technology push', in which key component technologies were developed to the point where viable optical systems could be configured. These systems were capable of entering the segment of the users' corridor associated with long distance telecommunications. The 'push me pull you' relationship, between system developments and the needs of the system user was then instrumental in extending the market for the light-wave regime into shorter-distance telecommunications applications (i.e. from the trunk network to the junction network).

Moreover, while telecommunications represented the 'forcing ground' which has promoted the development of successive generations of optical fibre communications systems, there has also been a strong sequence of pushes and pulls which have moved these systems sideways, into sections of the communications corridor associated with data communications (e.g. linking computers and computer networks) and also into sensor systems and the monitoring/control of production processes.

As systems users have learnt what the optical regime is capable of achieving, they have gained a greater influence in the processes that determine the mix of performance characteristics in successive generations of systems.

2. *Competing technologies*. Optical fibres are in direct competition with coaxial cables although, in certain circumstances, they are beginning to emerge as a viable alternative to some telecommunications applications which have previously been based on microwave or satellite links.

3. *Complementary technologies*. Testing and maintaining optical systems requires new equipment and new skills. In particular the need to train optical engineers to do work previously done by electrical engineers has tended to mitigate against the more rapid diffusion of optical systems.

4. *The legislative and regulatory environment*. In the case of optical fibre systems, this category of factors shaping the long period niche depends more than anything else on the issues arising from standardization of systems.

5. *Relative prices*. Until now, exogenous changes in prices have not had much effect on the long period niche for optical fibre communications technology. Nevertheless, it is worthy of note that the basic input to glass is in plentiful supply and traded in more stable market conditions than is copper.

Strategic approaches to innovation in optical fibre communications systems

Although the optical fibre communications regime is relatively new, in a number of cases component technologies have been developed by firms with knowledge bases that were previously associated with more established areas of technological expertise. These firms had experience in such things as semiconductor electronic devices, glass manufacturing, applied optics, test instrumentation for copper-based communication systems, and the manufacture of copper cables. Thus there was a considerable diversity in the technological pedigrees of firms who have moved into the optical fibre communications regime. It is this diversity, coupled with the nature of the inducement to innovate, that has influenced both the 'angle' at which firms have entered the regime (i.e. the degree to which they had to change technological direction) and the level of momentum associated with the development effort of individual firms.

In addition to firms who have changed direction to enter the optical fibre arena, there have also been start-up companies. These companies have, in general, been formed by entrepreneurs who have gained appropriate knowledge in an established organization and spun off to exploit a market opportunity. In the UK, these opportunities have tended to be concerned mainly with configuring systems for short-haul data communications markets. However, by contrast, the USA features a number of firms established to manufacture high technology, high value added optical sources and related families of components.

This case study which has now covered firms in every area of the technology with the exception of test instrumentation, has revealed strategic problems in both the acquisition of an appropriate knowledge base and its practical articulation. This problem of articulation has involved both the flow of knowledge within the organization and the efficiency with which that knowledge is translated into appropriate technological hardware. The current thrust of our research is concerned with tabulating the various combinations of circumstances in which the articulation of the firm's knowledge base either adds to or detracts from revealed competitive performance.

Conclusion

We have argued in this chapter that the rate and direction of technical change is a key element in the competitive process. We have sought to illustrate this by analyzing trajectories of technological change and technological variety within three case studies. In each one we have endeavoured to present the technology not only in terms of a sequence of innovations but also in terms of the evolution of key performance characteristics. We contend that it is these performance characteristics that are evaluated by the economic environment and which determine the pattern of emergence of dominant designs.

However, the nature and basis of the processes by which users select performance characteristics are no more fixed than technology. Over time, user requirements change as a result of advances in a given technology, changes in competing complementary technologies, new legislation or regulatory controls, and shifts in relative prices. These movements in the user's corridor of requirements are of paramount importance because they continually reshape the size of the long period niche for a technology and hence its economic weight.

New technological developments arise from opportunities to satisfy new user requirements, to find improved solutions for given problems, and to improve efficiency of production. These developments can only come to the market through the medium of firms, for it is firms that articulate specific design configurations and compete over time by improving the performance of those chosen configurations. It is our hypothesis that differences between firms, arising from their respective knowledge bases, strategies and resources are at the very heart of the competitive process. Choice implies variety and this is the essential characteristic of the competitive environment. Competition is therefore driven by variety and operates on the differences between the products and processes articulated by firms according to how these differences are evaluated by the economic environment.

We have found the choice of the technology as a unit of analysis an interesting and creative concept to investigate and understand the stimuli for technical change, the environment in which it occurs, and the agents which bring it about. However, we recognize that technological development may well be highly contingent on many non-technological factors and, in consequence, we would welcome views on the extent to which our analysis is justified as a useful framework within which to explore competitiveness and the momentum of technological change.

Notes

1 This point has been articulated most effectively by McNulty (1968: 642): 'Perfect competition, the only conception of competition to be

found in the corpus of economic theory, which is free of all traces of business behaviour associated with "monopolistic" elements, means simply the existence of an indefinitely large number of non-competing firms.' It is also worthy of note that the force of McNulty's essay draws much from the Austrian school of economics and in particular from Hayek (1949), ch. 5.

2 See in particular, Nelson and Winter (1977) vol. 6, pp. 36–76, Nelson and Winter (1982), Rosenberg (1976) p. 110, Dosi (1982), vol. 11, pp. 147–62.

3 See, for example, the work of Gilfillan, (1935a, 1935b), Usher (1954). Empirically-based studies which demonstrate the value of sustained post-innovation improvements have been provided by Hollander (1965), Enos (1958), vol. 6, pp. 180–97, Georghiou *et al.* (1986).

4 The concept of a 'corridor' has been developed in Metcalfe (1985). A fuller discussion is contained in Georghiou *et al.* (1986).

5 This concept has been developed by Ray (1985).

6 Schumpeter (1939), vol. 1, pp. 101–2. The term 'creative destruction' was actually coined in a later work, Schumpeter (1943) Chapter 7.

7 A fuller discussion of these dimensions is presented in Ray (1985).

8 The concept of a simultaneous invention is a notable feature of a needs-driven model of technological development advocated by the sociologist, S. C. Gilfillan (1935a). In the model, Gilfillan argues that no invention can be left unfound when the time for its application is ripe, i.e. when it is needed. Thus, at any given point in time, organizations with similar needs can be expected to produce similar inventions.

9 The term 'Schumpeterian competition' is used here to describe the active rivalry by which one firm seeks to gain a competitive advantage over other firms. This conception of competition, which may be found throughout Schumpeter's published work, can be traced from the astute statements about competitive entrepreneurship that first appeared in Schumpeter (1911). This first appeared in German in 1911, with a 1912 publisher's copyright. An English translation, which was made from a third edition of German text, was published by Harvard University Press in 1934.

10 Brunner, F. X., 'Dyestuffs for chemical carbonless copy papers', Basle: CIBA-GEIGY Ltd.

11 Kao and Hockham (1966), vol. 113, no. 7, pp. 1151–58.

12 Botez and Hershowitz (1980), vol. 68, no. 6, pp. 689–729.

References

Botez, D. and Hershowitz, G. J. (1980) 'Components for optical communications systems: A review', *Proceedings of the IEE* vol. 68, no. 6: 689–729.

Brunner, F. X., 'Dyestuffs for chemical carbonless copy papers', Basle: CIBA-GEIGY Ltd.

Dosi, G. (1982) 'Technological paradigms and technological trajectories', *Research Policy* vol. 11: 147–62.

Enos, J. (1958) 'A measure of the rate of technical progress in the petroleum refining industry', *Journal of Industrial Economics* vol. 6: 180–97.

Georghiou, L., Gibbons, M., Metcalfe J. S., Ray, T. and Evans, J. (1986) *Post-Innovation Performance: Technological Development and Competition*, London: Macmillan.

Gilfillan, S. C. (1935a) *The Sociology of Invention*, Chicago: Follett Publishing.

Gilfillan, S. C. (1935b) *Inventing the Ship*, Chicago: Follett Publishing.

Hayek, F. A. (1949) *Individualism and Economic Order*, London: Routledge & Kegan Paul, ch. 5.

Hollander, S. (1965) *The Sources of Increased Efficiency: A Study of Du Pont Rayon Plants*, Cambridge, Mass: MIT.

Kao, K. C. and Hockman, G. A. (1966) 'Dielectric fiber surface waveguides for optical frequencies', *Proc. IEE* vol. 113, no. 7: 1151–8.

McNulty, P. J. (1968) 'Economic theory and the meaning of competition', *Quarterly Journal of Economics*, vol. 82: 642.

Metcalfe, J. S. (1985) 'On technological competition', ESRC Workshop on New Technology, Cumberland Lodge, Windsor, 28–29 May 1985.

Nelson, R. R. and Winter, S. G. (1977) 'In search of a useful theory of innovation', *Research Policy* 36–76.

Nelson, R. R. and Winter, S. G. (1982) *An Evolutionary Theory of Economic Change*, Cambridge, Mass: Harvard University Press.

Ray, T. E. (1985) 'The process of technological change at firm level', PhD Thesis, CNAA.

Rosenberg, N. (1976) *Perspectives on Technology*, Cambridge: Cambridge University Press, p. 110.

Schumpeter, J. A. (1911) *The Theory of Economic Development: An Inquiry into Profits, Capital, Credit, Interest and the Business Cycle*, English Edition (1934), Cambridge, Mass: Harvard University Press.

Schumpeter, J. A. (1939) *Business Cycles* 1, 101–2.

Schumpeter, J. A. (1943) *Capitalism, Socialism and Democracy*, London: Unwin, ch. 7.

Usher, A. P. (1954) *A History of Mechanical Inventions*, revised edn. Cambridge, Mass: Harvard University Press, first published 1929.

Index

NB References are to the United Kingdom unless otherwise stated.

200